FROM STREET TO SCREEN

STUDIES IN THE CINEMA OF THE BLACK DIASPORA
Michael T. Martin and David C. Wall, *editors*

FROM STREET TO SCREEN

Charles Burnett's *Killer of Sheep*

Edited by
Michael T. Martin and
David C. Wall

INDIANA UNIVERSITY PRESS

This book is a publication of

Indiana University Press
Office of Scholarly Publishing
Herman B Wells Library 350
1320 East 10th Street
Bloomington, Indiana 47405 USA

iupress.org

© 2020 by Indiana University Press

All rights reserved

No part of this book may be reproduced or utilized in any form or by any means, electronic or mechanical, including photocopying and recording, or by any information storage and retrieval system, without permission in writing from the publisher. The paper used in this publication meets the minimum requirements of the American National Standard for Information Sciences—Permanence of Paper for Printed Library Materials, ANSI Z39.48-1992.

Manufactured in the United States of America

Library of Congress Cataloging-in-Publication Data

Names: Martin, Michael T., editor. | Wall, David C., editor.
Title: From street to screen : Charles Burnett's Killer of sheep / edited by Michael T. Martin and David C. Wall.
Description: Bloomington, Indiana : Indiana University Press, [2020] | Series: Studies in the cinema of the Black diaspora | Includes bibliographical references, filmography, and index.
Identifiers: LCCN 2020000321 (print) | LCCN 2020000322 (ebook) | ISBN 9780253049544 (paperback) | ISBN 9780253049537 (ebook)
Subjects: LCSH: Burnett, Charles, 1944—Criticism and interpretation. | Killer of sheep (Motion picture) | African Americans in motion pictures. | Motion pictures—United States—History.
Classification: LCC PN1997.K43526 F76 2020 (print) | LCC PN1997.K43526 (ebook) | DDC 791.43/72—dc23
LC record available at https://lccn.loc.gov/2020000321
LC ebook record available at https://lccn.loc.gov/2020000322

1 2 3 4 5   25 24 23 22 21 20

for
Leah Wise
and
Andrea DeHaan

CONTENTS

Acknowledgments   ix

Killer of Sheep: Charles Burnett and the Poetry of
Oppression / David C. Wall and Michael T. Martin   1

Part 1: Situating *Killer of Sheep*: Time / Place / Circumstance

  1 Cinema and Black Liberation / David E. James   49

  2 Struggles for the *Sign* in the Black Atlantic: Los Angeles
Collective of Black Filmmakers / Michael T. Martin   65

  3 Charles Burnett: A Reconsideration of Third Cinema /
Amy Abugo Ongiri   89

  4 Charles Burnett: Consummate Cineaste /
Michael T. Martin   99

Part 2: Reading *Killer of Sheep*

  5 Toward a Geo-Cinematic Hermeneutics:
Representations of Los Angeles in Non-Industrial Cinema—
Killer of Sheep and *Water and Power* / David E. James   121

  6 An Aesthetic Appropriate to Conditions: *Killer of Sheep*,
(Neo)Realism, and the Documentary Impulse /
Paula J. Massood   146

  7 Neorealism Meets the Blues in Charles Burnett's
Killer of Sheep / Keith Mehlinger   167

8	*Killer of Sheep* / James Naremore	182
9	*Killer of Sheep* / Jeffrey Skoller	202
10	*Revenons à nos moutons*: Regarding Animals in Charles Burnett's *Killer of Sheep* / Sarah O'Brien	214

Screenplay	245
Biography and Filmography	267
Index	269

ACKNOWLEDGMENTS

Any undertaking of this kind is always collaborative and always reliant upon a whole slew of folks beyond just the editors of the volume. As we have gone through the process of putting the collection together many people have committed time and energy in countless ways, and it is to all those people that we must extend our thanks for their support, encouragement, and pertinent criticism. However, we must accord particular gratitude to both Gary Dunham, director of Indiana University Press, and Lesley Bolton, project manager, for their sterling support and guidance. We also thank Pete Feely of Amnet for his exacting labors on proofing the manuscript. We also want to acknowledge the quality and range of scholarship by the contributors both to *Killer of Sheep* in particular and, more generally, to Black Film as a whole. We must also thank the artist Jamie Lancaster for her work. Her understanding of the film's intent is compellingly captured in those images that are on the book's cover as well as inside the volume. And of course, we are indebted to Charles Burnett, not only for creating such an extraordinary film as *Killer of Sheep*, but for his enduring commitment to the cinematic arts. Finally, as series editors, we would like to extend our heartfelt thanks to Indiana University Press for their continued and unwavering support of the series *Studies in the Cinema of the Black Diaspora*.

Michael T. Martin and David C. Wall

FROM STREET TO SCREEN

KILLER OF SHEEP

Charles Burnett and the Poetry of Oppression

David C. Wall and Michael T. Martin

*K*ILLER OF *S*HEEP IS AN UNASSUMING YET DEEPLY compelling meditation on laboring Black life, family, and community. Though the extant literature on director Charles Burnett's most well-known film is quite substantial, it is comprised largely of disparate essays, interviews, film reviews, and commentary. However, given the recognition and importance accorded this film in the annals of American cinema in general and Black film in particular, it seems odd that no book-length study has been published. To remedy this conspicuous gap, the editors have compiled this volume in order to bring together a collection of writing that will give some representative sense of the enormous breadth and variety of scholarship that *Killer of Sheep* has occasioned. As well as work that historicizes *Killer of Sheep* in the context of the tumultuous social upheavals of the 1960s and '70s and in relation to cinematic formations such as Free Cinema documentary, Italian neorealism, and Third Cinema movements, we have included analyses of the film's spatiotemporal hermeneutics, its containment and expression of memory and trauma, its formal and thematic embodiment of the blues, and less known and rarely discussed, its relationship to the broader politics of animal rights. As we have with other volumes published in the *Studies in Cinema of the Black Diaspora* series, we have also included the screenplay. Taken together, these materials will provide readers a wide-ranging and incisive critical companion to the film.

Killer of Sheep is a unique artifact in the history of American film, if for no other reason than it is the only MA thesis project selected for the National Film Registry by the Library of Congress.[1] Completed in 1973 as the culmination of Burnett's studies at UCLA, it was screened a few years later at a handful of local theaters but was never initially intended for formal theatrical distribution.[2] Indeed, it was for that reason that Burnett did not attempt to secure the expensive rights to the extensive music used on the film's soundtrack, thus delaying its commercial release in the United

States until 2007, thirty years after its first release. As Burnett himself said, "it was made for a small group of people and I never imagined it would go beyond that."[3] But this "quiet gem of a movie"[4] has of course gone way beyond that and is now considered one of the great achievements of American independent cinema. As well as its induction into the National Film Registry in 1990, as part of the first cohort of films to be given that honor, it was adjudged by the National Society of Film Critics as one of the one hundred essential American films and has been called both "a foundational work of black cinema"[5] and "one of the most insightful and authentic dramas about African American life on film."[6] Clearly, *Killer of Sheep* alone would have been enough to cement Burnett's place in the pantheon of American directors. But he has followed it with an enviably long and wide-ranging career as a director, screenwriter, and producer that has encompassed features, shorts, documentaries, television shows, and made-for-television movies.

Burnett (fig. I.1) has received grants, awards, and accolades from numerous organizations over the years, including the Film Society of Lincoln Center, the Rockefeller Foundation, the NEH (National Endowment for the Humanities), and the MacArthur Foundation's "Genius" award. In 2017, along with director Agnes Varda, actor Donald Sutherland, and cinematographer Owen Roizman, he received the Academy of Motion Pictures Governor's Award, the "honorary Oscar" bestowed upon individuals for a significant lifetime's achievement in cinema.[7] But notwithstanding this long and lauded career, Burnett remains largely unknown to a wider public beyond the world of independent cinema. Descriptions of Burnett as "the nation's least-known great filmmaker,"[8] "the most influential filmmaker you've never heard of,"[9] and "the greatest living black American filmmaker"[10] correspond with the odd position he has in American film, attesting ironically to his singular importance and yet relative anonymity. Indeed, Sukhdev Sandhu's apt description that, prior to its release on DVD in 2007, *Killer of Sheep* had "occupied a shadowy existence on the margins of mainstream cinema"[11] might equally well apply to Burnett himself.

The reasons for his relative obscurity are of course many and complex. And although as Burnett wryly says of himself, "being the most famous filmmaker that no one's heard of is kind of strange,"[12] it is a situation he is by no means entirely ungrateful for; as Michael Sragow puts it, Burnett has "found a certain freedom outside the mainstream."[13] Asserting that the director has "no desire to be Spike Lee," he quotes Burnett as saying that "I want to be able to walk down the street and observe people without

Fig. I.1

people observing me." But the life of an independent filmmaker, even one as accomplished as Burnett, is a constant struggle to get any project off the ground. This was even more the case when Burnett began his career as a filmmaker in the late 1970s, prior to the emergence, a few years later, of a kind of institutionalized independent industry represented most powerfully by the concurrent rise to prominence of the Sundance Film Festival and the Miramax company. As Peter Biskind demonstrates, it was the remarkable success of Bob and (the now disgraced) Harvey Weinstein's Miramax that firmly established an indie crossover culture, resulting in the emergence of an independent mainstream market.[14] Though never matching the economic success of Miramax, companies such as October Films, New Line, and Zeitgeist demonstrated that there was a profitable indie/arthouse market to be exploited. In response to this, mainstream Hollywood studios began developing their own "prestige indie" divisions, such as Sony Classics, Orion Classics, and Fox Searchlight. In time, the success of such independent companies resulted in their perhaps inevitable integration into the very behemoths they had originally challenged.

Similarly, Burnett's interstitial location between the independents and mainstream occasioned such films as *My Brother's Wedding* (The Samuel

Goldwyn Company, 1990), *The Glass Shield* (Miramax, 1994), *Nightjohn* (Disney Channel, 1996), and *The Wedding* (Oprah Winfrey Productions, 1998). However, a consequence of his precarious life as a director has led Burnett to claim, "I never really call myself a filmmaker because of the fact that it's so infrequent that I do it."[15] This statement is doubtless symptomatic of the life of any independent filmmaker. But the fact that from the mid- to late 1980s onward there was a clear market for indie films suggests that someone like Charles Burnett might have an easier time generating funds for his projects. However, American independent companies remained no less skewed to an overwhelming whiteness in their production and marketing than the major studios, with a small handful of notable exceptions, including Spike Lee and Julie Dash, having occasionally broached the broader crossover markets. But the very fact of their notable exceptionality underscores the broader point.[16]

In this way, then, it is not possible to understand Burnett's life and career outside of the complexities of race at work across the broad landscape of American cinema and, further, to consider that his access to the mainstream is framed not only by the fact that he is a Black director but also that he refuses to traffic in the narratives of blackness with which White Hollywood is comfortable. As Bernard Weinraub puts it, "Charles Burnett has struggled quietly to make films about the black experience in the United States, only to see his work ignored by movie studios and remain largely unnoticed by most moviegoers, perhaps because his films have no gangs or guns."[17] This has been the case from the very beginning of his career. Indeed, one of the motivating factors in his making of *Killer of Sheep* was "a reaction against studios and what they were making"[18] as "a response to the kinds of film that . . . I couldn't identify with."[19] Most immediately, this was a reaction against the dominant tropes of early 1970s blaxploitation in which the urban milieu functioned as an arena of spectacle for the acting out of all manner of racial, social, and sexual pathologies. There were complex and varied reasons as to why Black audiences—especially the targeted demographic of young Black men—might have responded positively to the kinds of images proffered throughout the blaxploitation genre. As the publicity material and movie posters for the blaxploitation genre routinely and ubiquitously demonstrated, and as Ed Guerrero asserts, one immediate pleasure offered by films such as *Shaft* (1971) (fig. I.2a), *Super Fly* (1972) (fig. I.2b), and *The Mack* (1973) (fig. I.2c) was an "assertive, sometimes violent, black manhood" that could "exude a sexual expressiveness long denied blacks on the

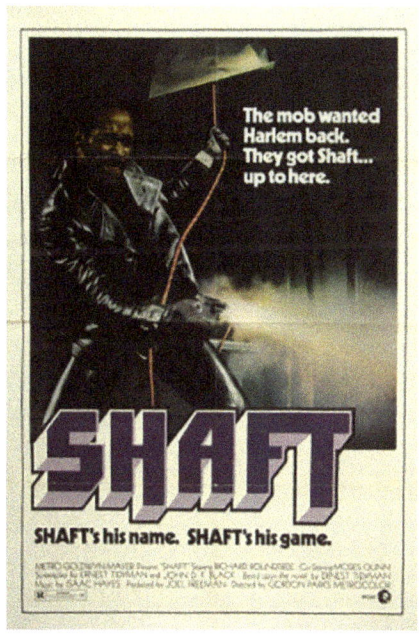

Fig. I.2(a–c)

screen."[20] Situated in the broader context of racial politics of the mid-1960s to early 1970s that saw repeated urban rebellions in major cities, a concomitant radicalization of the civil rights movement, and the assassination of both Malcolm X and Martin Luther King Jr., blaxploitation seemed to offer not a collective but a personal corrective for an audience that had become "increasingly dissatisfied with the emasculated and isolated characters"[21] played by Hollywood's greatest African American star of the time, Sidney Poitier. Melvin Van Peebles's independently produced *Sweet Sweetback's Baadasssss Song* (1971) is often cited as the progenitor of blaxploitation, and it is indeed hard to imagine a more aggressive rejection of the kind of White mainstream characterization of blackness offered by Poitier's John Prentice in *Guess Who's Coming to Dinner* (1967). A myriad of independent films of the broader period, from Shirley Clarke's *The Cool World* (1963) and Michael Roemer's *Nothing But a Man* (1964) to Ivan Dixon's *The Spook Who Sat by the Door* (1973) and Bill Gunn's *Ganja and Hess* (1973), offered alternative readings and renderings of Black American life that functioned in counterpoint to both the standard assimilationist fantasies of White Hollywood and what would become the deep problematics of blaxploitation. (In the case of *Spook*, there was even a vision offered of the potential for the revolutionary mobilization of the lumpenproletariat.) But *Sweetback*, notwithstanding its invocation of a reliance upon and avowal of its relationship to "the community," offers only an individualized vision (fig. I.3.). In this sense, though there is an argument to be made that Van Peebles's vision of racial politics possessed a certain radical import, it was roundly criticized for its presentation of "sterile daydreams and a superhero who is ahistorical, selfishly individualist with no revolutionary program."[22] On top of this, its sexual politics are deeply regressive, with the film's female characters functioning entirely in (both literal and figurative) service of heterosexual hypermasculinity. Taken together, it was those very elements of individualism and aggressive masculinity, devoid of even the merest gesture toward any kind of broader political radicalism or project, that came to define blaxploitation.[23]

Killer of Sheep, what Sukhdev Sandhu describes as a "quotidian, West Coast take on a Samuel Beckett play,"[24] served as Burnett's own corrective to the corrosive materialism and celebration of hypermasculine "superspade" violence that defined Hollywood's visions of Black life. As Armond White puts it, the film "counters the trashy distortions prevalent in seventies blaxploitation movies by staring solemnly at the reality of unrelieved misery and oppression."[25] In her essay in this collection, Amy Abugu Ongiri

Fig. I.3

similarly asserts that while in *Killer of Sheep*, "violence is important, it is never postulated as a solution . . . either thematically for the characters or as catharsis for the audience."²⁶ And *Killer of Sheep* does not exist in isolation. Burnett's entire career has indeed been a resistant refusal to traffic in the "typical corrupted Hollywood devices"²⁷ that White describes. At the same time, we can read it equally well as no less a critical response to the kinds of paternalistic White liberal fare that Hollywood had been producing since the late 1940s, from *Pinky* (1949), through *The Defiant Ones* (1958) and *Guess Who's Coming to Dinner* (1967), and on through *Driving Miss Daisy* (1989).

The challenge of Burnett's refusal is not only in cinematic terms—in his disruption of dominant visual codes—but also in its ideological and political intent through his instantiating a set of representations that refute the assertions, politics, discourses, and images that determine dominant representations of Black life both within and without the frame. And the radical import of *Killer of Sheep* is as a much more profoundly counterhistorical film than any of the early blaxploitation fare or its varied reiterations of the neo-blaxploitation of the 1990s, such as *Boyz n the Hood* (1991), *New Jack City* (1991), and *Menace II Society* (1993). In an industry predicated on perpetuating such a narrow range of representations, Burnett's films, then, are profoundly and equally out of step with the types of "Black" film that have their roots in either the violence-laden tropes of blaxploitation or in patronizing White liberal evocations of "inclusion." This refusal has its roots in his graduate work at UCLA and the emergence of what has come to be known—somewhat controversially—as the LA Rebellion. A motley group of about fifty filmmakers-in-training of color (aka "The Los Angeles School of Black Filmmakers") at UCLA endeavored to hone their craft as they strove "to perform the revolutionary act of humanizing Black people on screen."[28] Their collective project, according to one of its members, Ben Caldwell, was to "emancipate the image" from ensconced stereotypical and derogatory portrayals in American cinema and popular culture and within Black radical traditions that foreground agential authority and its inscription in the long struggle for representation and a Black futurity. For a detailed discussion and further elaboration of this cinematic formation and its thematic concerns and practice, see Michael T. Martin's chapter and extensive interview with Burnett in this collection.

* * *

Like all great films, *Killer of Sheep* is a complicated and multivalent cinematic text that offers rich rewards for the spectator-critic. And its combination of poetic lyricism and political engagement is unusual in that the film's commanding social critique is articulated in profoundly nuanced and subtle ways. Consider that *Killer* is a film about violence but from which physical violence is almost entirely absent. Similarly, it is a film about race but in which race remains almost entirely unremarked. It is also a film about innocence but set seemingly in a world of cynical despair. These initial examples of the deeply contradictory nature of the text contain within them the structural features of both formal and thematic determinants that shape the narrative and which we elucidate in detail throughout this chapter. In these general terms, we discern five organizing

Fig. I.4

principles around which consideration of *Killer of Sheep* is constituted and assessed.

- The most significant of these principles is the historical fact of violence. As we go on to discuss at greater length, Burnett refuses to traffic in those banal representations of Black violence that permeated (as they continue to do) American film. But violence is certainly central to *Killer of Sheep* as it threads its way through the warp and weft of everyday life. There are no gang fights, no explosions, and no shootings to witness. Nonetheless, in counterpoint, a serial violence is manifest in the slaughterhouse, as it is ubiquitous in relationships between characters and between children at play in decaying asphalt environs. Though the film begins with a young boy being slapped across the face by his mother as his father screams at him, violence is not always physical and more often than not is implied or off-screen. Consider, too, that the mechanical and routinized slaughter of sheep is never explicitly shown, nor is a planned killing alluded to by two hoods who solicit Stan's complicity in their criminal scheme. In fact, the most overt expression of physical violence portrayed is that of the children at play in desolate places in the neighborhood. Nevertheless, as we shall demonstrate, violence is present and constant in multiple forms.

- The second organizing principle at work in *Killer of Sheep*—deeply related to violence—is the structural nexus between race and class. Indeed, we contend that class is the most obviously and anomalously understudied, yet salient, subject of study in *Killer of Sheep*. Race is of course present in every single frame of this film. Not only in diegetic terms inasmuch as the film is self-consciously representing features of the Black American experience attributable to historical circumstance and everyday life, but also extra-diegetic in that American viewers' sense of race (conscious or otherwise) engages with their viewing of the film. And yet, to return to within the frame of the film itself, we would argue that race remains entirely unremarked by its being masked and subsumed by the experience of class. In this sense, the film is providing an ontology of blackness in that it is attempting to articulate and depict a state of material and conceptual "being" that is Black without having to foreground its salience and determinacy. The film invites the viewer to acknowledge the consequences and circumstances of what that ontological state of blackness means within the American polity and most especially, then, as it is articulated through the structures of class. As we go on to demonstrate, race intrudes explicitly at only one point in the film, when a White grocery store owner engages with her Black clientele, but the registers of class are explicitly articulated throughout.
- Such class registers marked by place and circumstance in *Killer of Sheep* correspond to and inform a third organizing principle, which is that of the centrality of the family. In classic Marxist terms, the film's protagonist, Stan, personifies the proletariat. It is the material conditions of his labor and relationship to his employer that are no less than determinate, at once the cause of, and alienating effect in, his relationship with his wife and children. However, beyond his family, all of his social and economic relationships derive from, and pivot on, the nature of his labor and class position in the production line at the slaughterhouse. The crisis of masculinity, then, that we elucidate in some detail later in this essay is as much a crisis of class, signifying as it does at a second-order level the inability of Stan to fulfill his duties as a man precisely because of the enervating emasculation of his entrapment within the workplace. Stan is alienated from his labor as he is alienated from his family; yet the family stands as the bulwark against Stan's near total estrangement from

himself, his family, and social reality itself. It is the familial discourses that emerge from history and from the Black South in the form of folkways, sayings, and invocations of a past life that form the thin thread preventing Stan's complete dislocation. While they are sitting together in the kitchen, Lacey asks Stan: "When was the last time you been in church?" Stan replies: "Back home. Ever since then I've done a lot of things but I haven't done nothing yet that would make the devil blush." These are by no means wholly resistant—and Stan's son's invocation of "mot dear" is seen as a troubled and disrespectful abuse of the terms—but it is there, nonetheless, as a pattern of saying and seeing that is, at least in part, outside of the system of capitalist modernity as the traces of that other—Southern, agrarian, simpler—life keep intruding through the fabric of the hypermodernity of life in Los Angeles. As Jeffrey Skoller's essay demonstrates, those shards and specters of the historical and geographical past intrude on the apparent spatiotemporal contemporaneity of this hypermodern megalopolis as the characters are largely excluded from participation in the processes of consumerism. Though Stan functions as brute labor in his daily life, Gene and Lacey are excluded even from that involvement in the capitalist production, and none of them partake as consumers. As David E. James explains, this outsidedness is accentuated by the spatial and geographical boundaries of Watts. This, in turn, is further emphasized by the old-fashioned entertainments that structure the social lives of both children and adults, from the little girl playing dress up with the doll, to the trip to the horse races, the grown-ups dicing at the party, and, perhaps most evocatively, the child's spinning top. Though he is both alienated and enervated, nevertheless it is to the family that Stan always returns, and it is the family that offers what little comfort he appears to derive. In this way, the film appears to suggest that, against the vagaries and imperatives of capitalist production, survival and the raison d'être for life itself are to be found in the family. The term *Black family* has a curious dysfunctionality in American culture, especially in a post–World War II media landscape that has consistently portrayed this unit in extremely circumscribed ways related almost ubiquitously to poverty, crime, and deprivation. In short, the Black family becomes something that is by definition broken and in need of rehabilitation. In keeping with the cultural labor performed by all manner of Black representations across the American landscape, frequently even the most well-meaning analyses and assessments of the social problems of race have served to pathologize the

Black family by constituting it solely as an object of examination, dissection, and diagnosis. On the surface it might appear that *Killer of Sheep* is trafficking in this same kind of "social problem" narrative. True enough, Burnett refuses to shy away from representing the day-to-day privations of diminished material circumstances or indeed the perniciousness with which poverty, as a condition of life, is able to bore its way into the most intimate spheres of interpersonal and domestic life. And yet, *Killer of Sheep* is a testament to the fact that the characters are the consequence rather than the cause of such conditions. This is not a film about moral failing but of the systemic failures of a social democratic market capitalism, we would argue, as it relates to an alienated and enervated urban working and (lumpen) underclass. It is, further, a film that demonstrates that in spite of the inordinate difficulties, pressures, and instabilities to which it is subject, the Black family powerfully endures with a dignity absent from mainstream cultural representations.

- Our fourth organizing principle within the film is the relationship between the individual and the community. In consideration of this, we assert that in *Killer of Sheep*, the strength of the family resides with women. Stan's wife appears not only as the moral center of the family but, in some distinctive ways, of the entire narrative of the film. That she remains unnamed throughout is, thus, an interesting anomaly. This refusal to individuate her through naming could be read as deeply marginalizing. However, we would suggest that in his refusing to name her, Burnett signifies her function as an archetype of the strong-willed and deeply principled matriarch who exists at the cultural and historical center of Black American life. In this sense, Stan's wife can simultaneously occupy two distinct narrative roles—that of the fictional character within the story of the film and that of a larger emblematic role outside the frame, within the broader context of historical actuality. Written within this gesture toward a shared history of the endurance of Black womanhood is also a history of the gendered link between the family and the broader community. The film articulates this in a number of interesting ways, not least of which is its representation of the nexus between the individual and community that is mediated by gender. Most notably, in the film's penultimate scene, a young woman is brought into a supportive and welcoming community of "elders" who react with unreserved joy about the new life she is to bring by her pregnancy into this tight-knit, loving, and life-affirming community. This sense of female solidarity stands apart from that of the

Fig. I.5

men, who are much more likely to interact in pairs and in violent settings (in its myriad forms) (fig. I.5.) as the most frequent determining conduit for their interactions. These distinctions drawn by Burnett point to a further tension between gender and community that is more critically focused on the male characters, for whom self-involved needs inevitably trump the broader community's wellbeing. This is rendered apparent by the pair of hoods who attempt, as noted earlier, to suborn Stan as a participant in their scheme to rob and murder. At the same time, Burnett employs this moment in an interestingly contradictory way. Though Stan refuses their entreaties, there is an implied understanding that, notwithstanding Stan's objections to their scheme, he would never betray them even as he refuses to take part himself.

- This critical relationship that pertains between the individual and the community is expressed most powerfully through Burnett's choice of sheep as the structuring metaphor of the film, our fifth organizing principle (fig. I.6). The complex multiplicity of relations, reactions, and resistances that inhere in *Killer of Sheep* are centered on this most potent cultural signifier. In seeking to address Burnett's

Fig. I.6

use of the image of the sheep, even the most cursory consideration reveals the pervasive and commonplace presence of sheep within our language universe. We speak of lambs to the slaughter, we count sheep to sleep, we might as well get hanged for a sheep as a lamb, and, of course, there is the ever-persistent baleful presence of the black sheep. Consider, too, how in biblical terms, sheep signify innocence and passivity, though perhaps more importantly for our purposes, they are social creatures who coexist without preying on each other, although of course they, too, have a hierarchy and possess the herd instinct to simply follow. Clearly, Burnett wants to signify by the title of the film and more specifically by selecting sheep rather than other animals, say chickens, pigs, cows, that we consume and with which, as humans in the industrialized world, we have a similar relationship. Thus, the immediacy and familiarity of the sheep in popular discourse make it a particularly useful and powerful image. The sheep embodies and expresses a myriad of discourses that carry the burden of history for Black America, including the notion of an internal colony corralled in a designated space of containment for slaughter, Black-on-Black violence, the absence of class consciousness or any direct challenge to oppression, the oppressive and alienating nature of surplus labor within capitalist relations, and the nature of innocence, experience, and redemption. Burnett's political deployment of this metaphor, then, is complicated. We can read it as a call for a sense of communal responsibility upon which the common good and indeed survival of the group depend and a rejection of the forces of individualism and predation on others. Those forces of predation are represented most strongly by the two hoods and the White grocery store owner, whose drive is not for survival of the broader community but for individual survival through the accumulation of power through the extraction of surplus. At the same time, it must be acknowledged that as a potent and multivalent symbol, a counter-reading leads us to the sheep as representing inertia and lack of agency, and as such Burnett may very well be pointing to a problematic that asserts a seeming passivity of the Black community in relation to capitalism, class hierarchy, and racism, that suggests it is not dissimilar to that of the sheep whose fate is to be literally consumed as the Black community's labor is consumed for others in the food chain. In other words, the sheep's commodification, literal slaughter, and consumption within the marketplace functions as a mirror for the material exploitation of the Black community's labor as it too is absorbed and exploited within the system of market capitalism. The profitable rendering of the live bodies of the sheep into carcasses to be consumed becomes another powerful metaphor for the functioning of the Black body, speaking to its literal as well as metaphorical death. This reading demands that we accept, then, that the sheep Stan slaughters evoke Black complicity in their own grim fate. But, as always with Burnett, it is neither that simple nor that straightforward. The endurance of Stan and the broad panoply of characters who populate this world refute any simplistic characterization of them solely as victims. Even the two hoods, notwithstanding the misguided criminal nature of their intentions, are refusing to accept their designation as victims in their efforts to assume an autonomous power over the immediate material circumstances of their own lives. That this might then fold back into an abdication of any kind of responsibility to their community, thus allowing the exploitation of Black America to continue at the systemic level and serving to even further disempower them on the individual level, is again illustrative of that complexity and contradiction that are nuanced features of Burnett's work. One of Burnett's chief concerns throughout his career, and most evident in *Killer of Sheep*, is that of the Black child's relationship to adulthood.

Fig. I.7

Watts in the mid-1970s is a world in which children, as they grow to maturity, are defined by ever more limited options. Stan's son is a case in point that illustrates the child's ill-defined vision and performance of adult masculinity. In the violence of his environs, will he become just another alienated worker like his father, or will he turn to crime, as his still-innocent playing morphs to regression and violence in the truncated experience of the world he inhabits? Perhaps it is the sheep that tells us most clearly and distressingly of what fate has in store for him (fig. I.7).

* * *

With these five organizing principles as a working model for analysis, we next turn to situating *Killer of Sheep* in correspondence with the formal, aesthetic, and political concerns of the neorealist tradition in cinema. The film's emergence out of the LA School and its resistance to Hollywood aesthetic and narrative conventions have meant that historians and critics have been drawn (perhaps inevitably) into situating *Killer of Sheep* in social and cinematic contexts outside of the American mainstream. The most frequent and dominant mode of those contextual readings has been that of Italian neorealism. There is a good deal of debate about both the origins and characteristics of neorealism. Though it is most usually understood as having emerged in 1945 with Roberto Rosselini's *Roma città aperta* (*Rome, Open City*), Susan Hayward suggests that it was in fact Luchino Visconti's 1942 release, *Ossessione* (*Obsession*), that was "the herald of this movement."²⁹ As with all distinct styles, frequently the "rules" of neorealism were more honored in the breach than the observance, and it was a term that evolved to comfortably embrace films as distinct from one another as Vittorio de Sica's *Ladri di biciclette* (*Bicycle Thieves*, 1948) and Visconti's *Senso* (1954). Nevertheless, it largely conformed to a set of recognizable working precepts: the negotiation of the everyday material realities of working-class life in postwar Italy (and by extension the rest of Europe). In formal stylistic terms, this meant the invocation of a kind of documentary sensibility obtained by the use of grainy black-and-white film stock, nonprofessional actors, naturalistic dialogue and lighting, and local settings and a focus on the quotidian. This formal aesthetic strategy was deployed in order to portray as realistically as possible the social and material reality of a proletarian existence, mired in poverty, pessimism, and despair, as well as the failure of the bureaucratic state apparatus to address all and any associated social problems. As a set of discursive formulations, the politics and poetics of neorealism was not cynical, but rather expressed the fundamental "truth" that the industrial worker under capitalism is always, and of systemic necessity, subject to powerfully oppressive economic and bureaucratic forces far beyond their control.

In considering the employment of a documentary-like verisimilitude as a mode of representation that foundationally structures the social realist text as an authentic expression of the life of "the people," it makes perfect sense for readings of *Killer of Sheep* to assert that "Burnett turned to Italian neo-realism, for its aesthetic as well as sociological qualities,"³⁰ that "stylistically and visually, *Killer of Sheep* shares much in common with Italian neo-realist productions,"³¹ and that "*Killer of Sheep* is a masterpiece of . . . neo-realism."³² Indeed, Paula Massood's trenchant essay analyzes the film's relationship to neorealism and its documentary impulse, testing the extent to which *Killer of Sheep* might be classified as an example of a neorealist text. Massood's conclusion is that though the correspondences between the two are profound, there is an ambivalence at the heart of a neorealist reading tending, as it does, toward that other radical and resistant cinematic form to emerge out of the 1960s, Third Cinema. However, while there may be aesthetic and even political congruities between *Killer of Sheep* and the fundamentals and trajectories of such films as *Barren Lives* (Nelson Pereira dos Santos, 1963), *The Battle of Algiers* (Gillo Pontecorvo, 1966), and *The Hour of the Furnaces* (Fernando Solanas and Octavio Getino, 1968), these similarities serve to elide the central principle of Third Cinema's call to mobilization and action. Like other neorealist films, while *Killer of Sheep* points—with often surgical precision—to societal problems, it offers no direct call for systematic change either within or without the frame. It is Massood's concentration on the documentary tradition that is perhaps more insistently imperative and something to which we shall return as we argue that though the Italian neorealist context is important, it is no more so than the emergence of British social realism in the 1960s and the Free Cinema documentary movement that preceded it.

Further, *Killer of Sheep*—this most "European" of American films—frequently and consistently disrupts the generic conventions of neorealism in complex and fascinating ways. Its utilization of soundtrack music is largely diegetic, although it frequently also functions extra-diegetically in a classical Hollywood style; though it employs much of the visual language of neorealism, it simultaneously roots itself in the semi-magical—the children at play, the dog mask, the root spirituality of the pregnant woman, the invocation of ancient wisdoms from the South and the past—from a preindustrial and bucolic world. As Bishetta D. Merritt puts it, "the characters in *Killer of Sheep* . . . have one step in the rural south and one in modern Los Angeles."[33] In its subtle invocations of the pastoral, this expresses a kind of inchoate subcutaneous resistance to the urban. Stan himself is a profoundly ambivalent character caught between agrarian Southern roots (frequently though obliquely invoked throughout) and the hyper-modernity of the Los Angeles from which he is excluded. Stan and his family lead what we might describe as a proto-rural existence—with its folk wisdom, its ties to the animal world for sustenance, and its semi-barter economy—within the boundaries of this futuristic megalopolis that denies them all the possibilities contained in that promise of the future. This ambivalent incongruent situatedness between the pastoral and the urban is reflected in those city spaces that are made rural, such as the empty, concrete fields of open play and the road to the racecourse. Indeed, as David E. James points out in his chapter "Toward a Geo-Cinematic Hermeneutics: Representations of Los Angeles in Non-Industrial Cinema," the spatial locations of *Killer of Sheep* bear almost no trace of the thriving, modern city of Los Angeles at all: "No business districts, no supermarkets, no luxurious high-rise apartment or office buildings, no technicolor sunsets, no homes of the stars." He goes further: "Indeed, there are almost no cars; and those few that are not so permanently disabled that they have been reinvented as street furniture are at best unreliable. And so nothing can happen."³⁴ When modern Los Angeles does intrude, it does so in ways that are aggressive and highly masculine—such as the brutal mechanical efficiency of killing in the slaughterhouse—and in counterpoint to the nurturing feminine embrace of the pastoral as embodied in the memory and folk wisdom of Stan's grandmother. As James Naremore asserts, "One of [Burnett's] recurring themes is the country versus the city, expressed through family traditions or manners that once helped enslaved or segregated communities survive but were later threatened by urban discrimination."³⁵ In considering this connection between the country and the city, it needs to be noted that images of the factory, street, home, and family are constantly intercut, establishing a reciprocal relationship that allows for each to embody the other both metaphorically and metonymically. These distinct spatial and geographic domains share a set of aesthetic and political features so that what takes place in one domain is mirrored, shadowed, reflected in all other domains. They share the same structures and discourses though articulated in the forms appropriate to each of the separate domains. At the same time, each of these domains also expresses qualities that exist outside of the spatio-temporality of the modern city. The empty urban lots of crumbling buildings and the boundary-marking railroad with its occasional engine and lonesome whistle recall and evoke images of the South, with children playing across its empty tracks, while the decrepit interior of Stan's Los Angeles home is not recognizably different from that of a rural shack.

The film's correlation of these sites asserts an aesthetic, political, and social equivalency to be drawn in terms of both class and race. Just as the intimacy of the private home reflects and articulates conditions as they exist on the factory floor, so life for the Black underclass is no different in supposedly cosmopolitan southern California than it is in backward rural southern Mississippi. This mapping of spatial and geographic linkages mirrors that of the linkages between present and past, as it anticipates a future not unlike its present. For Jeffrey Skoller, these "legacies of events from the past actually inhere in the present, invisibly inflecting daily life with a force that is powerfully intangible." The most powerful of these intangible forces from the past, and which remains ever present but never remarked upon, is of course that of slavery, the most Southern, agrarian, and rural of institutions, and it is through "Burnett's formal style of real time observed through the continuous take" that "we are able to sense the specters of [that] past trauma that creates such affect in the present."³⁶

Fig. I.8

Made around the same time as *Killer of Sheep*, Burnett's short film *The Horse* shares similar thematic (if not aesthetic) concerns. Shot in full color, its narrative of a young Black boy waiting for his father to arrive to put down an aging horse is an elegiac and poignant meditation on time and modernity as it simultaneously works as a subtle commentary on the Black American experience. Set in the deep rural countryside, outside of the spatial and architectural markers of modernity, the film's temporality is difficult to place. Similarly, and equally undetermined, is our relation to the characters on the screen. Along with the boy, there are four White men who clearly know each other, though as viewers we have no real sense of who they are or the nature of their specific relationships. As they wait together on the porch of a broken-down shack, the boy remains at a distance from them (fig. I.8). The film's beautifully languorous opening is an extremely long shot in which we see the fields, the shack, and a dusty road along which a pickup truck approaches. In the field we can see a horse and a young boy toward whom strides an older man. We then cut to the shack and meet the White men. The purpose of their gathering together is unspecified, though it emerges incrementally over the course of the film. This indeterminacy

Fig. I.9

is underscored by the fact that the two most significant characters—the boy and his father—are absent from the screen for almost the entirety of the film. They appear in any significant way only toward the film's end, when following the father's arrival and loving embrace with his son, we then shortly register an off-screen gunshot as the father completes his task (fig. I.9).

What is to be made of this enigmatic vignette, with terrible and shocking violence in the context of a glorious pastoral idyll with evening sunshine, fields of undulating grain, and warm, summer languor? It appears especially from a distance in that opening long shot to be a world utterly beautiful, in harmony, and at peace. But the closer we get, the more unsettling it is. The men are edgy. One of them plays a foolishly dangerous game with his knife. The boy is there but separated from them. There is an innocence and gentleness to the boy opposed to the gruff, impatient, and nervous intensity of the White men. The boy leads the old horse lovingly away for his father to kill. In the context of this apparent idyll, the death of the horse is shocking in its straightforward brutality. Further, it is undertaken by a Black man at the behest of the horse's White owner, as the other White men stand, looking on impassively. The horse and the father equate to a single fact, which is their utility and service on behalf of Whites (not unlike the sheep and Stan in *Killer of Sheep*). As with Stan's son in *Killer of Sheep*, Burnett in *The Horse* gestures an implied future in which the lot and station of his father will follow the young boy and thus be reproduced into manhood. In doing so, he is employing a metaphor for Black deferment to serve as the conduits for, as well as the victims of, White devised and directed violence and which might just as well serve as a metaphor for the entirety of the American project in a land that looks so glorious from a distance but up close is marked by the most shocking violence (as to underscore the point recent events of US immigration policy of "zero tolerance" substantiate).

The ambiguities, disjunctions, and contradictions that characterize *The Horse* are reflective of Burnett's insistent drive throughout his career to create films that ask profound questions without necessarily offering any pat or predictable answers in the tradition of Third Cinema. This early short also, and not incidentally, serves as another rejection of the prevalent and attenuated repertoire of images through which Hollywood represented Black America.

* * *

But perhaps most powerfully, notwithstanding the pessimism that a suffocating banality of oppression structures their everyday life as they adjust to rather than mobilize against those forces to which they are subject, there is a deep vein of humor running throughout and a resistance born of their simply continuing and surviving. In this way, we can read *Killer of Sheep* in the tradition of the social realism of the British New Wave of the 1960s and, perhaps even more especially, in the Free Cinema documentary movement that predated it.

Free Cinema emerged out of a series of film screenings put on at the National Film Theatre in London between 1956 and 1959 and featured work by a number of directors who would go on to have significant success as central figures in the "kitchen sink realism" of the so-called British New Wave. There was no great stylistic consistency to the Free Cinema directors, but they possessed a shared desire to make films outside of the influence of major studios. Their focus was very much on everyday working-class experience as evidenced by films such as *Every Day Except Christmas* (Lindsay Anderson, 1957) about traders and laborers at Covent Garden market, *We Are the Lambeth Boys* (Karel Reisz, 1959) about the lives of south London teenagers, and *Enginemen* (Michael Grigsby, 1959) about Manchester railway workers.

Fig. I.10

Free Cinema was made up almost entirely of documentary—a notable exception was Lorenza Mazzetti's *Together* (1956), a fictional narrative about the lives of two deaf-mutes in London's East End—and committed not only to the depiction of realism but deliberately and self-consciously to the depiction of a "poetic realism" of "theatrically inspired stylization."[37] Further, the Free Cinema manifesto stated a "belief in freedom, in the importance of people and in the significance of the everyday."[38] This might in a general sense be a fair way of describing Burnett's own philosophy of cinema, but there is a much closer and more direct relationship to British documentary through Basil Wright. As Ntongela Masilela says, "The poetic realism of the early films of the Los Angeles school, reminiscent of the British documentary film movement of the 1930s . . . is inseparable from the imagination of Burnett. The connection is not coincidental: Wright, a leading figure in the British documentary movement, was one of Burnett's teachers at UCLA in the 1960s, and persuaded Burnett to pursue film studies."[39] Though Masilela is referring to an earlier decade in British filmmaking, the Free Cinema movement of the 1950s drew on the poetic sensibility of the 1930s while rejecting what they saw as filmmakers' class-bound parochialism, and *Killer of Sheep* works as a fascinating amalgam of the poetic sensibility rooted in

Fig. I.11

the 1930s and the starkly realist traditions of the 1950s. The film is replete with examples of the colliding of the grimly realistic and floatingly poetic. Consider the repeated juxtaposition of images of Stan in the slaughterhouse accompanied by its hauntingly beautiful soundtrack or the scenes where Stan's young daughter wears her dog mask (fig. I.11). These scenes play no necessary part in advancing the realist narrative of social deprivation but tell us something deep and moving through the visual poetry of cinematic language of the reality of that existence. Naremore's analysis of the opening scene that "takes on thematic or poetic rather than narrative importance"[40] applies equally in all these instances. But nowhere is this poetic realist sensibility more powerfully expressed than in the scene when Stan and his wife dance slowly together to Dinah Washington's mournful rendition of "This Bitter Earth" (fig. I.12). The camera's meditative stillness, combined with Washington's extraordinary lament, offers a brief moment of intimacy that is profoundly expressive of their relationship but can also stand independently outside of the broader narrative. With an extraordinary economy of visual language, as Stan's wife holds her husband and gently traces with her hands across his naked chest and back, the unshifting camera allows us to perceive this most intimate of moments while never cutting to an invasive close-up. In this way, reflecting the struggle of Stan's estrangement, the

Fig. I.12

camera allows us to be both intimately close and yet simultaneously distant observers. It is giving us an optic into the externalization of Stan's interior life while debunking the view that to the poor and dispossessed, intimacy is lost. This is a critical point to be drawn from Burnett's radical reimagining of the possibilities for representing Black family life on the American screen. The necessity to institutionally determine and delimit the parameters of the "Black family" has been central to the American polity since the founding of the United States by virtue of the fact that it was inseparable from the issue of slavery. Once the Constitution affirmed the legitimacy of slavery, thereby assuring it would form a foundational structure of White nationhood, the familial circumstances of enslaved Africans was wholly determined by that same resolution. In its prohibitions on marriage and indifference to the separation of family members, slavery was designed to facilitate the wholesale destruction of the Black family. Indeed, as the abolitionist movement gained ground through the first half of the nineteenth century, one of its principle attacks on the "peculiar institution" was precisely that its tearing apart of mothers from children, husbands from wives, and siblings from siblings was an affront to the notion of "family" as asserted in the Christian Bible.

Whether from the perspective of the pernicious racism of slaveholders of the early nineteenth century or the most well-meaning of liberal commentators of the late twentieth century, this instituting of the Black family as a "problem" to be dealt with has remained a constant in American life. Perhaps its most famous iteration was in Daniel Patrick Moynihan's landmark publication *The Negro Family: The Case for National Action* (1965), a critical corollary to Lyndon Johnson's War on Poverty program. (See Paula Massood in this volume.) In its influence and intention, the Moynihan Report is both emblematic and instructive of the broader social problems of poverty, deprivation, and benign neglect suffered disproportionately by Black Americans; as it did its work of sociological investigation, it reaffirmed the Black family as a problem to be solved and retrenched its ubiquitous availability for examination, dissection, diagnoses, and assessment to White audiences. The constituent feature of this pathologizing of Black life is that, both implicitly and explicitly, the right to privacy is stripped away. This assumed right to look into the intimate interiority of pathologized Black life has its own corollary in the criminalization of blackness and the fundamental loss of privacy that is the structural feature of carceral disciplinary regimes. The consequences of structural and systemic racism, then, become situated almost entirely within the social and economic environments. The sensitivity with which Burnett presents Stan dancing with his wife foregrounds the profound intimacy, as affirming as it is redemptive, of the moment and jolts us into an awareness and acknowledgment of the fact that racism can perform its most pernicious and venal work at the very heart of the most intimate of relationships.

In this way, *Killer of Sheep* shares something with Michael Roemer's *Nothing But a Man* (1964) in that it strives to capture the interiority of an invidiously intrusive system that insinuates itself into the most human sentiments and practices of everyday life. As Naremore puts it, the film dramatizes the "quotidian struggles of a working-class Black family, its attempts to reproduce itself and raise its children against almost impossible odds."[41] Again as with Roemer's own neorealist examination of Black life in America, and again unlike Third Cinema, *Killer* contains no explicit reference to the broader political landscape of the time or indeed the pervasive and pernicious legacies of slavery and Jim Crow, and there are no overt gestures toward racism as an explicit motive force. But, of course, it is present implicitly in every frame of the film. The forces of oppression and violence are arrayed not in the presence of racist cops on the streets, but on the fields of interiority. And arrayed in these arenas, it is those interior spaces of subjectivity where the struggle is undertaken at its most difficult and profound.

It is in this sense that we might think of *Killer of Sheep* as in the Gramscian tradition, rooted as it is in a sociopolitical analysis determined by culture as much as it is by economics, unlike the more rigid materialist/economic reading of society that de Sica offers us in *Bicycle Thieves*. And while we can read *Killer of Sheep* as a film about oppression in ways similar to *Bicycle Thieves*, it is also (unlike *Bicycle Thieves*) a film about the utterly quotidian, and yet extremely powerful, ordinariness of resistance.

* * *

As alluded to earlier, the critical mass of analysis undertaken on *Killer of Sheep* clearly centers on its neorealist credentials and its determination to address and correct the ubiquity of Hollywood's misrepresentations of Black characters and life. While central to understanding the aesthetic and political dimensions of the film, it has at the same time meant the elision of one of the film's most fundamental undertakings, which we noted above is its complicated and often contradictory representations of gender. Just as Burnett's project in *Killer of Sheep* was, at least in part, an effort to redress the egregious misrepresentations of race in Hollywood cinema, so too was it an effort to problematize and locate the issue of gender within the larger frame of class oppression under those social and economic conditions determined by capitalism. Though some critics have addressed the issue tangentially within other arguments, the largely understudied and unremarked factor of masculinity, we argue, is equally central to the film's aesthetic discourse, modes of address, and representational strategy. And fundamental to this dynamic is the critical centrality of violence as it relates to the structures of masculinity that permeate *all* structures of social, cultural, and economic life.

From the very first moment of the film's opening scene of the young boy roundly slapped by his mother as his father intones "you will soon be a goddamn man!," masculinity is defined and yet problematized throughout. Indeed, Stan's interior life is adumbrated by his inability to perform masculinity, what Richard Brody calls the "idea and impossible ideal of being a man."[42] Two centrally traditional arenas in which the masculine ideal could be exercised and realized are rendered unavailable to Stan; he is unable to engage in any significant or sustained sexual intimacy with his wife and his function as the breadwinner for his family provides him with a job that is deeply enervating. Death is the corrosive element at the heart of his profound ennui. Stan must of necessity kill in order to stay alive, as it were, literally as well as figuratively. As "both the butcher and the butchered,"[43] he is victim of what Nathan Grant contends is a "miasma" of "disaffection for everything he had previously come to know as real, as genuine" and, as a consequence, a series of "emasculations effected from without."[44] Stan's relationship, then, to violence is complicated and contradictory as it fundamentally structures negotiations of social relations, family dynamics, and the workplace.

In "The Turning Point of Who Shall Be Master: *Killer of Sheep*, Naming, Gender, and the Gaze of African American Women," Sean Davis Watkins argues that Burnett, "while challenging the stereotypes of black men," unintentionally "demonstrates the lack of recognition that women faced in domestic, activist, and employment spheres," and in so doing, "Burnett conspicuously reifies the relegation of women into that silent and domestic sphere."[45] However, though it may be true that the film situates women largely in the domestic sphere (there is one notable exception), they are by no means rendered silent. Indeed, as the film engages with more normative notions of masculinity, it presents an inversion of conventional Hollywood representations in depicting a social and cinematic world populated by agential women who refute dominant stereotypes. Male power is almost always exercised through violence, and we sometimes see women behaving on occasion in similar ways, though always toward men and never other women. They also on occasion perform masculinity, from the mother at the beginning slapping the young boy across the face to the woman who takes a gun to her feckless boyfriend (fig. I.13a) or the teenage girls who maul the boy on his bicycle (fig. I.13b).

Nowhere is this "inversion" more pronounced than in the character of the White woman who owns the local grocery store. She is overbearing and aggressive toward her Black male employee, who appears intimidated as he is pushed back from the counter to make way for her. Unable to authorize the cashing of a check, he must perforce defer to her. In this same scene, the woman flirts with Stan, lasciviously caressing his arm and wrist as she promises to protect him should he choose to work for her. This discomfiting scene not only pointedly establishes sex as a currency of exchange but in doing so also refutes the trope of the Black male as sexual aggressor, as it inverts the expected male/female dynamic and reaffirms the expected racial

Killer of Sheep | 29

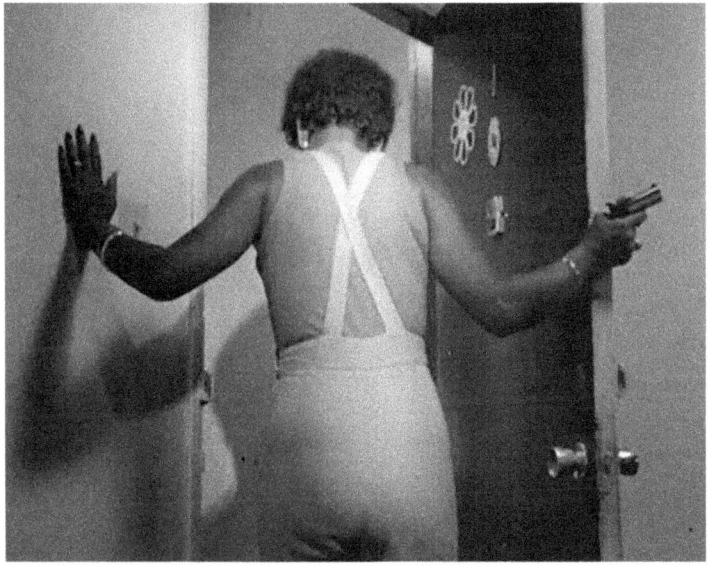

Fig. I.13(a–b)

dynamic in which Whites assert social and sexual power over Blacks. In that sense, it cannot be understood outside of both the broader contexts of American history of miscegenation and blaxploitation's reliance upon the aggressive sexuality of the Black buck evoked in such films as *Mandingo* (1975) that centralized the buck figure as an object of sexual desire for White women.

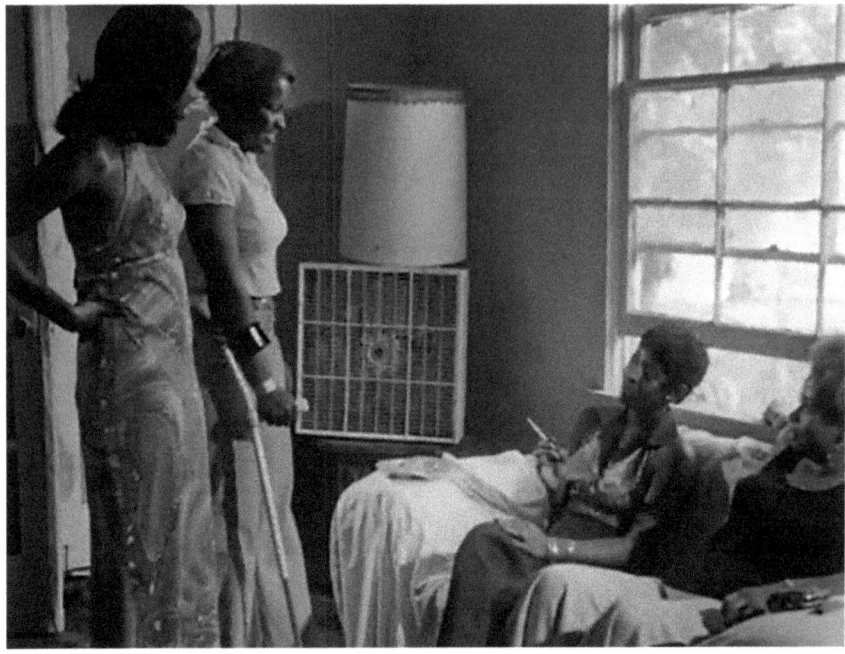

Fig. I.14

But this is not some trite assertion that the world is inverted because women—Black and White—are somehow being transformed into men. While men appear largely ineffectual throughout the film—the repeated progenitors of hapless ideas and aborted schemes, constantly fixing things that can never be fixed—women's power assumes multiple forms as they stand outside of Hollywood's overdetermined frames of Black feminine representation. In the film's penultimate scene, when the young woman comes to the house to announce that she is pregnant, it is hard not to read the scene as a vision of a compelling and powerful female life force, shared among a community of other women, taking joy in the pregnancy and the new life it anticipates (fig. I.14). As might be expected, Burnett complicates this by having this scene of powerful feminine life-giving joy before immediately crossfading to Stan in the slaughterhouse, the only place in which he is able to exercise his masculine duty, which is one of killing and destruction.

The film's most powerful female figure is of course Stan's wife. The first time we see her is as a figure of authority and disapproval, standing in the kitchen door and filling the frame, with Stan looking small in the medium

Killer of Sheep | 31

Fig. I.15

distance and filling the top left-hand corner of the screen. But the critical point at which the multiple discourses of gender, masculinity, and violence collide is when the two hoods come to Stan in an effort to persuade him to join them in a robbery, searching as they are for someone who "wouldn't blush to murder" (fig. I.15). Though Stan is angry and insulted and refuses to become a party to their scheme, it is his wife who decisively intervenes. With Stan shoeless and seated on the stoop and the two hoods dressed in black leather jackets standing over him, his wife, framed by the screen door in back, emerges from the house: "Why you always wanna hurt somebody?" One of the men replies, "That's the way nature is. I mean, an animal has his teeth and a man has his fists. That's the way I was brought up." Stan is being offered a redemptive masculinity—abominable though it is—while his wife upbraids the hoodlums, furiously asserting that there's more to being a man than "just using your fists." In this exchange, Burnett's camera shifts from a medium shot of Stan's house with him in the frame, sitting on the stoop with his wife, and the two hoods standing in front of him (fig. I.16a), to a closer shot of only the hoods and Stan's wife (fig. I.16b). In the next shot,

Fig. I.16(a–b)

Fig. I.16c

Stan's wife has shifted to now entirely obscure Stan (fig. I.16c). We know he is present, but he is rendered invisible behind his wife, who continues to argue with the hoods about what it means to be a man. She then turns to Stan—who we still can't see—and says, "Are you going to sit here and let them do this?" As Nathan Grant puts it, "For Stan, who sits on his stoop in despair and confusion, the challenge from his friend—'Be a man, Stan, if you can'—is layered with levels of indeterminacy that practically demand someone come to his rescue."[46] That person is his wife. In this way, the camera speaks of and to the politics of gender and renders Stan figuratively, as well as literally, invisible.

In engaging with gender in this way, Burnett is grappling with what it means to be a man. In doing so, he is offering two compelling and entirely contradictory readings. One interpretation might be that though Stan is beaten down, and struggling, and in constant existential crisis, Burnett is suggesting that Stan is, arguably, a hero in many ways. Just as Samuel Beckett's anonymous, eponymous narrator in *The Unnamable* says, "You must go on. I can't go on. I go on," Stan goes on. His heroism here is essentially rooted in the heroism of postwar existentialism and a perseverance in the

Fig. I.17

face of a meaningless and oftentimes malevolent universe, the systemic power of which is seemingly overwhelming (with the parallels to race in America all too obvious). Crushed by a life "as bounded by invisible threads of hopelessness as that of the sheep he slaughters each day,"[47] Stan nevertheless endures and persists. This is his heroism, and it is in the act of perseverance that Stan's being as a man is to be found and signified.

Another reading, however, is to suggest that a hero is to be engaged against the circumstance of their oppression; to act with intent to alter the conditions in which one endures. To endure is to invoke the silence of the sheep before and during their slaughter rather than struggle against it. Such is the character of Duff, who in *Nothing But a Man* (1964) resolves to return with his son to wife Josie in the violence of where they reside, saying to Lee at the grave site of his father, "I guess I'll make me some trouble in that town" (fig. I.17).[48] In this sense we must be drawn to reading Stan as at least partially complicit in his own circumstances. His refusal or inability to act renders him politically impotent, a state that mirrors of course the enervation of his sexual potency and energies.

* * *

Killer of Sheep is a profoundly—and self-consciously—contradictory text, not least in the way that it is at once artfully poetic in its imagery while simultaneously starkly realist. Nowhere are the contradictions and paradoxes more deeply emphasized than scenes in which Burnett deploys the juxtaposition of sound and image. As has been commented upon by numerous critics and reviewers, Burnett's use of music in *Killer of Sheep* is of absolutely critical importance and is striking in its power to both delineate and confound. Indeed, the music in the film is, as Naremore argues, "as important as imagery."[49] As Keith Mehlinger's chapter elucidates, the formal structure of the film is fundamentally rooted in music, with its neorealist aesthetic sharing with blues music "the visceral power of both modalities [in] their universal themes of human struggle." In further consideration of the formal and material qualities of Burnett's "lo-fi" 16mm feature, Mehlinger pushes the formalist analogy even further as he "liken[s] the experience of watching this film to that of listening to a vinyl LP with all the pops and scratches in the right places." Its layered structuring throughout serves as a recurrent mode of ironization in its constant employment as distanced and knowing commentary on the scenes in which it appears. An obvious example of this is the scene in which Paul Robeson's haunting rendition of "What Is America to Me?" is employed to contrast the lofty ideals contained within the lyrics with the material reality of Black life in America, as we watch the unknowing children at play (fig. I.18a). This scene is mirrored by an immediate and sharp cut to the slaughterhouse, with sheep quietly awaiting their fate as Robeson now sings "Going Home" (fig. I.18b). Mehlinger argues that this constant use of music as a suture between scenes—a series of match cuts through audio—echoes the call-and-response of early blues, thus helping to further concentrate the aesthetic and political and ideological spatiotemporal linkages discussed above.

Structured as it is by the ubiquitous juxtaposition of image and sound, there is a constant dialectic at work through the collision of race and class, class and gender, race and gender. But we can think beyond the dialectic to a trialectic, with each of those discursive categories unable to be understood outside of its complex defining relationship to the others. Contradiction is built into this triangulation, demanding as it does an acknowledgment that our understanding is never rooted in either/or but always each/also. At the center of it all, and characteristic of Burnett's unending impetus to "embrace contradiction ... enthusiastically,"[50] is the profound counterpoint evinced between Stan's gentle character and the terrible violence of his job.

The relationship between Stan and the horrifying violence of his work points to a fundamental contradiction at the heart of *Killer of Sheep*, as mentioned above, and one incidentally that furthers Burnett's connection to the British social realist tradition, that this is a film that is simultaneously

Fig. I.18(a–b)

about race and yet somehow not about it. In other words, it is present in every frame and yet remains unremarked. It is a film about class—race intrudes most obviously during the scene in the liquor store when Stan gets a check cashed—but otherwise race in the form of blackness is an a priori state. It simply *is*. The situatedness of race in this way moves the spectator unexpectedly, in that the film (as part of its broader resistant strategy) foregrounds our self-consciousness of race as we bring it to bear on the screen. In other words, all the markers of blackness that we might expect to see in a mainstream Hollywood "Black" film are absent, and the specific circumstances of what it means to be Black in America are never articulated or expressed. We are left with having to consider our own assumptions and expectations in relation to what is presented within the frame.

To reiterate, in *Killer of Sheep*, the most powerful and explicitly articulated significations are that of class, not only in terms of the representation of material circumstances but in conversations around the nature of poverty and work. This is expressed most pointedly in the scene when Stan reacts indignantly to his friend Bracy's teasing accusation that Stan thinks he is middle-class: "Hey, I ain't poor! I give things away to the Salvation Army and you can't give things away to the Salvation Army if you're poor." Stan tells Bracy that if he wants to "see somebody's who's poor" he should "go around look at Walter ... sitting over an oven with nothing but a coat ... eating nothing but wild greens picked out of a vacant lot." This exchange is at once desperately sad and mordantly comic. (One wonders, for instance, to whom Walter would send us if he wanted us to see who is *really* poor.) This deformed notion of class consciousness is worked through repeatedly and often in similarly darkly comic form; each comic set piece again relies on contradiction and inversion in turn. Consider the scene in which two young men are escaping with a stolen television and the ways in which the scene switches constantly and artfully between the genuine discomfort and threat felt by the old man witnessing the theft and the comic ineptitude of the burglars; consider also the bathetic comic inversion of the scenes in which Stan and Gene purchase a car engine only to see it fall from their truck as soon as they leave with it (figs. I.19a, I.19b, I.19c, and I.19d) or the deftly constructed comic contradictions when some of the characters, dressed in their Sunday best and heading to the racecourse for the day, must return defeated and deflated when Gene's car gets a flat. But the best example of this employment of comic contradiction and paradox comes with the visual gag where we see a group of people sitting in a car outside of the grocery

Fig. I.19(a–d)

Fig. I.19(a–d) (*continued*)

Fig. I.20(a–b)

store. We suddenly see the person in the passenger seat just lean through where the front windshield should be and grab a can of beer that had been sitting on the hood. The gag works because of our assumption that there was glass where the windshield should be. We see one thing, but suddenly, in a compelling visual joke, the film reveals our assumption to be illusory and, through this contradiction, shows us entirely the opposite (figs. 1.20a and 1.20b). Not only is the car obviously one of the most powerful cultural signifiers in American life, its history entwined with that of the discourses of modernity, progress, and utopian visions of the American dream, but, by virtue of that very fact, it carries an especially compelling symbolic charge in *Killer of Sheep*. And Burnett returns repeatedly to the car as a trope of underdevelopment as well as disrepair. Much of the film is spent with various of the characters trying to fix cars, adjust them, and get them working again, all of which result in failure. The scene described above, when Stan, Gene, Lacey, and their wives attempt a day out at the racecourse, is, then, simultaneously both comic and deeply serious. With the car limping along on a rim, thus denying them the utilization of this most quotidian of American symbols of freedom and movement, the equally quotidian dream of escape from the drab reality of everyday life is denied them.

* * *

As with that classic of British social realism, Mike Leigh's *Kes* (1969), in which a young kestrel is employed in multiple ways simultaneously as the embodiment of freedom, youth, and hope as well as cruelty, imprisonment, and ultimately, as the symbol of hope crushed, *Killer of Sheep*'s characters possess much greater reserves of resistance than mere sheep. Similarly, the use of sheep as a metaphor is equally contradictory. Though Naremore argues that the film "implicitly compares the children in Watts with the sheep going to slaughter,"[51] it is surely more complicated than that. Are the children really just powerless victims? Is Stan? His wife? His friends? It is another pertinent example of the need to avoid a binary reading. The slaughter of innocents may be one way to read the metaphor, but it is contradicted at every turn by multiple other forms, not least of which are those powerful biblical resonances related to innocence and slaughter that perhaps return us to our earlier discussion about the Southern Baptist tradition, folkways, and the rural/urban dichotomy.

The central importance of the image of the child is intimately connected to the central importance of the image of the sheep. There are obvious corollaries between the two, united perhaps most obviously in their cultural labor as embodiments of innocence. But other animals are present in myriad other and no less interesting relationships to the children. Not least is the scene in which the young boys on their bikes in the street are suddenly and viciously attacked by two dogs (fig. I.22). This jarring moment serves to remind us again that the children are undertaking two important functions in the narrative. They allow us to witness the play of untouched

Fig. I.21

innocence, but they simultaneously function as a kind of knowing chorus, a prism through which the troubled, tainted, corrupted world of adulthood is brought into the grimmest and starkest relief. In this way, the children, these "silent, sometimes amused witnesses,"[52] embody the contradictions that run throughout the film in all forms.

The most striking "silent witness" among the children is Stan's daughter, who repeatedly and literally just stands and watches while wearing a dog mask. Considering the central importance of animals within the political, thematic, and formal structure of the film, this is surely no coincidence. The boundary established between human and animal in the slaughterhouse is aggressively policed, with the extreme violence employed by Stan and the other workers being a dramatic assertion of the complete otherness of the sheep. Stan's daughter's wearing of the dog mask presents a collapsing of this boundary, a crossing point between the human and the animal that perforce troubles those categorical definitions of difference upon which the human racial subject is predicated. That race is by definition otherness, this cannot help but speak to the ontological status of blackness and whiteness. But in doing so, it equally cannot help but to assert the fundamentally

Fig. I.22

unstable nature of those categories, pointing to their essence as performed identities. With her innocence as yet seemingly untrammeled by the privations and predations of class and race, Stan's daughter is able to play with those categories in a way that the adults surrounding her are unable or unwilling to do. In our turn, we cannot help but think of the deep ontological crises of Ralph Ellison's invisible man who survives, indeed thrives, of the very malleability of racial categorization as he aggressively and deliberately plays with his identity and subjectivity, deploying his own masks for strategically resistant purposes. The child's gazing into the camera (at us) behind the mask is an expression of her visible invisibility. It also echoes the gaze of the sheep, which, in Sarah O'Brien's chapter, functions as the "starting point" for her analysis of the film. As she puts it, *Killer of Sheep*'s "distinctive engagement with a constellation of boundaries—between sound and image, waking and dreaming life, human and animal—works to loosen the visual field"[53] to allow us to make increasingly complex connections between the visual, spatial, and discursive fields upon which both humans and animals exit. It is also, and most importantly, yet another instance of Burnett's making contradiction and paradox central to our understanding of his film.

Notes

1. Joining the works of other notable directors with multiple selections, such as Alfred Hitchcock, Billy Wilder, Spike Lee, and Martin Scorsese, Burnett's 1990 feature, *To Sleep with Anger*, was selected for inclusion on the National Film Registry in 2017.
2. The fact that *Killer of Sheep* was completed in 1973 but not screened publicly until 1977 means that, depending on the specific source, both dates are sometimes used to denote the year of the film's production. The editors of this volume have not altered the individual authors' usage.
3. Michel Martin, interview with Charles Burnett broadcast on National Public Radio (NPR), October 17, 2007.
4. Cliff Thompson, "The Devil Beats His Wife: Small Moments and Big Statements in the Films of Charles Burnett," *Cineaste* 23, no. 2 (1997): 24–27.
5. Tre'vell Anderson, *LA Times*, November 9, 2017.
6. Dave Kehr, "Shadows of Watts in the Light," *New York Times*, March 25, 2007.
7. In his article "Charles Burnett Honored for Black Misery," *National Review*, November 15, 2017, Armond White argues that the honorary Oscar bestowed on Burnett was not a sincere effort to laud the brilliance of his work but yet another "attempt to make film culture's liberal racists feel good about themselves" and, as such, was "an offense to Burnett's seriousness and genuine artistry."
8. Bernard Weinraub, "A Film Director Collects Honors, but Not Millions," *New York Times*, January 30, 1997.
9. Martin, interview with Burnett, 2007.
10. John Patterson, *The Guardian*, September 18, 2004.
11. Sukhdev Sandu, "Charles Burnett: We Thought that Killer of Sheep Could Help to Change the World," *Daily Telegraph*, June 20, 2008.
12. Martin, interview with Burnett, 2007.
13. Michael Sragow, "An Explorer of the Black Mind Looks Back, but Not in Anger," *New York Times*, January 1, 1995.
14. Peter Biskind, *Down and Dirty Pictures: Miramax, Sundance, and the Rise of Independent Film* (New York: Simon & Schuster, 2004).
15. Weinraub, 1997.
16. The recent emergence to prominent critical and commercial success of Black directors such as Barry Jenkins (*Moonlight*), Ava DuVernay (*Selma, 13th, A Wrinkle in Time*), Jordan Peele (*Get Out*), and Ryan Coogler (*Creed, Black Panther*) might suggest that there is some shift taking place within Hollywood as to the general viability of Black creators, voices, and stories. Whether this indicates any permanent reorientation of the mainstream American film industry remains to be seen.
17. Weinraub 1997.
18. Martin, interview with Burnett, 2007, page x.
19. Ibid.
20. Ed Guerrero, *Framing Blackness: The African American Image in Film* (Philadelphia, PA: Temple University Press, 1993), 78.
21. Paula Massood, *Black City Cinema: African American Urban Experiences in Film* (Philadelphia, PA: Temple University Press, 2003), 82.
22. Guerrero 1993, 89.
23. Lerone Bennett was unwilling to concede any radical element to *Sweetback* at all. In his 1971 essay, "The Emancipation Orgasm: Sweetback in Wonderland," he argued that the film

merely replicated images of deprivation associated already ubiquitously with blackness and that, notwithstanding the film's assertions, "nobody ever f***ed his way to freedom." "The Emancipation Orgasm: Sweetback in Wonderland," *Ebony* 6, no. 11 (September 1971): 106–116.

24. Sandhu 2008.

25. Armond White, "Sticking to the Soul," *Film Comment* 33, no. 1 (1997): 38–41.

26. Amy Abugo Ongiri, "Charles Burnett: A Reconsideration of Third Cinema" (chapter 3, this volume).

27. White 1997, 41.

28. Allyson Nadia Field, Jan-Christopher Horak, and Jacqueline Najuma Stewart, eds., *L.A. Rebellion: Creating a New Black Cinema* (Oakland: University of California Press, 2015), 1.

29. Susan Hayward, *Cinema Studies: The Key Concepts* (Abingdon: Routledge, 2000), 201.

30. Joel Karamath, "Black Sheep Blues: Interview with Charles Burnett," *Electric Sheep* (summer 2008): 6–13.

31. Chris Norton, "Black Independent Cinema and the Influence of Neo-Realism," *Images: A Journal of Film and Popular Culture*, no. 5, www.imagesjournal.com/issue05/features/black.htm, accessed April 20, 2018.

32. Monona Wali, "Life Drawings: Charles Burnett's Realism," *The Independent*, October 1986, 18–21.

33. Bishetta D. Merritt, "Charles Burnett: Creator of African American Culture on Film," *Journal of Black Studies* 39, no. 1 (2008): 109–128.

34. David E. James, "Toward a Geo-Cinematic Hermeneutics: Representations of Los Angeles in Non-Industrial Cinema" (chapter 5, this volume).

35. James Naremore, "Killer of Sheep" (chapter 8, this volume).

36. Jeffrey Skoller, "Killer of Sheep" (chapter 9, this volume).

37. Erik Hedling, "Lindsay Anderson and the Development of British Art Cinema," in *The British Cinema Book*, 3rd ed., Robert Murphy, ed. (London: BFI/Palgrave-MacMillan, 2009), 40.

38. Quoted in James Chapman, *A New History of British Documentary* (Basingstoke: Palgrave-MacMillan, 2015), 225.

39. Ntongela Masilela, "The Los Angeles School of Filmmakers," in *Black American Cinema*, Manthia Diawara, ed. (New York: Routledge, 1993), 107–117.

40. Naremore "Killer of Sheep" (chapter 8, this volume).

41. Ibid.

42. Richard Brody, "The Cinematic Blues of Charles Burnett and Billy Woodberry," *New Yorker*, https://www.newyorker.com/culture/richard-brody/the-cinematic-blues-of-charles-burnett-and-billy-woodberry, accessed May 5, 2018.

43. Manhola Dargis, "Whereabouts in Watts? Where Poetry Meets Chaos," *New York Times*, March 30, 2007.

44. Nathan Grant, "Innocence and Ambiguity in the Films of Charles Burnett," in *Representing Blackness: Issues in Film and Video*, Valerie Smith, ed. (London: Athlone Press, 1997), 135–155.

45. Sean Davis Watkins, "The Turning Point of Who Shall Be Master: *Killer of Sheep*, Naming, Gender, and the Gaze of African American Women," unpublished MA thesis, Kennesaw State University, 2016.

46. Grant 1997, 142.

47. Aida A. Hozic, "The House I Live In: An Interview with Charles Burnett," in *Charles Burnett: Interviews*, Robert Kapsis, ed. (Jackson: University Press of Mississippi, 2011) 75–94.

48. See David C. Wall and Michael T. Martin, eds., *The Politics & Poetics of Black Film: Nothing But a Man* (Bloomington: Indiana University Press, 2015), 264.
49. Naremore "Killer of Sheep" (chapter 8, this volume).
50. Terrence Rafferty, "Invisible Man," *GQ* (March 2001): 239–243.
51. Naremore "Killer of Sheep" (chapter 8, this volume).
52. Ibid.
53. Sarah O'Brien, "*Revenons à nos moutons*: Regarding Animals in Charles Burnett's *Killer of Sheep*" (chapter 10, this volume).

PART 1.
SITUATING *KILLER OF SHEEP*: TIME / PLACE / CIRCUMSTANCE

1

CINEMA AND BLACK LIBERATION

David E. James

> Mourn for us sold out and chained to devil pictures.
> *Amiri Baraka*

THE INTEGRAL ROLE OF BLACK ARTS IN THE creation of the natural and national identity that nourished the civil rights and Black Power movements can hardly be overestimated. Though in instances like post-Coltrane jazz, the popular and indeed revolutionary aspirations of the most avant-garde artists may have outstripped their social base,[1] in general, Black dance, theater, writing, and music combined aesthetic and political vanguardism in cultural practices whose origins in popular traditions were reciprocated by their availability for popular use. Distinguishing Black art from that of other races, the similarities and frequent interdependencies between achievements in these different mediums made possible the definition of a specifically Black aesthetic, even as the clarification of the African origins of Afro-American culture made available pragmatic conceptions of art of the kind that have been suppressed by idealist aesthetics in the West since culture became commodified.

The Black aesthetics of the late sixties transcended the split within the Black movement between cultural nationalism and the materialist understanding of the situation of racial minorities within capitalist social formations. They were radical, not because they invoked ironic inversions, stylistic switches undetectable from the outside, subversive adaptations of hegemonic forms, or other formal qualities that reflected ghetto life (though they certainly presupposed these), but because they stressed a populist functionalism.

"Tradition teaches us, Leopold Senghor tells us, that all African art has at least three characteristics: that is, it is functional, collective and committing or committed . . . And by no mere coincidence we find that the criteria is not only valid, but inspiring. That is why we say that all Black art, irregardless of any technical requirements, must have three basic characteristics which make it revolutionary. In brief, it must be functional, collective and committing. . . . Black art must expose the enemy, praise the people and support the revolution."[2] Given the privileged position that, since Lenin, the cinema has occupied in pragmatic aesthetics, it would not have been illogical to anticipate a large investment in the cinema by Black artists in the sixties and the development of film as a Black art, one capable of participating in the creation of a revolutionary Black subject committed to political struggle. But apart from one or two notable exceptions, film played a marginal role in the Black movement, and, if anything, the sixties marked the culmination of the decline of the Black cinema, whether it be defined rigorously in terms of Black control over all stages of production or more generally so as to recognize any Black participation or responsiveness to Black needs.[3] The failure of Black people to develop a film practice responsive to their political needs directly reflects the intrinsic conditions of the medium and its hegemonic use, and it does so in a way that makes that failure exemplary for a materialist understanding of film and of minority cultural interventions generally.

On the one hand, the double integration of the dominant film industry into the institutions of the capitalist state—the contribution of its narrative and formal codes to bourgeois ideological reproduction and its own economic determination as itself a capitalist enterprise—allowed only one role for the proletariat, that of consumer. The industrial function ensured that the lack of representation of Blacks in the cinema would be reciprocated by their lack of representation in film; the imprisonment of Black people as consumers of commodity film culture reproduced their imprisonment in the proletariat.

On the other hand, traditional Black cultural practices were both outside the institutions of cinema and also, characteristically, antipathetic to the conditions of film. As Amiri Baraka pointed out, only those nonmaterial aspects of African culture—"music, dance, religion [that] do not have *artifacts* as their end product"[4]—survived the diaspora and slavery. When these performing arts entered into industrial production, Blacks did successfully engage technology—in popular song, for example. But the general unfamiliarity of film technology and its antipathy to their cultural traditions reinforced the general difficulty the proletariat has in obtaining access to the means of industrial commodity production, making it especially difficult for Blacks to break through that fetishization of advanced technology by which Hollywood naturalizes the industrial practice. It would not have been impossible for Black filmmakers to inflect an avant-garde practice of their own with Black motifs or qualities and thereby to inscribe blackness as a filmic function (as indeed the underground so often had done and as Bill Gunn did to some extent with the anomalous *Ganja and Hess* in 1970); but to make such an endeavor the focus or vehicle of popular resistance would have meant repeating the beats' attempts to wrest a community practice out of industrial functions, at a time of great political urgency and without the resources of a subculture in which film was the privileged medium or in which independent distribution was feasible.

Not until the increased Black enrollment in higher education in the seventies did an ongoing independent Black cinema emerge in university and semi-academic milieus; the work of UCLA film school graduates like Haile Gerima (*Bush Mama*, 1975), Larry Clark (*Passing Through*, 1977), Charles Burnett (*Killer of Sheep*, 1977), Ben Caldwell (*I and I: An African Allegory*, 1977), and Julie Dash (*Four Women*, 1978) typifies the independent momentum and social responsibility attained by what was initially an artificially nursed practice. But, ironically, the increased enrollment of Black students in film schools that generated this alternative film culture followed from the same liberal thrust that had destroyed the only previous instance of a genuinely Black cinema. The liberal commitment to integration that continued the anti-racist rhetoric of the World War II era did produce an increase in the visibility and participation of Black people in the industry; and an industrial genre of Black problem pictures through the mid-sixties, from *A Raisin in the Sun* (1961) and *To Kill a Mockingbird* (1963) to *Guess Who's Coming to Dinner* (1967), preached a reform of race relations on a personal if not a systemic basis. But the gains made as a result of NAACP and government pressure to bring Blacks into the mainstream destroyed what before the war had been a sizable Black feature industry, which, though almost invariably White-financed, was still Black-controlled and in some cases entirely Black-operated for the exclusive patronage of Black people.[5] With the failure of the independent Black production companies after the thirties, subsequent Black cinema was White-funded and almost entirely White-written and White-directed. In this independent cinema, two groups, corresponding to the liberal integrationist and the radical separatist phases of the Black movement, may be distinguished.

The first group developed from the social intersections between the beat subcultures and Black bohemianism, from the attempts by the underground to model film practices on jazz,[6] and from the reformist milieu of the New American Cinema Group; this group of films is best illustrated by Shirley Clarke's *The Cool World* and Michael Roemer and Robert Young's *Nothing But a Man*, both of 1964. The sensitivity and courage of these new-realist dramatizations of Black life in the urban North and the rural South, respectively, exhibit the liberal hope of changing social injustice through knowledge and goodwill. Clarke's use of cinema verité strategies—handheld camera, cutaway shots to details of the environment, rapid and unpredictable editing—for what is mostly a staged drama allows her to texture her story of a Harlem teenager's fall into crime with both the energy and the aimlessness of slum life. The more extended narrative of *Nothing But a Man* details a young Black laborer's attempt to maintain his marriage in the face of systemic and apparently ineluctable racism that attacks all aspects of his life—racism in the prejudice of his bride's middle-class parents, in the virtually complete disintegration of Black family life, and especially in employment, which can be secured only at the price of abject self-negation. Largely unsentimental and free from studio stereotypes, the film demonstrates how racism is useful for capitalism and how it produces sexual violence. In its final depiction of the hero's determination not to allow social forces to destroy his resolution, it looks forward to the Black militance of the next years. Both films fairly represent the prison walls around the Black community, the absence of social opportunity for people trapped in the ghetto, and the psychic damage these inflict. In both, the White world appears as a suffocating horizon peopled by gargoyle caricatures, imprisoning an accurately but sympathetically portrayed Black world that includes models of dignified and courageous Black people. *Nothing But a Man* is especially anomalous—and, in fact, virtually unique—in portraying a Black woman with respect.

Despite their real achievements, both films remain refinements, however more subtle and courageous, of the problem films of the late fifties,[7] their formal limits reproducing the limits of their liberal ideology. They strain the industry's narrative and representational codes, but they cannot pass beyond them any more than they can conceive of alternatives to humanist appeals on behalf of the social plight of the Black people they present as sensitive and courageous but essentially impotent and condemned. They cannot envisage structural social change any more than they can envisage the transcendence of the illusionist narrative film. The importance for the civil rights legislation of the mid-sixties (the Civil Rights Bill of 1964 and the Voting Rights Act of 1965) of the liberal social currents from which these films emerged cannot be overestimated; but the year after they were released, riots in Los Angeles, New York, and Newark and the assassination of Malcolm X revealed a social urgency they could not address.

With the failure of reform to keep pace with the explosion of desire after 1964, integrationist demands and nonviolence gave way to the nationalist aspirations of SNCC and Stokely Carmichael and to the anti-racialist, revolutionary program of the Black Panther Party. As liberal reformism was left behind, films like *The Cool World* and *Nothing But a Man* were no longer ideologically or formally possible. Increasingly militant action demanded the speedy circulation and mass accessibility of the newsreel documentary, but like the Black community at large, the Black Power leaders had neither experience in filmmaking nor access to means of production and distribution. So, continuing a tradition that began with *Troublemakers* (1966), Norman Fruchter and Robert Machover's film about community organizing in the Newark ghetto, radical Black films in the era of the assassination of Martin Luther King Jr., the publication of Eldridge Cleaver's *Soul on Ice*, and riots throughout the country were made by radical White filmmakers.

Exemplary of this tradition were the collaboration of San Francisco Newsreel with the Oakland Black Panther Party on three films (*Black Panther*, 1968; *Mayday*, 1969; and *Interview with Bobby Seale*, 1969); the Los Angeles Newsreel's (finally aborted) project, *Breakfast for Children*; Third World Newsreel's early seventies films about Black prisoners *(Teach Our Children*, 1973, and *In the Event Anyone Disappears*, 1974); and various ad hoc productions of a similar documentary/agitational nature, such as Leonard Henney's *Black Power, We're Goin' Survive America* (1968) and the collaboration of Stewart Bird and Peter Gessner with the League of Black Revolutionary Workers that produced *Finally Got the News* (1970). Working on such films typically proved educational for the White filmmakers; for example, making *Black Panther* radicalized San Francisco Newsreel and turned it away from the counterculture toward Marxist-Leninism, while later the integration of Third World Newsreel within the proletariat approached the conditions of a truly popular practice. Of the films made by White radicals in cooperation with the Black Panthers, the most substantial were *The Black Panthers: A Report* (1968), Agnès Varda's documentation of Black protest during the imprisonment and trial of Huey Newton on a charge of murdering an Oakland policeman, and *The Murder of Fred Hampton* (1971), Mike Gray Associates' documentation of the Chicago Panthers that focused on the murder of two of them by the Chicago police.

Both films attempt to explain and vindicate the Panthers, and apart from a single voice-over remark by Varda noting that the Panthers want Newton freed "without even raising the question of his possible guilt," both are entirely without qualification or assessment of the justice of the Panthers' cause, of the correctness of their methods, or of the fact of the police program to eradicate them. This is not to say that either film emerges directly from the processes of Panther political activity or that either allows an absolutely unmediated transmission of the Panther's own discourse. Despite Varda's sympathy, locutions like her claim that Stokely Carmichael is "the leader of all Afro-Americans," as well as being incorrect, ring with a cultural unfamiliarity that in other aspects of the film—for example, the awkwardness in interview technique, a touristic lingering on an item of dress or mannerism—tends to objectify Black people, almost producing them as the exotic natives of an ethnographic documentary. While the makers of *Fred Hampton* are closer to the Panthers, the film's poor sound quality, its grainy images, and its generally low production values interpose a scrim between the Panthers and their audience—though this impediment can translate into a suggestion of financial exigency that reciprocates the Panther's own economic marginality. These interventions are, however, minor, and by and large both films are successful attempts by White radicals to make themselves, their skills, and their access to the apparatus the vehicle for a discourse that is essentially the Panthers' own; they are the means by which the Panthers can obtain a presence in alternative cinema or a voice in the media at large that by themselves they would not be able to secure. Since their audiences, comprising immediately adjacent groups in the Black community, White American radicals, and Third World sympathizers in general, were predisposed to be sympathetic, the filmmakers' task was as far as possible to allow the Panthers to speak for themselves. Thus their speeches—at rallies, in conversation among themselves, and also in direct address to the camera—make up the bulk of the films, supplying both their ideological stance and their formal organization.

In *The Black Panthers*, an interview with Newton in jail supplies a center of authority from which radiate other ratifying discourses—those of Eldridge Cleaver and Stokely Carmichael at a rally in Newton's support, of lesser-known figures from the Oakland community, of more or less casual presences at the rally, and finally of Varda herself. In support of these mutually corroborating speeches, the film produces illustrative images. For example, the recitation of the 10 Point Plan, almost a generic convention of Panther films, which, as in Newsreel's *Black Panther*, usually is simply inserted while the camera tours the ghetto streets, is here formally integrated. At the "Free Huey" rally that the film concentrates on, Bill Brent, a captain in the party from Oakland, introduces himself. This provides the motive for a survey of Oakland with voice-over information about its size and population, the nature of its police force, and the formation of the Panthers up to Newton's arrest. Returning to the rally, the camera allows Brent to provide details of the incarceration of Newton, who is himself introduced in a jail interview. His complaint that prison officials intercept his reading materials includes mention of Mao Zedong's writings, which prompts a series of cutaways revealing young people at the rally reading the *Little Red Book*. Back in the cell, the camera records Newton describing some of the features of the party: it is a Marxist-Leninist program, and its members are practical revolutionaries who identify with the armed struggle of colonized people throughout the world. Then the film returns to the rally for a speech by Stokely Carmichael about the war being waged upon Blacks in the United States. The camera picks out Brent again in the crowd to allow him to explain the 10 Point Plan, but his recitation is interrupted by cutaways to community people who extend his references: a young woman discusses his demands for education; when he comes to the draft exemption for Blacks, several young men amplify his remarks; and when he demands the release of all Blacks in jails, the camera returns to Newton's jail cell. As well as providing the editorial logic for a densely textured and thematically coherent film, this constant interweaving of many voices, each explaining the Panther position with illustrative and corroborative material from their constituency, produces ideological consistency. The Panther spokespeople are seen to speak with the voice of the community, accurately representing its interests, and, conversely, the community is seen as deriving its own self-consciousness from the Panthers' analysis.

With almost no voice-over narration, *Fred Hampton* is constructed from inter-Panther dialogue and direct address by Panthers; it admits non-Panther discourse only to discredit that discourse. The first part of the film is built up around situations inside the Black community—speeches at rallies, meetings between Panthers and representatives of other groups, visits to a Panther breakfast program and a community medical center—but after this community is violated by the murders of Hampton and Panther defense captain Mark Clark, the diegesis is similarly penetrated by the mendacious discourse of the establishment. The press conferences held by Illinois state's attorney Edward V. Hanrahan, the accounts of the shoot-out in the *Chicago Tribune*, and the inconsistent accounts of the police officers involved are all as much in conflict with each other as with the evidence the Panthers produce, and they are totally discredited by a federal grand jury. The ease with which the Panthers prove their propositions verifies their argument that the state is set to destroy Black dissidents, demonstrates the accuracy of their social analysis, and so justifies Hampton's own exhortations that his audience "live for the people . . . struggle for the people . . . die for the people."

One film liberating Huey Newton's discourse from incarceration and the other redeeming Fred Hampton's from the murderers' guns, neither can be faulted for infidelity to the Panther position; making it their own, they gave it a public dissemination wider than the limited circulation of the Panther's public speeches and the *Black Panther* newspaper and more honest and sympathetic than the version of the Panthers sensationalized by the media. Where the films became problematic—and the reason for their unpopularity on the left and within sectors of the Black community[8]—was in their failure to confront the contradictions of the Panthers' position, especially as these were duplicated and exaggerated in the sensationalized, reified Panther image constructed in the mass media.

Although the Panthers' class analysis of the situation of Blacks and their identification of the Black struggle with Third World liberation were superior to rival analyses by cultural nationalists and liberal integrationists, their assumption of a Leninist vanguard role and their decision to militarize resistance to the state finally destroyed them. Whether or not American Blacks constituted a colonized society, without the resources of the Vietnamese or the Algerians, they were not to throw off the *colon* by Vietnamese or Algerian methods; the promulgation through the media of the image of the urban guerrilla, quite eclipsing the breakfast and education programs, only ensured that the Panthers' most adventurist gestures, but not their legitimate grievances, were brought to public attention. So while the various African revivals, the leather jackets and the dark glasses, and all the other accoutrements of the outlaw uniform distinguished Panther militancy from the integrationist programs of the civil rights period and stimulated recruitment by providing a role-model alternative to the self-deprecation that Frantz Fanon and Paulo Freire both diagnosed as the essential mechanism of oppression, the audacity corresponded to no viable method of achieving political power. The paramilitary posture simply polarized public response to the point where the White community's fear and the state's anger permitted a systematic, illegal police offensive against them.

Like Fred Hampton's prediction that he would not die by slipping on a piece of ice but in the service of the people, the aggression and paranoia of the Panthers' rhetoric could be validated only by the destruction of its speakers. Thus both films appropriately emphasize the fury that the police reserved for *images* of the Panthers; Varda's, for example, ends with a shot of the Panthers' devastated Oakland headquarters and dwells on posters of Newton riddled by police bullets. But neither is capable of critical attention to the social function of those images or of self-critical attention to their own role in the dissemination of those images. In their inability to deal with the disparity between the claims of the Panthers' image and their actual political potential, *The Black Panthers: A Report* and *The Murder of Fred Hampton* participate in their errors; their spectacularization of the Panthers did nothing to avert the group's destruction. The failure of these films to negotiate the contradictions in such highly politicized representation is all the more striking since it prefigures parallel ambiguities in a slightly later industrial genre—one that exploited a debased form of Black militancy to preempt a genuinely Black cinema—blaxploitation.

The financial success of Ossie Davis's *Cotton Comes to Harlem* in 1970 spawned a plethora of generic remakes aimed specifically at the Black market: the western was represented by Sidney Poitier's *Buck and the Preacher* (1972), for example, and the musical by *Lady Sings the Blues* (1972). The most successful of these was the gangster movie. This new film noir featured a Black, urban outlaw hero—usually a drug dealer and a pimp—pitted against the Mafia and a corrupt White police force. A sister genre mobilized an equally ferocious heroine who, ironically, took an equally ferocious revenge on ghetto drug pushers. *Shaft* (1971), *Shaft's Big Score* (1972), *Shaft in Africa* (1973), *Across 110th Street* (1972), *Slaughter* (1972), *Slaughter's Big Rip-Off* (1973), *Superfly* (1972), *Superfly T.N.T.* (1973), *The Mack* (1973), *Trick Baby*

(1973), and *Truck Turner* (1974) are representative of the former; *Coffy* (1973), *Cleopatra Jones* (1973), and *Foxy Brown* (1974) are representative of the latter. The first films in these genres were independently produced by Blacks, but they were always studio-distributed; once they proved to be financially viable, the studios took control of production. *Superfly*, for instance, was independently written and financed by Blacks, with Warner Brothers purchasing it for distribution, but the sequel was produced inside the studio.[9] Though the fourteen examples mentioned above all had Black stars and extensive Black casts, ten of them were White-written, White-produced, and White-directed, with only Gordon Parks's direction of the two *Shaft* films and the first *Superfly* and Ron O'Neal's direction of the second *Superfly* interrupting the shutout.

Blaxploitation did provide the Black proletariat with something no previous film had: heroes from the community, resourceful and powerful enough to take on and defeat their predators. But the value of those role models was almost entirely countered by the films' displacement of attention away from the political analysis of the situation of Black people and from the possibilities of improving it by systemic social change. By presenting the traumas of the ghetto empirically as local criminal issues, blaxploitation spoke directly to its audience's everyday experience but not to what determined it. The genre's conventions—the redress of wrong by the superhero vigilante rather than by community control; the portrayal of corruption as a police or Mafia aberration rather than as endemic and structural; the backhanded glorification of heavy drugs, prostitution, and other forms of self-destruction that sublimated resentment rather than channeling it in socially useful directions; and a chauvinist, macho anti-intellectualism—allowed for a vicarious release of anger in ways that challenged the power of neither the state nor its local institutions. Despite the popularity of blaxploitation, its regressiveness and its instrumentality to the bourgeois state was widely recognized in both the popular Black press and radical film journals.

While almost all blaxploitation films were entirely cynical formula productions, some remain of interest, either because, like *Across 110th Street*, they take the conventions to such hyperbolic extremes that they subvert the genre's mechanism of gratification or because, like Melvin Van Peebles's *Sweet Sweetback's Baadasssss Song*, they struggle against the limitations of the genre strongly enough to rupture its ideological closures. *Sweetback* is especially illuminating, since in the trials of its hero, it dramatized the tensions between the genre's need to depoliticize the Black condition and Van Peebles's own political commitment—a tension that recurs on the formal level in his attempt to use strategies developed in the underground to force the industrial vocabulary toward a more authentic Black dialect. The film may be understood as a meta-generic meditation on the difficulty of making over the Hollywood film as the vehicle of a Black cinema.

Van Peebles retained the full roster of generic motifs: "a detailed and graphic social anatomy of the black underworld that established credibility; a carefully segregated point of view, which unfortunately misfired because no white character was allowed a shred of humanity; a set of symbols and gestures that bore a great freight of outlaw meaning; and a ritual of mayhem that almost orgasmically released upon the film audience the picaresque urban outlaw as a mythic black redeemer."[10] While carrying some of these conventions almost to the point of caricature (making Sweetback himself a professional stud, for example), he also attempted to align them with the politics of Black liberation. In distinct contrast to the genre's suppression of political self-consciousness demanded by the entertainment industry function (*Superfly*'s ridicule of political activists is typical), Van Peebles makes Sweetback's response to Black Power the motive of his actions and the condition of his heroism. The implications of Sweetback's transformation from a child into a man and then from a woman into a man in the opening scenes are completed by his decision to intervene in the police attack on the radical Moo Moo. Saving Moo Moo awakens him from his social passivity; he acquires speech, and, shortly after, day breaks for the first time in the film. By jeopardizing his life for Moo Moo, he is freed from his degradation as a sexual spectacle and freed for his role as a political outlaw. His recognition that his people's future lies with the young radical is endorsed by representatives of the Black community—by the preacher, for example, who applauds him for having saved "the young bud" that the police would have picked off. First as Moo Moo's protector and then as his heir (for the end suggests that after recovering his strength in Mexico, he will return to the struggle), he receives the support of the Black community and of other racial and sexual minorities.

On the basis of such a reading, Huey Newton was able to declare *Sweetback* "the first truly revolutionary Black film made"[11] and Sweetback himself "a beautiful exemplification of Black Power."[12] While it overstates the case and entirely ignores the film's relentless sexism, the argument is not without some justification, for the narrative does supply a logic to the hero's growth from the renegade stud of blaxploitation to the militant of the documentary tradition; the latter role model is used as a critique of the former, and there is the suggestion that Sweetback's sexual potency carries the stigma of his political impotence. But the implications of such a bildungsroman form cannot be elaborated through the full register of narrative motifs. Sweetback cannot finally transcend his blaxploitation machismo; neither, despite the terroristic pretensions of his name, can Moo Moo be more than a cipher. Without charisma or initiative, he provides no politically useful role model, and his absolute dependence on Sweetback undermines all the claims for his importance. Incapable of appropriating film presence, the proffered example of Black Power is incapable of asserting himself in either aesthetic or political terms.

These thematic tensions, which subvert the militance *Sweetback* wants to endorse and cause the film to fall back into the generic codes it wants to distinguish itself from, recur in Van Peebles's attempts to expand the formal vocabulary of the commercial feature. The general absence of shot/reverse-shot patterns and other standard tropes, the often ungrammatical lighting patterns, and the grainy image—all following from the low production costs—by and large harmonize with the decrepit ghetto slums, rhyming with their decay rather than producing spectator distance. In this, as in many of its motifs, *Sweetback* recalls contemporary independent feature productions, especially Roger Corman's and Russ Meyer's biker and soft-core exploitation films, but it goes well beyond these in its assertion of authorship. Independently produced by Van Peebles (though perhaps with completion funds from Bill Cosby), it was also written, directed, edited, and scored by him, and it starred him in the title role. This insistence on personal vision links it with the underground in terms of its auteur control over all stages of its production and with the trance film especially in terms of its structure.

Like the picaro heroes of Curtis Harrington's *Fragments of Keeping*, Kenneth Anger's *Fireworks*, or Stan Brakhage's *Reflections on Black*, Sweetback wanders through an urban nightmare of demonic antagonists and sexual hyperbole, seeking the resolution of psychosexual confusion. This structural subjectivity is reciprocated by parallel formal invocations of the late sixties' psychedelic underground, especially the color solarizations, multiple superimpositions, loop printing, and other forms of image manipulation associated in Los Angeles with Pat O'Neill and Burton Gershfield (and, in fact, some of the effects in *Sweetback* were done by a small company run by O'Neill). Used to punctuate crises like Sweetback's initial beating of the police and his sexual triumph over the motorcycle gang leader, such optical effects skew the film toward the first person, though the subjectivity does not distinguish the artist from the community so much as affirm the commonality of his highly charged vision; it inscribes blackness. The same is true of the other main stylistic trait, the construction of a phantasmagoric mosaic out of short shots of the cityscape and brief, documentary-style interviews with people from the community; in these visual jazz riffs, the continually moving and zooming camera creates a vertiginous run through the ghetto that establishes the reciprocity of Sweetback's vision with the community's. Other underground conventions that destroy diegetic unity and narrative transparency, such as the use of Black music and the quasi-surrealist chorus of voices that follows Sweetback through his desert miasma, similarly fix the individual hero, especially in his crisis, as tile surrogate for a whole culture.

It is appropriate to approach *Sweetback* as psychomachy, as the dramatization of deep personal conflicts in which the tension between the political and the sexual is only the summary vocabulary for a whole series of social and libidinal bifurcations across which the Black self in its historical uncertainty is stretched. In this trauma, Sweetback recapitulates the condition of an entire people; but *Sweetback* does not. It is set against itself in contradiction: its reenactment of the social relations of capitalist culture is at odds with those of its avowed thematic project. As a commodity in exploitative social transactions, even Black social transactions, it does not derive from the praxis of the community, but only from the isolated entrepreneurial determination of a single man. His attempt to make the production methods and marketing operations of capitalist cinema the vehicle for social reform are abrupted at the point where market functions enclose revolutionary desire. Unlike Black music, Black cinema could find no authentic place in the Black community, neither as popular expression nor, especially, as a model of production capable of popular imitation. As a commodity, its function is finally that of every other industrial film, every other exploitation film. *Sweetback*'s opening credits, which affirm "The Community" as its stars, speak this contradiction, for what they propose as its stars are really its marks. Concealing the commodity relations by which it works to sustain the capitalist cinema, its very celebration of blackness, of blackness given voice, is inevitably alienated and so can do no more than preoccupy the vacant space of a genuine community culture—a Black revolutionary cinema.

The virtual absence of cinema from the most progressive social movement of the sixties must be understood as the interdependence between the establishment media's refusal to portray the radicalization of the Black movement honestly and the parallel failure of Blacks themselves to develop a film culture adequate to their needs. This relation provides a particularly clear instance of the historical and social determination of cultural production. Parallel conditions among other ethnic groups forestalled any substantial cinematic contribution to their struggles in the sixties as well. Hollywood did continue the modification of its portrayal of Native Americans that had been developing since World War II, and there were a few instances of successful collaboration between independent filmmakers and Indian groups, such as that between Carol Burns and the Survival of the American Indian Association, which produced the Newsreel-distributed *As Long as Rivers Run* (1971). Yet Sol Worth's remarkable 1966 experiment of introducing the apparatus to the Navajo, however fascinating the films are and however invaluable the critical perspectives on cinema that it makes available, was of little use to the Navajo themselves. Nor could collaboration between White radicals and the Latin community in Newsreel films like *Los Siete* (1969), *Rompiendo Puertas* (*Break and Enter*, 1970), *El Pueblo Se Levanta* (*The People Are Rising*, 1971), and *G.I. Jose* (1974) produce anything with the social momentum of the Chicago Guerrilla Theater or Fresno's El Teatro Campesino or New York's Soul and Latin Theater. Apart from isolated instances, the gap between the politically disenfranchised and economically marginal ethnic minorities and the material conditions of cinema, along with the antipathy of ethnic arts to the material conditions of film, precluded any substantial role for the medium in ethnic political contestation. Cultural traditions aside, it is clear that the virtually unalloyed commodity consumption that occupies the position of these absent ethnic cinemas is a matter of class rather than ethnicity per se. With the exception of students, women, and sexual minorities, those sixties dissident groups who theorized themselves politically, especially ethnic minorities, prisoners, and GIs, were all predominantly from the working class. Their inability to produce cinema for their own purposes should be thought of as an aspect of the absence of a working-class cinema. Like its constitutive instances, this more general failure has implications for cinema as a whole, clarifying the dominant cinema's integration in capitalism—its intrinsic and inevitable reiteration of economic and social subordination and impoverishment. But these general issues also reflect the condition of the working class in this period, the repression of historical self-consciousness and materialist thought in general. By the end of the sixties, a class understanding of the United States was available to inform attempts to produce a working-class cinema. But both class knowledge and proletarian film were shaped by the war in Vietnam.

Notes

1. Though even here the lack of a mass Black audience for avant-garde jazz does not discredit other political functions. Kofsky, who has argued the relationship between Black nationalism and modern jazz most thoroughly, quotes Archie Shepp as claiming that jazz is "anti-war, it is opposed to Viet Nam; it is for Cuba; it is for the liberation of the people" (Frank Kofsky, *Black Nationalism and the Revolution in Music*, New York: Pathfinder Press. 1970, 64). While this assertion may better represent the feelings of the musicians than it does the concrete function of the music, still in its resistance to commodification and its modernist pursuit of its formal possibilities, jazz came closer than any other art form to reconciling negation with commitment.

2. Ron Karenga, "Black Cultural Nationalism," in *The Black Aesthetic*, Addison Gayle, Jr., ed. (New York: Athlone 1972), 32.

3. In the most extensive collection of essays from the period defining the Black aesthetic (Gayle 1972), not only is there no section on film, but film is mentioned only three times, in each case to note the absence of a satisfactory Black film. Most commentators prefer to reserve the term *Black cinema* for productions entirely controlled by Blacks, but they admit the unfeasibility of doing so. On Black film as genre, see especially Cripps (1978, 1–13) and Murray (1973, xi–xv). In addition to providing the best account of the independent Black feature industry of the twenties and thirties, Cripps also records the extraordinary case of the traveling preacher, Eloise Gist: "She ranged over the South during the great Depression, spreading her revivalist faith through motion pictures shot only for the specific narrow purpose defined by her own faith and spirit. Nowhere from script to screen did any white hand intrude, or any white eye observe. Neither white financing in the beginning nor white appreciation at the end affected her pristine black fundamentalism. Her films were naïve, technically primitive, literal depictions of black Southern religious folklore that brought faith to life, much as an illuminated manuscript gave visual life to Christian lore in the Middle Ages" (Cripps 1978, 4). Cripps is interested naturally in Gist's work as the best example of "pure" Black films; this purity notwithstanding, Gist's appropriation of the medium for devotional practice and her total integration of it into a life's work is unequaled in recorded film history, though it is approached by the utopian functionalism that history allowed to Dziga Vertov. Though Clyde Taylor claims that a "new black cinema was born out of the black arts movement of the 1960s" (Taylor 1983, 46), all the examples he gives are from the mid to late seventies, which substantiates my claim that independent Black film developed from the educational reforms produced by the movement rather than from the movement itself.

4. Amiri Baraka, *Blues People: Negro Music in White America* (New York: William Morrow, 1963), 16.

5. See especially Thomas Cripps, *Black Film as Genre* (Bloomington: Indiana University Press, 1978, 13–63). Edward Mapp, *Blacks in American Film: Today and Yesterday* (Metuchen,

NJ: The Scarecrow Press, 1972) excludes from this discussion as atypical Black films by Black producers (the Birth of a Race Company, Ebony Pictures, and even Oscar Micheaux), but otherwise his is an exhaustive inventory of the changing portrayal of Blacks by Hollywood and by independent White productions. Save only *A Raisin in the Sun* (1961), *Nothing But a Man* (1964), and *The Learning Tree* (1969), he records unrelieved failure to treat everyday Black life with seriousness or dignity and especially to address the issues of the Black Power movement.

    6. Although the tradition of the representation of Blacks by the underground goes back through Ron Rice's *The Queen of Sheba Meets the Atom Man* (1963), Jonas Mekas's *Guns of the Trees* (1961), and John Cassavetes's *Shadows* (1959) to Lionel Rogosin's *Come Back, Africa* (1959) and Sidney Meyers's *The Quiet One* (1948), throughout Blacks are used as metaphors for White desires or fears. Even an instance of substantial Black control over the profilmic, such as Shirley Clarke's *Portrait of Jason* (1967), sensationalizes and spectacularizes its subject. Still, together with its use of Black music, the underground's representation of Black people made it a major moment in Black cinema; its reproduction in the medium of film of the formal and social qualities of jazz is even more significant in indicating the terms by which a popular Black film could have been developed, given a different situation for the medium in Black society generally. The link between the bohemian underground and the lost Black cinema is, of course, Amiri Baraka; if his *Dutchman* (1967), made in England, had been a popular success, some of the energy of the revitalized Black theater might have gone into film.

    7. Though, as Mapp notes, Clarke recycles the same stereotypes about Blacks—the vicious criminal, the absent father, the petty thief, the stud—that populate most racist films (Mapp 1972, 94–95).

    8. *The Murder of Fred Hampton* was especially unpopular; invoking Jean-Luc Godard's distinction between radical filmmaking and the filming of radical politics, *Cinéaste* suggested that "in its portrayal and advocacy of revolutionaries as gun-slinging, death-defying desperadoes [it] will thus be seriously counter-productive (Crowdus 1973, 51). Godard, incidentally, warmly recommended Varda's film at showings of his own, very different treatment of Panthers, *One Plus One*—a film that itself depicts the Panthers as gunslinging desperadoes.

    9. B. J. Mason, "The New Films: Culture or Con Game," *Ebony*, 28, no. 2 (1972), 62.

    10. Cripps 1978, 133–34.

    11. Huey P. Newton, *To Die for the People* (New York: Random House 1972), 113.

    12. Ibid., 139.

2

STRUGGLES FOR THE *SIGN* IN THE BLACK ATLANTIC

Los Angeles Collective of Black Filmmakers

Michael T. Martin

> I am concerned with the reality of black people and our situation. Because not only does the black population not have its reality reflected in media—because we are not empowered to give expression to what we know and feel—but the larger audience and the larger public in this country are also not aware.
>
> *Billy Woodberry*

> We think with words. To be able to think together, we have to first agree on the terms we use... The importance of the word is determined by the space in which it is uttered and by the reason why it is uttered.
>
> *Joseph Gai Ramaka*

FORTY YEARS HAVE ELAPSED SINCE BLACK INDEPENDENT FILMMAKERS in Los Angeles came to prominence, time enough to engage anew with hindsight and study the oeuvre of a distinctive association of filmmakers-in-training, raconteurs whose vision, reflexivity, and contributions to a second Black creative renaissance are remarkable—indeed legendary. My project for this essay is to perform a clearing exercise that parses this cinematic formation and illumines the *habitas* of its practice and enduring legacy to this day among veterans of the group. Revisiting the earliest works by three of the group's best-known members—Charles Burnett, Julie Dash, and Haile Gerima—I seek to discern the depth and social relevance of their extraordinary work in real time and futurity and within the framework of what David C. Wall and I call *cine-memory*.[1] By *cine-memory* we mean a conception of history as an active and dynamic process that speaks to the past and present as it mobilizes for and gestures Black futures.

However you consider this Los Angeles assemblage of nascent filmmakers, you will find in the historiography of its formation and the evolution of Black independent cinema—if nothing else—material evidence of the filmmakers' enduring presence and, perhaps more importantly, an undeterred claim of agential authority. Collecting utterances, creative work, and the documentary record is to conceive an archive; constituting such a body of work, however, as Stuart Hall remarks, "represents a significant moment, on which we need to reflect with care, it occurs at that moment when a relatively random collection of work, whose movement appears simply to be propelled from one creative production to the next, is at the point of becoming something more ordered and considered: an object of reflection and debate."[2] For Hall, the embodiment of the archive marks closure of "a kind of creative innocence" and the start of self-awareness of an artistic movement in which "the whole apparatus of 'a history'—periods, key figures and works, tendencies, shifts, breaks, ruptures—slips silently into place."[3] And thanks to the interlocutors of this intellectually groundbreaking project and the intervention of the UCLA Film & Television Archive, what was once a collection of "dead works" is now a living archive-in-progress. In its "heterogeneity," Hall further explains, "the multiplicity of discourses, not only of practice but of criticism, history and theory, of personal story, anecdote and biography, are the 'texts' which make the archive live."[4] Consider that one strand among such discourses concerns the branding of the group. What's in a name, self-referential or otherwise? The title of this essay—"Struggles for the *Sign* in the Black Atlantic; Los Angeles Collective of Black Filmmakers"—makes claim to a historical, transnational, and cultural activity less the reference, admittedly compelling, although ambiguous and contentious) to "LA Rebellion." The designation is not unproblematic and, indeed, is consequential for conceptualizing the group and situating them in correspondence to parallel, yet distinctive, cultural and artistic movements of the period whose practices embodied shared ideological and political convictions. I prefer Ntongela Masilela's term LA *School* and in this essay use the less precise LA *Collective* or *Collective*.[5] These designations point to a *tradition*, no less compelling and transformational than *rebellion* is revolutionary. By tradition, I mean an (artistic) heritage marked by particular thematic concerns, points of view, and stylistic sensibilities. Did the LA Collective constitute a movement, as *rebellion* suggests?[6] Arguably yes, absent programmatic enunciations or a declaration or two of a vision and mission notwithstanding. Yet, the term *collective* better suggests the ways in which the filmmakers are linked by organizing principles of a working practice, artistic sensibility, and politics tied to other and preceding Black and Third World oppositional practices and a corpus of creative work that activates cine-memory to recuperate the past and imagine Black futures.

The LA Collective responded to a long history of screen racism crystallized in American cinema in D. W. Griffith's epic of antebellum strife, *The Birth of a Nation* (1915). Griffith's genius was to elevate White supremacy to existential cause—immutable, insoluble, and permanent—and, in the drama of the historical epic that is *Birth*, to affirm patriarchy and White reign in the planter aristocracy and nascent industrial bourgeoisie. In a recent essay, Wall and I describe this national project in which Griffith was so invested as involving the creation of a racist regime of historical memory:

> *Birth*, notwithstanding its claims to reality and truth, is an egregious distortion of history whose purpose is not to offer an objective view of the south during the Civil War and Reconstruction but to socially, culturally, ideologically, and historically legitimize and valorize a racial hierarchy rooted in the presumption of white superiority... *Birth* is fundamentally a film about memory. Indeed, it relies upon the nature and function of memory to perform its emotive and seductive work... It lays claim to a kind of racial memory intended to provide a shared, yet wholly personal experience of whiteness, one that would be immediately and intimately familiar and recognizable to its intended audience. In its strategic employment of character, narrative, and plot... the film labors to provide a collective memory, rooted not in nationality but in race.[7]

Griffith, then, does two devilish things that signify the ideological project of *Birth*: First, he parses race, precipitated by the crisis of the Civil War and its aftermath, to fashion a Black social class, unlike that for Whites and traces of which endure to this day in the cinematic and historical world. Second, he pivots the nation's renewal on the preservation of White supremacy and patriarchy, despite disagreement between family members, because for Griffith the personal is inseparable from the familial, which is to say the nation.

Against *Birth*, we find the long history of struggle to reinscribe Black Americans in the nation as subject peoples in the struggle for the sign—and a Black futurity. For the record, the LA Collective's lineage can be traced to the fraud "stillbirth" of *The Birth of a Race* (John W. Noble, 1918), a commercially and aesthetically failed attempt to answer Griffith's racist drama with redeeming representations of Black personages across history to the present. For film historian Marc Ferro, *The Birth of a Race* marks the "first historical *counter-film* in American cinema in which African Americans incarnate a new vision in history."⁸ Consider, too, that from 1909 to 1948, more than 150 independent companies made, distributed, and exhibited "race movies," that distinctive aggregate of films with all-Black casts shown largely in segregated theaters. In the first half of the twentieth century, such films constituted by all manner of genre and to varying degree counter-historical readings of the American experience—racinated. Moreover, comprised of a range of visual and narrative styles and autism no practices, they anticipated—as they bore traces of—a Black American cinematic tradition.⁹

Where in this struggle is the LA Collective? Situating it is necessarily historical and invokes two parallel traditions. First, the Black radical tradition posits racism as a systemic practice that engenders inequality while legitimizing White privilege in virtually all sectors of American society: economy, culture, judiciary, education, and so on. That tradition's roots and iterations of resistance trace to slavery and colonialism, the Civil War and Reconstruction, the rise of the United States as an imperial power at the close of the nineteenth century and during the aftermath of World War II, Jim Crow, and the emergence of transnational corporations under "late" capitalism. Within this tradition, variants of Pan-Africanism—Marxist and otherwise—cohere with Black internationalism and identify with similar formations in the African diaspora, as it gestures solidarity with decolonizing and postcolonial struggles in the global South.¹⁰

The other tradition is cinematic and features two formations, distinct yet imbricating ideologically informed practices. In the United States, after the "race movie" period described above, Black independent cinema was comprised of at least two wings in the 1960s: the seminal documentary work by East Coast filmmakers, among them William Greaves, Madeline Anderson, and St. Clair Bourne; and, discovered in the Harvard Film Archive, the collaborative filmmaking initiatives between Larry Neal—a key figure in the Black arts movement—and Amira Baraka, Edward Spriggs, and James Hinton.¹¹ Both groups adhered to, if not enunciated, a defining ethos and cinematic practice affirming these imperatives: that "film must have utility and social purpose; it must endeavor to give voice to protagonists who otherwise are marginalized and silenced; and must resist and debunk the received notion that Black people are unable to manage their own affairs."[12] What registers here is not stylistic or aesthetic sensibility, but rather the social advocacy function and deployment of film on behalf of Black self-empowerment.

Such tenets resonate and broadly correspond with Third Cinema—that theorized and counter-historical reading of hegemony and underdevelopment that evolved during the 1960s and early 1970s and that privileged the documentary as the cultural form and genre for struggle preferred by adherents, in contrast with the LA Collective's emphasis on narrative fiction. What can be said of this militant approach to cinema and filmmaking? In counterpoint to dominant paradigms of Hollywood and European "art" cinemas of a kind, search cinema labels to resist and challenge the *ancien régime* in its twentieth and now twenty-first century incarnations, along with the inequality and poverty they sustain. The early programmatic texts upon which Third Cinema is premised, and which some LA members read and endeavored to adhere to, are largely derived from Latin American theorist-filmmakers, who, Robert Stam has observed, searched "for production methods and a style appropriate to the economic conditions and political circumstances of the Third World."[13] For Julianne Burton, these texts were "written by filmmakers whose theoretical propositions derive from the concrete practice of attempting to make specific films under specific historical conditions," as—and it is important to emphasize—members of the LA Collective themselves tried to do.[14] And it is also important to specify and elaborate the key texts of this movement for, in no small measure, they were espoused and adopted, selectively, by members of the collective.

Influenced by the Caribbean theorist Frantz Fanon, the foundational declarations of Third Cinema include Argentines Fernando Solanas and Octavio Getino's "Towards a Third Cinema" (1969), which calls for clandestine, subversive, "guerrilla," and "unfinished" cinema that radically counteracts the hegemony of Hollywood and European production and distribution practices. They conceive of cinema, especially in the documentary mode, as an instrument of social analysis, political action, and social transformation.[15] In *An Esthetic of Hunger* (1965), Glauber Rocha, a founder of the Cinema Novo movement in Brazil, inverts the social reality of underdevelopment and dependency into a signifier of resistance and transformation rendered by the oppressed through violence as authentic and empowering. Bolivian Jorge Sanjinés delineates in *Problems of Form and Content in Revolutionary Cinema* (1978) the thematics of recovery of identity, culture, and history in peasant communities and struggles. And the fourth major polemic of this movement engages with postrevolutionary concerns ten years into the Cuban revolution. Authored by Julio García Espinosa, *For an Imperfect Cinema* (1969) rejects the technical perfection of Hollywood and calls for "an authentically revolutionary artistic culture" where filmmaker and (active) spectator are coauthors engaging with the problems and strategies of ordinary people.[16]

Together, these claims, cast as polemical declarations, foreground an "active cinema for an active spectator" and constitute the social and ideological foundations of the New Latin American Cinema.[17] They also advance a conception of cinema as a transformational social practice that reflexively "incorporates in itself a discourse on its social and material conditions of production"[18] and what Tomás Gutiérrez Alea asserts is "genuinely and integrally revolutionary, active, stimulating, mobilizing, and—consequently—popular."[19] Eloquently summarized by Kim Dodge, the aesthetic and political project of Third Cinema is, above all, to interrogate "structures of power, particularly colonialism and its legacies"; contribute, at the cultural level, to the "liberation of the oppressed, whether this depression is based on gender, class, race, religion, or ethnicity"; engage "questions of identity and community within nations and diaspora populations"; "dialogue with history to challenge previously held conceptions of the past, to demonstrate their legacies on the present, and to reveal the 'hidden' struggles of women, impoverished classes, indigenous groups, and minorities"; "challenge viewers to reflect on the experience of poverty and subordination by showing how it is lived, not how it is imagined"; "facilitate interaction among intellectuals and the masses by using film for education and dialogue"; and "strive to recover and rearticulate the nation, using politics of inclusion and the ideas of the people to imagine new models and new possibilities."[20]

While Ana M. López cautions that these writings "signaled a naive belief in the camera's ability to record 'truths,'" members of the LA Collective were cognizant of and inspired by them and the transformational practice they implied.[21] Indeed, elements of this radical conception of cinema are demonstrably evident in the collective's work, perhaps most notably in Haile Gerima's enduring, influential, and affecting films made during and after the UCLA period.

The LA Collective's gestation as a distinct formation occurred during the tumultuous decade of the 1960s, a period of political ferment in postwar

America during which integrationist struggles for civil rights and nationalist strategies for self-determination gave rise to corresponding oppositional gestures of artistic practice and innovation for cultural renewal. As Masilela says, the intellectual and cultural commitments of the first "wave" or first cohort of the collective were "inseparable from the political and social struggles and convulsions of the 1960s."[22] Their thematics and practice were shaped by the Black radical and Third Cinema traditions outlined above.

The LA Collective's cinematic corpus clusters along and is differentiated by several overlapping motifs. Together, both films and motifs intersect in unexpected and remarkably salient ways to reconstitute the Black subject. This includes (1) women's lived experiences, subjectivities, and agential authority;[23] (2) family and community histories;[24] (3) social consciousness, activism, and protest gestures;[25] (4) the project of recuperating the past;[26] and (5) personages and celebratory evocations of diasporic spirituality and folklore.[27]

To explore these themes, the collective developed a radical stance concerning what their film education should entail. With economy and aplomb, Toni Cade Bambara distills the collective's position toward their filmmaking practice, with important attention to issues of cultural history and memory.

> Their views differed markedly with the school's [UCLA's] orientation:
> - accountability to the community takes precedence over training for an industry that maligns and exploits, trivializes and invisibilizes Black people;
> - the community, not the classroom, is the appropriate training ground for producing relevant works;
> - it is the destiny of our people(s) that concerns us, not self-indulgent assignments about neurotic preoccupations;
> - our task is to reconstruct cultural memory not slavishly imitate white models;
> - our task leads us to our own suppressed bodies of literature, lore, and history, not to the "classics" promoted by Eurocentric academia;
> - students should have access to access to world film culture—African, Asian, and Latin American cinema—in addition to Hitchcock, Ford, and Renoir.[28]

These principles, stated by those who testified on the collective's behalf, constituted the raison d'être of the collective's mission and responsibility. Though derived from different sources and enunciated with different inflections by members of the group, such principles were constitutive of a shared oppositional practice evidenced and substantiated in the collective's creative work, which I illustrate through close-ups on Charles Burnett, Julie Dash, and Haile Gerima in part 2 of this essay.

In contradistinction to Hollywood, and however varied the motifs, all filmmakers in the LA Collective deployed *cine-memory* to foreground and memorialize thematic concerns. Constituting a "form of repository or archive, memory recuperates, documents, and parses experience. It comprises images, sounds, meanings, gestures, and aural utterances" in order to illumine and critique the present in the past.[29] In this sense, the project of cine-memory is to parse lived experience and to interrogate domination in order to imagine a futurity. Cine-memory comprises three classes of sign and corresponds to the Latin American programmatic texts of Third Cinema noted earlier, as well as Teshome H. Gabriel's three-stage model of cultural decolonization—"unqualified assimilation," "return to the source," and the "fighting or combative" phases, derived from Frantz Fanon's seminal account of the master/slave dialectic.[30]

Class 1 cine-memory, evidenced by a film like *The Birth of a Nation*, affirms received notions and discourses and the ideological assumptions of the audience, valorizing their beliefs and expectations. It portrays the hegemonic order as natural rather than as part of culture and economy. By rendering the past, it masks ideology that normalizes the "reality" it expresses. Events appear fixed, simplistically framed, and analytically wanting. Hollywood has pioneered this form of historical reconstruction by dehistoricizing events in both past and present. Trajectories of race, class, and gender are particularly elided by personalized depictions that distance, in fact remove, audiences from the processes and dynamics of history. *Birth*, for example, naturalizes Black inferiority and the inevitability of Black subjugation under White rule.

Classes 2 and 3 of cine-memory, in contrast, are evident in the LA Collective's filmmaking. Class 2 cine-memory works to recuperate the past and in the service of renewal, identity, culture, and nation and infers comparisons between historical struggles. (As discussed below, Gerima best exemplifies this trajectory.) It labors to reconstitute the narratives of such struggles and transform how history and the present are read by audiences. Films of this ilk of cine-memory serve, as Tomás Gutiérrez Alea claimed before his death, "to deepen the understanding of our past and revindicate the best traditions of struggle."[31]

Class 3 cine-memory is the more complex of the three classes. Its purpose is to inspire activism in real time in the actual world; as such, memories foreground the future as indeterminate and work in a film's narration to transform consciousness and, in the tradition of Third Cinema, enable audiences to imagine outcomes of historical struggles in the project of world making.[32]

While the three classes of cine-memory are a feature of narration, classes 2 and 3 are essential to a radical-militant film practice because they destabilize and challenge normative readings of history and the social order. And, in varying ways, *all* LA Collective members have deployed such cine-memory in their work, among them the three filmmakers of the close-ups that follow.

Close-Ups

In this part, I address key themes and how they were engaged in narrative by the LA Collective as well as the political-theoretical assumptions that—particularly in the first cohort ("wave")—influenced and shaped the filmmakers' understanding of and relationship to Black and other communities of color in the United States and internationally. Recall the period of the collective's formation during the late 1960s and early 1970s: a moment of political and cultural upheaval and indeterminacy in the United States and world affairs and, correspondingly, of artistic renewal and invention. Inspired by these transformations, the strategic deployment of cine-memory by some of these filmmakers was the means to recuperate the past, mobilize in the present, and gesture futurity.

To illustrate these concerns, I present the following "close-ups" of three members of the collective—Charles Burnett, Julie Dash, and Haile Gerima. Burnett and Gerima are associated with the first cohort; Dash, the second.[33] While distinctions—aesthetic, stylistic, and otherwise—merit consideration for understanding each cohort's evolution and differences, this is not a subject for elaboration here. However, between the two cohorts, several differences stand out: arguably, in the first, urban settings and working-class family dramas, and in the more schematic films, the relationship between systemic domination and insurgency, are apparent (consider Gerima's *Bush Mama*, 1975, and *Ashes & Embers*, 1982, and Larry Clark's *As Above, So Below*, 1973); while in the second, films appear less didactic and confrontational. I chose these three filmmakers because during their training period, their work was influential, illustrating the defining themes that preoccupied members of the collective and shaped the tradition associated with this grouping of filmmakers. The source films I discuss are their first student works, the Project One and Two (if extant) by each filmmaker and in particular their thesis projects. I ask two questions: Who is the protagonist and for whom does she/he speak? And what is the setting for and circumstance of the story? Personage/group and setting/circumstance constitute the factors in play. By *personage/group*, I mean the central characters in the narrative and for whom they signify at the group level (by gender, race, nationality, etc.). *Setting* suggests the physical space the characters inhabit (cityscape, pastoral environment) that evokes place in the story, while *circumstance* connotes the situation that drives the story. Through these factors protagonists are constituted, emblematic, and located in time and space, while calling attention to the filmmaker's concerns and politics. Considering these factors also renders discernable similarities between the films and filmmakers, flagging the traditions they elaborated and the cultural memory they mobilized in the service of reconstituting the Black subject.

Close-Up: Charles Burnett

Charles Burnett is one of the pioneer members of the group, and his body of work makes it clear that his cinematographic formation crystalized and was honed, his style and aesthetic evolved, and his political convictions matured.[34] Burnett's Project One film is untitled and not extant. In Allyson Nadia Field's overview of the Project One films of the collective, she describes Burnett's offering this way: Shot on "a Bolex with a Switar lens, borrowed from his TA, using regular 8mm Kodak color film," the film's subtext is "interracial sex" and features the artist Michael Cummings, who, cast as a Black artist, "chokes his white nude model after making love to her." Importantly, Field goes on to say that, along with *69 Pickup* (1969) by Thomas Penick—also a member of the collective—both films "challenge white patriarchal norms, [yet] their acts of resistance actually serve to reinforce those same norms through a form of racialized misogyny."[35] To Burnett's credit, intelligence, and self-awareness, this backward position, articulated in writings by Eldridge Cleaver and others as revolutionary, was not repeated in films that followed, although a young White woman—as an object and measure of status between Black men—appears in Burnett's next film, *Several Friends* (1969).[36] We can see how in subsequent works he develops more nuanced strategies for reframing the kind of compliant construction of the past associated with class 1 cine-memory. That is, rather than employ such a seemingly crude rejection of interracial sexual taboos (in contrast to Griffith's version of Black-on-White rape), Burnett's next works ponder more deliberately and methodically how Black people have come to the stultifying stasis that makes their lives.

His first 16mm student film, *Several Friends* chronicles the quotidian experience of Black urban life in two movements; in each, the car stands as metaphor for both stasis and mobility. In the first movement, the opening scene depicts an unspoken and powerfully realized counterpoint, along a decrepit street, between a Black child and a Black inebriated soldier. One reading of this scene imagines the child's future in the soldier's hapless and vulnerable condition. The scene also alludes, by the child's seemingly unmoving affect, that such encounters are not uncommon in the neighborhood. Next follows a verbal exchange, replete with racial epithets, as four Black adults in a parked car muster coins to purchase wine from the liquor store down the street. The site of both scenes is presumably South Central Los Angeles, damning the Black community in a testimony of the physical and moral state of decay there. A fight breaks out between two drunken Black men before the liquor store. Observing, the woman in the car calmly says, "Hey, what they doing down there, fighting going on . . . I mean it's possible that something can done about it, you know . . . Yet and still I mean, if anything can be avoided, why not avoid it?" Consider what purchase the Black woman's proposed intervention immediately calls to mind: Why does she propose to intercede and not the Black men in the car?

The second movement transitions to a house in the neighborhood. A Black man sleeping on a couch is awakened by the arrival of the mother, also Black, of his two children, who walk off and out of the frame. The point made—he has family. The couple argues, and the music in the background attests to his affection for her. Cut to the preparation of chicken at the local butcher shop—a scene Burnett later refashions for the slaughterhouse in *Killer of Sheep* (1977). Cut back to the house, where the men converse as they repair a car propped on wooden crates in lieu of wheels and the woman is hanging clothes to dry. Another couple arrive—an interracial couple. The youthful White woman asks for and goes to the bathroom, while two men praise her companion's good fortune and new status. Cut to their departure, back to repairing the car, relocating the washing machine and other chores, and the arrival of another Black man and friend who urges them to prepare for that evening's tryst with other women. Together the film's two movements signify the impossibility of escape from the blight of the neighborhood and community. The car—mode of mobility—requires repair (endless repairs, and that is the point made clear by Burnett); and it is absent an essential part—the wheels—while in the house the banality of the everyday occurs, the characters transition to the fixed and ever-demanding maintenance work that signifies the stasis of their existence.

Burnett describes his Project Two film, *The Horse* (1973), as a "kind of allegory of the South."[37] The film is marked by counterpoint, as in *Several Friends*; a Black child caresses an old horse whose utility has passed and who is fated to be shot later in the day by the child's father, as four White men await his arrival in order to witness the execution. In a distinctive style, unlike the gritty realism of *Several Friends*, Burnett deploys camera, color film stock, voice, and the occasional punctuation of music in a pastoral setting to quietly, unobtrusively, and sparingly reveal the boy's agony and the indifference of the men. This powerful, understated, and understudied, if at all critically studied, film merits a close reading—further still, an essay of its own.

Consider the opening scene, one Burnett would later refashion for *Namibia: The Struggle for Liberation* (2007), of a rural expanse, a boy (Will) beside a horse, an abandoned house in the background, each framed like a still yet moving photograph of three protagonists: boy, horse, setting. Cut to the arrival of the men. They exit the car in the heat, calmly reconnoiter the house, and claim space on what remains of the porch. Cut to the man prostrate on that porch, who tests his luck in a close-up when the descending pocketknife barely escapes his face; cut back to the horse and boy walking off in the direction of the windmill in the background, horse absorbing life from the trough, perhaps sensing it will be his last gulp before death. Later the boy's father arrives. They embrace affectionately, affirming paternal ties unlike in *Several Friends*, which registers no notice of them. Cut to the gun, animated as it is taken from its sheath of paper and loaded by one of the men, not by the boy's father, which alludes to his complicity and maybe necessity but not choice in this matter. In the final scene, witness the boy close his eyes and cover his ears, awaiting the gun's discharge and the horse's death. In this profoundly haunting account, horse and father equate to a simple fact: their utility and service on behalf of Whites, which Burnett alludes will be the boy's lot in manhood. In one reading suggested by the interface between the White men and Black father, mediated by the horse's pending death and death itself, Burnett points to the lesson that *all* Black youth must learn and endure—that life, like the story, is circumstantial and at best tentative.

These initial efforts to constitute a film style grounded in "home truths" and the community Burnett knows all too well by experience as unforgiving are poignantly and sparingly realized in his thesis project and neorealist masterwork *Killer of Sheep*. A deeply meditative and haunting work of fiction, as it is haunted by the subject of its address—filmed in Watts, though the setting could be any urban space in America—the film testifies on behalf of a Black laboring class and lumpenproletariat who, displaced, hover in isolation and a debilitated community. *Killer* can be characterized as the Black American's encounter with collective trauma and "social death." And where intimacy and desire are negated, reduced to elemental forms of emotional and material subsistence, Stan and family endure without prospect. Burnett's frame is itself contained by the very material and spatial limitations exacted upon the lives of his characters. This he purposefully and dramatically revisits with damning effect through compelling scenes of children adrift in what passes for their playgrounds—alleys, abandoned and gutted buildings, a treeless savanna bounded by concrete. His approach is eminently neorealist and economical, like the lives of the characters he depicts, and is distinguished by a nonlinear narrative punctuated by surreality to underscore the alienation of the workplace. *Killer*'s realism is uncompromising. Indeed, the scopic regime of Burnett's intrusive and unforgiving camera captures starkly contrasting hues of black and white, perfectly expressing the everyday lives of ordinary people in a setting not unlike that of a cityscape after the apocalypse, where the survivors have little other than themselves and their own ingenuity to rely on.

Stan is emblematic of Burnett's central concern: the Black working class who have been left to fend for themselves in a decayed and decaying postindustrial wasteland. As in real life, Stan, with whatever dignity he can still muster, parses the circumstance of near subsistence, along with his wife and children. Burnett then renders the Black family with his full consideration and without condescension as he displays the underbelly of urban America and all it portends for the Black laboring underclass: cement, debris, the alienating workplace of the production line in the slaughterhouse, the banality of each day, and the longing for something better that escapes them and will always and inevitably remain unattainable. In this regard, Burnett deploys class 2 cine-memory in a neorealist style to foreground the actuality and banality of community life and labor; to render visible and immediate, by gestures, spoken utterances, and the camera's intrusiveness, the disfigurement of Black urban life.

Close-Up: Julie Dash

Julie Dash, like other LA Collective members, consciously resisted the visual and narrative culture of Hollywood and, as Clyde Taylor puts it, portrayed Black women as having "an existence for themselves."[38] Unlike Burnett, she drew on her stock of class 2 cine-memory to recuperate Black women's pasts, enabling them to act on their own behalf while, not unlike Gerima, she also constituted such women as a spiritual and life-rendering force for renewal.

Dash's first three films made before and during the UCLA period illustrate this claim and are foundational to her sustained interrogation of Black women's lives and subjectivities. Beginning with *Four Women* (1975), set to jazz singer and composer Nina Simone's commanding evocation of slavery's legacy on Black women in the song of the same title, Dash renders and subverts as she signifies Black female archetypes. Casting the choreographer and dancer Linda Young, who, like a chameleon, enacts each stereotype of Aunt Sarah, Safronia, Sweet Thing, and Peaches in cadence with the song's lament, Dash, like Simone, foregrounds the resilience, rape, miscegenation—and because of it, sexual commodification—and resolve, and bitterness that are Black women's, for want of a better word, bequeathal. The sound of flailing whips and the moans of a dispossessed people off-camera render in Young's dance—at once poetic and haunting, beautifully choreographed and powerfully performed—the immorality, hypocrisy, and brutality of Western civilization. *Four Women* also stylistically foregrounds Dash's experiment with the aesthetic registers of movement, sound, and camera that she would later deploy with poetic and dramatic effect in her masterwork, *Daughters of the Dust* (1991), which without pause or conditions situates Black women at the epicenter of all manner of things past, present, and future.

For her Project One film, *The Diary of an African Nun* (1977), Dash set the story in Uganda, depicting the crisis of a nun whose declining fidelity to Christ is occasioned by solitude, cultural displacement, and disbelief. *Diary* is adapted from a short story by Alice Walker, and Dash's reasons for making the film are complex and revealing of the subtexts that inform the film.

Field notes that among several motivations, Dash was inspired by "the striking image of the nun's habit and a photograph ... of several white women nuns surrounded by a group of Black children."[39] The "inner turmoil" of Walker's protagonist echoes that of other Black women figures in Dash's work who are conflicted about serving White interests and how they lock the women into White-defined historical roles of servitude and invisibility.

For example, in Dash's thesis project, *Illusions* (1982), set during World War II in Hollywood, the protagonists, Mignon Dupree, a film executive passing for White, and Ester Jeeter, a Black singer dubbing for a White Hollywood star, render circumstance and reason for Dash's critique of White patriarchy in the Hollywood studio system. Engaging with the polemic of "passing" while affirming Black women's solidarity, *Illusions* foregrounds the centrality of women—Black women—in the narrative and visual frame, endowing them with agential authority from subject positions that the women can identify with and the rest of us believe in. Indeed, the film is an instructive refutation and counterpoint to Hollywood Black representations of both sexes over the preceding decade in blaxploitation films.[40]

Close-Up: Haile Gerima

Unlike other veterans of the LA Collective who were unable to make many films, Haile Gerima has a substantial oeuvre for an independent Black African filmmaker. His work is deeply compelling, committed, and theorized and, in its address, consistently interrogative of Black peoples' dispossession and location in the world political economy. Born in Gondar, Ethiopia, Gerima has chronicled struggles in the Black Atlantic by time, location, and notably, gender. From his earliest films of the UCLA period to his most recent award-winning *Teza* (2008), as a "Third Worldist," Gerima debunks and lays waste to local and global narratives of domination. His project, unashamedly instructive, is without pretense the denunciation of all manner of inequality and the systemic causes of violence, racism, and patriarchy that beset African peoples on a world scale; Gerima calls for Black and other colored communities to stand fast and resist. In this way, his films exemplify the transformative feature of class 3 cine-memory by calling for activism in real time. In my view, no other filmmaker in the collective has emphasized and sustained the critique of domination as rigorously and without pause as Gerima, for which his reputation and standing among cineastes of political cinema are assured.[41]

Gerima's Project One film, *Hour Glass* (1971), sets forth the trajectory and purpose of his work to this day. *Hour Glass* posits a simple truth that the counterpart to college basketball in antiquity was manifest in Roman stadiums where men endured mortal combat for the pleasure and profit of others. Certainly, Gerima's analogy is not without precedent. "Bread and circuses," as a strategy of domination and appropriation, take many forms throughout history, and with this framing device and the revolutionary texts by Frantz Fanon and others, Gerima weaves a montage to raise a young Black male college basketball player's consciousness. The intersectionality of sports and the commodification of Black youth as raw material and cannon fodder are rendered immediate and compelling, as the player's deepening social awareness, suggested by the film's title, evokes the idea that social change follows in historical time.

Child of Resistance (1972), Gerima's Project Two film, is still more adamant and denunciatory than *Hour Glass*.[42] Experimental in its temporal and narrative registers and disjunctive editing, *Child* works, in the character of a Black woman imprisoned for her political convictions and activism, to condemn the "white man's world," asserts Alex James.[43] The film is set for the most part in a jail cell—and what can be more emblematic of Black dispossession—with the audience "looking down on her as the camera pans back and forth from an uncomfortable distance; her eyes follow the camera's movement . . . with a chilling look of pure disdain. This feeling of disdain and anger is the mood that drives the entire film."[44] At the close of *Child*, the protagonist, speaking from deep within her person, implicates as she admonishes, "Wake up Black men. Wake up!" Here, too, Gerima's call is to Black men, but unlike in *Hour*, this project is a work of agitprop ostensibly to shame Black men to activism, and the means to do that is Black women, who themselves are at the vanguard of struggle.

Gerima's thesis project film, *Bush Mama* (1975), is no less an indictment of state policy and American racism than Burnett's take on the Black working class—anatomized and without prospect—or Dash's on Hollywood hegemony, Dupree's passing, and Jeeter's artistic appropriation. Gerima theorizes a self-empowering alternative to the community's malaise by locating the community within global and colonizing formations. Gerima does not cast the individual as the protagonist of historical activity; rather, it is in the circumstance of the individual that systemic levers of domination are revealed as signifiers for collective action. By situating Black Americans and other communities of color in correspondence to and in conversation with international historical struggles, Gerima renders these struggles within a larger global and civilizational frame. In *Bush Mama*, he evokes the US war and occupation of Vietnam and the Angolan peoples' war of independence against Portuguese rule; he also references the Cuban revolution, which for many in the LA Collective was a source of inspiration, example, and solidarity.

In *Bush Mama*, Gerima's Black community is not a discrete site of poverty and decay. Rather, it constitutes a distinctive formation—an internal colony—within the matrix of late twentieth-century global capitalism. And, too, the political status of inhabitants is more or less similar to other colonized peoples under corresponding conditions of dependency and underdevelopment in the global South. By gesturing a Third Worldist approach to and schema of underdevelopment and oppression, Gerima conjoins Marxist and Pan-African concepts that resonated with Black audiences at the time of *Bush Mama*'s release. In the character of Dorothy, we find the counterpart to Stan's wife in *Killer of Sheep* as well as a variant articulation of the historical subject of Burnett's and Gerima's mutual address—the Black working class and lumpenproletariat. Along with Gerima's theorizing of racial and class oppression, the practical in women's agency is manifested as both reproductive (biological) and political imperatives. This is evinced in the poster image of the Angolan mother/soldier who bears arms against the "Portuguese masters." The association between motherhood and nation personified by this iconic image at once affirms women's agency in historical struggles while arguably feminizing the nation—the Black nation—a concern that I have raised elsewhere about *Sankofa* (1993).[45]

Moreover, unlike Burnett and Billy Woodberry (*Bless Their Little Hearts*, 1984), for whom the political evocation of women is less apparent, in the character of Dorothy, Gerima without condescension or whiff of patriarchy invites women of color to partake as equals in the strategically important task of formulating a collective way forward, And Dorothy's character suggests a nascent self-conscious militancy whose end game is the realization of personal and collective self-determination. In *Bush Mama*, then, Gerima's stance is without equivocation: women are at once mothers, lover-companions, and freedom fighters in the struggles ahead.

By positing America's ghettoes as internal colonies while challenging audiences to contemplate women's essential role in nation building, *Bush Mama* performs agitprop, as *Child of Resistance* does. By design, *Bush Mama*'s denunciations and claims work to reconstitute the Black subject, renew solidarity with other anticolonial formations in the African diaspora and global South, and engage with the project of world making in the United States. And as Gerima himself declared in 1983 at the Third Eye Symposium—On Third World Cinema, "This cinema must initiate the dialogue of change."[46]

Comparisons between Burnett, Dash, and Gerima are suggested by the shared thematics evident between the films. For example, one comparison concerns the encounter of Black Americans with modernity in urban sites, a modernity we wrongly associate with cosmopolitanism. In *Illusions*, the misrepresentation of history and the psychic toll on Black women "passing," as it were, to be heard in a White and paternal Hollywood studio system are central. Nearly a decade later, in *Daughters of the Dust* (1991), Dash reframes the setting of Dupree's encounter with modernity by the crossing of the Peazant family from the Sea Islands to the mainland. This crossing is fraught with dangers that will test the fortunes and fate of the family in sites not unlike those in *Killer of Sheep* and *Bush Mama*, where predations await to rob them of their identities, along with their spirituality and folklore traditions, not to speak of their savings as well.

Class correspondences also appear in these films. Jeeter, the singer in *Illusions* who dubs for the White star, Leila Grant, is cast as a woman of modest education and means, like the women characters in *Killer of Sheep* and *Bush Mama*. Dash's Dupree in *Illusions* is an exception, however; she is less constrained by the determinations of class and locale, though the gravitas of her life and circumstance is as compelling as the women's in *Killer of Sheep* and *Bush Mama*. And while their sexualities appear heterosexual (less so in *Illusions*), the women "act" in their self-interest and refute regressive discourses about Black women's identities and agency as these concepts were articulated in, say, Black Power discourses. In the arc of these portrayals, especially for Dash and Gerima and unlike for Burnett, Black women are the purveyors of memory in whose agency the nexus, solidarity, and source for the reproduction of community are possible.

In the films discussed here, class 2 and 3 cine-memory work to refute held beliefs, substantiate and redress historical claims, "vindicate," as Gutiérrez Alea asserted, "the best traditions of struggle," and invite audiences, in the tradition of Third Cinema, to conjure and narrate their own outcomes for historical struggles. Class 3 cine-memory is the project of world making and is most apparent among the three filmmakers in Gerima's work.

Burnett, Dash, and Gerima are among the LA Collective's most prominent and influential members. Their Project One, Two, and thesis films provide a means by which to understand the collective's originary orientations, motivations, aesthetic concerns, and practice. Their films also express the core themes and trajectories of a self-conscious and evolving cinema that challenges hegemonic discourses and cinematic readings of Black subjectivity and life in America. Dash's "Afrofemcentric" orientation traces to *Four Women* and *The Diary of an African Nun* and, validating Black women and their representation in the narrative and visual frames, continues to drive and sustain her work to this day. For Burnett and Gerima, their address is engaged broadly through the trope of the Black family—for Gerima, the global African family—constituted by laboring peoples and community. Following *Killer of Sheep*, Burnett continued to mine the Black family and community in *My Brother's Wedding* (1983) and *To Sleep with Anger* (1990); more recently, he has turned to the historical in world affairs with *Namibia The Struggle for Liberation* (2007) and his in-development biopic on Algerian Abd El Kader.[47] More schematic than the others, Gerima deploys a transnational frame, associating, as noted earlier, the plight and underdevelopment of Black Americans with that of other diasporic and colonized people. Returning to his native land in his most recent film, Gerima engages with the themes of exile and displacement in the seemingly self-referential drama *Teza* (2008).[48]

What to say, then, of the LA Collective? The group was an iteration of Black independent filmmaking evolving parallel to and in real time with the East Coast, especially Boston and New York documentary formations (i.e., *Say Brother*, 1968–82, *Inside Bedford-Stuyvesant*, 1968–71, and *Black Journal*, 1968–70) and Black Arts movement film initiatives.[49] Its members were inspired by Black pioneers of the "race movies" era and partial to the project of Third Cinema while being ever mindful and expressive of the Black radical tradition. They were no less denunciatory of American complicity in all manner of racism and global capitalism than Third Worldist theorist-filmmakers were and are of the colonial and neocolonial project and continuing North/South antinomy. Absent a manifesto of their own, yet determined to resist Hollywood conventions, its promotion of blaxploitation and its popular appeal,[50] as well as its commanding cultural dominance internationally, the LA Collective contested representations, especially of Black masculinity and Black women's agency, along with (but less so) those of Black sexuality pervasive in popular culture.[51] As such, these filmmakers challenged ensconced and widely held accounts of Black identity and normativity.

And not to forget, albeit largely unremarked, they conversed (perhaps unknowingly?) with exilic and diasporic cinema, that emerging trajectory and international movement of filmmaking engaged with transnational migration, postcolonial and "minoritarian" subjectivities, and the émigré experience constituted and refracted in gendered and racialized narratives—what Hamid Naficy refers to in his seminal study of such films as "accented cinema."[52] Certainly Gerima's *Teza* fits the bill and, to a lesser extent, so does *Sankofa*, with its focus on identities defaced in the New World by slavery, Western modernity, and the imperatives of modern capitalism. A case, too, can be made for Dash's *Daughters of the Dust*, where the specter of the city awaits the descendants of slaves embarking en masse to the mainland. In this sense, the migration and circulation of peoples, cultures, and traditions, displaced and displacing—all that distinguishes a people from their host societies, in which faces signify difference and serve as passports—are the stuff of the Black Atlantic, past, present, and becoming.

In sum, was the LA group a collective, or movement, or rebellion, or motley assemblage of would-be filmmakers? With certainty, in our time and epoch, the LA Collective constituted one such artistic and compelling substantiation of a defining cultural struggle for the *sign* in the Black Atlantic and to whom we are—in historical terms—indebted.

Notes

1. This futurity is now witnessed in the "Black Radical Imagination," a collection of contemporary media works that C. C. H. Pounder describes as "a carefully selected body of work inquiring and responding to what it means to be Black in the 21st century." Sergio Mims, "Black Radical Imagination Screening Series comes to REDCAT in L.A. Next Month, 10–7," *Shadow and Act*, September 13, 2013, http://blogs.indiewire.com/shadowandact/Black-radical-imagination-screening-series-comes-to-redcat-in-la-next-moth-10-7. (Site discontinued.)

2. Stuart Hall, "Constituting an Archive," *Third Text* 15, no. 54 (2001): 89.

3. Ibid., 89.

4. Ibid., 92.

5. See Ntongela Masilela, "The Los Angeles School of Black Filmmakers," in *Black American Cinema*, ed. Manthia Diawara (New York: Routledge, 1993), 309. Kara Keeling notes, "There is disagreement among the L.A. Rebellion filmmakers themselves and among the scholars engaged with their work, about the aims, strategies, purview, and even the name of the movement, and there are those who question whether this diverse group actually

constitutes a movement per se." See her "School of Life," *Artforum International* 50, no. 2 (October 2011): 294. The LA Rebellion moniker was first coined by Clyde Taylor for historical and aesthetic concerns—see his "L.A. Rebellion: New Spirit in American Film," *Black Film Review* 2, no. 2 (1986): 11, 29—but what matters is whether the group constituted a movement. If so, what kind of movement and in relation to what other formations of cultural production and reversal?

    6. Collectives, including artistic ones, do not necessarily cohere along a particular mission or objective. They also work as loosely knit associations of shared interests, friendships, and motivations—common and individual—as Allyson Nadia Field suggests for the LA group.

    7. Michael T. Martin and David C. Wall, "The Politics of Cine-Memory: Signifying Slavery in the History Film," in *A Companion to the Historical Film*, Robert Rosenstone and Constantin Parvulescu, eds. (Malden, MA: Wiley-Blackwell, 2013), 446–47.

    8. Mark Ferro, *Cinema and History* (Detroit, MI: Wayne State University Press, 1988), 152. For the backstory to the film, see Thomas Cripps, *Slow Fade to Black* (New York: Oxford University Press, 1993), 70–76 (emphasis added).

    9. Pioneers Oscar Micheaux (Micheaux Picture Corporation) and George and Noble Johnson (Lincoln Motion Picture Company), among others, are in this tradition.

    10. For an overview, see Cynthia A. Young, *Soul Power: Culture, Radicalism, and the Making of a U.S. Third World Left* (Durham, NC: Duke University Press, 2008); Cedric J. Robinson, *Black Marxism: The Making of the Black Radical Tradition* (Chapel Hill: University of North Carolina Press, 2000); Penny M. Von Eschen, *Race Against Empire: Black Americans and Anti-Colonialism, 1937–1957* (Ithaca, NY: Cornell University Press, 1997); Thomas Borstelmann, *The Cold War and the Color Line* (Cambridge: Harvard University Press, 2001); Michael C. Dawson, *Black Visions: The Roots of Contemporary African-American Political Ideologies* (Chicago, IL: University of Chicago Press, 2001); Harry Haywood, *Liberation* (New York: International Publishers, 1948); Anthony Dawahare, *Nationalism, Marxism, and African American Literature Between the Wars* (Jackson: University of Mississippi Press, 2003); and Michael C. Dawson, *Blacks In and Out of the Left* (Cambridge: Harvard University Press, 2013).

    11. See Lars Lierow, "The 'Black Man's Vision of the World': Rediscovering Black Arts Filmmaking and the Struggle for a Black Cinematic Aesthetic," *Black Camera* 4, no. 2 (2013): 3–21. While some members of the LA Collective and Black Arts movement were aware of each other's existence and perhaps production, I am unable to discern the extent of such awareness of the influence each movement had on the other, if any.

    12. While I am referring to Madeline Anderson in the specific, these tenets were shared by other filmmakers. See Michael T. Martin, "Madeline Anderson in Conversation: Pioneering an African American Documentary Tradition," *Black Camera* 5, no. 1 (2013): 73–74.

    13. Robert Stam, "College Course File: Third World Cinema," *Journal of Film and Video* 36, no. 4 (fall 1984): 50–61.

    14. Julianne Burton, "Marginal Cinemas and Mainstream Critical Theory," *Screen* 16, no. 3–4 (1985): 4.

    15. Consider Peter Rist's essay, "The Documentary Impulse and Third Cinema Theory in Latin America: An Introduction," *CineAction* 18 (1989): 60–61.

    16. Michael T. Martin, ed., *New Latin American Cinema, vol. 1, Theory, Practices, and Transcontinental Articulations* (Detroit, MI: Wayne State University Press, 1997), 76.

17. See my two-volume collection, Michael T. Martin, ed., *New Latin American Cinema, vol. 1, Theory, Practices, and Transcontinental Articulations*, and *vol. 2, Studies of National Cinemas* (Detroit, MI: Wayne State University Press, 1997). For debates about Third Cinema, see Jim Pines and Paul Willemen, eds., *Questions of Third Cinema* (London: British Film Institute, 1989); Mike Wayne, *Political Film: The Dialects of Third Cinema* (London: Pluto Press, 2001); Anthony R. Guneratne and Wimal Dissanayake, eds., *Rethinking Third Cinema* (London: Routledge, 2003); Michael Wayne, "The Critical Practice and Dialectics of Third Cinema," *Third Text* 14, no. 52 (2000): 53–66; and Nicola Marzano, "Third Cinema Today," *Offscreen* 13, no. 6 (2009): 1–18.

18. Rist 1989, 61.

19. Tomás Gutiérrez Alea, *The Viewer's Dialectic* (Havana: Jose Marti Publishing House, 1988), 18.

20. Kim Dodge, "What is Third Cinema?," 2007, http://thirdcinema.blueskylimit.com/thirdcinema.html.

21. Ana M. López, "At the Limits of Documentary: Hypertextual Transformation and the New Latin American Cinema," in *The Social Documentary in Latin America*, Julianne Burton, ed. (Pittsburgh, PA: University of Pittsburgh Press, 1990), 407.

22. Masilela 1993, 107.

23. Consider Zeinabu irene Davis's *Cycles* (1989), *A Period Piece* (1991), and *Compensation* (1999); Alie Sharon Larkin's *The Kitchen* (1975) and *A Different Image* (1982); Barbara McCullough's *Water Ritual #1: An Urban Rite of Purification* (1979); O.Funmilayo Makarah's *Define* (1988); Julie Dash's early projects, *Four Women* (1975) and *The Diary of an African Nun* (1977), and her thesis film, *Illusions* (1982), followed post-UCLA by her masterwork, *Daughters of the Dust* (1991), and *The Rosa Parks Story* (2002); Haile Gerima's *Child of Resistance* (1972); and Bernard Nicolas's *Daydream Therapy* (1977).

24. Charles Burnett's first student project, *Several Friends* (1969), also *The Horse* (1973), his landmark thesis project, *Killer of Sheep* (1977), and *To Sleep with Anger* (1990); Haile Gerima's no less compelling thesis project, *Bush Mama* (1975); Billy Woodberry's second film, *The Pocketbook* (1980); and *Bless Their Little Hearts* (1984), examples of Black realism at their best. Others include Jamaa Fanaka's *Emma Mae* (1976) and *Penitentiary* (1979), the latter a prison metaphor for Black life and community; Alile Sharon Larkin's *Your Children Come Back to You* (1979); Carroll Parrott Blue's *The Dawn at My Back: Memoir of a Black Texas Upbringing* (2003); Jacqueline Frazier's *Shipley Street* (1981); S. Torriano Berry's *Rich* (1982); Shirikiana Aina's *Brick by Brick* (1982); and Larry Clark's Western and second feature, *Cutting Horse* (2002).

25. Haile Gerima's Project One, *Hour Glass* (1971); *Child of Resistance* (1972); thesis project, *Bush Mama* (1975); and in the post-UCLA period, his feature, *Harvest: 3,000 Years* (1976); and *Ashes & Embers* (1982). Also Larry Clark's *Tamu* (1970) and *As Above, So Below* (1973); Gay Abel-Bey's *Fragrance* (1991); Shirikiana Aina's *Brick by Brick* (1982); Melvonna Ballenger's *Rain (Nyesha)* (1978); Bernard Nicolas's *Gidget Meets Hondo* (1980); and O.Funmilayo Makarah's *Apple Pie* (1975).

26. Dash's *Illusions* (1982), which resonates with Iverson White's *Dark Exodus* (1985), a meditation on racial violence and migration in America, and *The Rosa Parks Story* (2002); Haile Gerima's *Sankofa* (1993), a powerful albeit flawed indictment of slavery and reconstruction of the Black subject; and Charles Burnett's *Selma, Lord Selma* (1999).

27. Among them, Haile Gerima's *After Winter: Sterling Browne* (1985); Ben Caldwell's *Babylon is Calling* (1983) and *I & I: An African Allegory* (1979); Don Amis's *Festival of Mask*

(1982); Larry Clark's *Passing Through* (1977); Carroll Parrott Blue's *Vanette's World: A Study of a Young Artist* (1979); Zeinabu irene Davis's *Trumpetistically, Clora Bryant* (1989); O.Funmilayo Makarah's *Creating a Different Image: Portrait of Allie Sharon Larkin* (1989); Barbara McCullough's *Shopping Bag Spirits and Freeway Fetishes* (1981); Elyseo J. Taylor's *Black Art, Black Artists* (1971); and Charles Burnett's *To Sleep with Anger* (1990).

28. See Toni Cade Bambara's delineation of the group's orientation in "Reading the Signs, Empowering the Eye: *Daughters of the Dust* and the Black Independent Cinema Movement," in *Black America Cinema*, Manthia Diawara, ed. (New York: Routledge, 1993), 119.

29. Martin and Wall 2013, 450.

30. See Frantz Fanon, "Racism and Culture," *Presénce Africaine*, no. 8/9/10 (1956): 15–18; and Teshome H. Gabriel, *Third Cinema in the Third World: The Aesthetics of Liberation* (Ann Arbor, MI: UMI Research Press, 1982), 7.

31. Gerardo Chijona, "Gutiérrez Alea: An Interview," *Framework* (England) 10 (1979): 29.

32. For elaboration, see Martin and Wall 2013, 445–67.

33. Although Dash is associated with the second cohort, recall that she completed two films before her thesis project, *Illusions* (1982), *Four Women* (1975) and *The Diary of an African Nun* (1977).

34. For an overview of Burnett's formation, aesthetics, and practice, see Charles Burnett, "Interview: Charles Burnett—Consummate Cineaste," by Michael T. Martin and Eileen Julien, *Black Camera* 1, no. 1 (winter 2009): 143–70.

35. Field describes *69 Pickup* as a story "about two Black men who pick up a white woman and then rob, sexually assault, and beat her."

36. See Eldridge Cleaver, *Soul on Ice* (New York: Dell, 1968).

37. Allyson Nadia Field, Jan-Christopher Horak, Shannon Kelley, and Jacqueline Stewart, *L.A. Rebellion: Creating a New Black Cinema* (Los Angeles: UCLA Film & Television Archive, 2011), 29.

38. Taylor 1986, 29.

39. See Allyson Nadia Field, "Rebellious Unlearning," in *L.A. Rebellion: Creating a New Black Cinema* (Berkeley: University of California Press, 2015), 83–118.

40. *Illusions* achieved acclaim, including awards from the Black American Cinema Society in 1985 and the jury prize for best film from the Black Filmmakers Foundation in 1989.

41. I am not uncritical of Gerima's work. See Michael T. Martin, "Podium for the Truth? Reading Slavery and the Neocolonial Project in the Historical Film: *Queimada! (Burn!)* and *Sankofa* in Counterpoint," *Third Text* 23, no. 6 (2009): 717–31.

42. In "Rebellious Unlearning," Field notes that *Child of Resistance* was inspired by Gerima's dream after witnessing Angela Davis handcuffed on television.

43. Alex James, "LA Rebellion ATL Tour Review: Haile Gerima's *Child of Resistance*," *Shadow and Act*, December 5, 2013, http://blogs.indiwire.com/shadowandact/la-rebellion-atl-tour-review-haile-gerimas-child-of-resistance. (Site discontinued.)

44. Ibid.

45. See Martin 2009, 724.

46. See Haile Gerima, "Afro-American Cinema," in *Third Eye: Struggle for Black and Third World Cinema*, Greater London Council Race Equality Unit, ed. (London: GLC Race Equality Unit, 1986), 22.

47. See Tambay A. Obenson, "Charles Burnett Heading to Algeria to Direct Biopic on Algeria's Greatest Hero, Abd El Kader," *Shadow and Act*, September 9, 2013, http://blogs.indiwire.com/shadowandact/charles-burnett-is-heading-to-algeria-to-direct-biopic-on-algerias-greatest-hero-abd-el-kader. (Site discontinued.)

48. See the recent close-up on *Teza*, guest edited by Greg Thomas, *Black Camera* 4, no. 2 (2013): 38–162; see page 48 for Gerima's identification with the character Anberber as displaced immigrant.

49. See Devorah Heitner's study of Black public-affairs television, *Black Power TV* (Durham, NC: Duke University Press, 2013), and my interview with Madeline Anderson about *Black Journal*, Martin, "Madeline Anderson in Conversation," 82–86.

50. An exception, asserts Field, was Jamaa Fanaka, criticized for "embracing aspects of exploitation cinema that put him at odds with many of his classmates."

51. For comparisons, consider Matthew Henry's take on recycled iterations of Black masculinity in the "hood" films of the 1990s. See his "He is a 'Bad Mother*$%@!#': *Shaft* and contemporary Black Masculinity," *Journal of Popular Film and Television* 30, no. 2 (2002): 114–19.

52. Hamid Naficy, *An Accented Cinema: Exilic and Diasporic Filmmaking* (Princeton, NJ: Princeton University Press, 2001).

3

CHARLES BURNETT

A Reconsideration of Third Cinema

Amy Abugo Ongiri

And every story will end badly.
Virginie Despentes

African American history as marked by violence has always been strikingly visual. In her assessment of the mix of violence and entertainment that creates "the abject fact of blackness," Elizabeth Alexander reminds us that "Black bodies in pain for public consumption have been an American spectacle for centuries."[1] From the blaxploitation boom of the sixties and seventies to the "hood" films of the nineties, African American visual culture has tended to negotiate the history of visuality and violence with strategies of embrace rather than refusal of violence as aesthetic. The work of Charles Burnett has largely bucked the conventions of representation of African Americans in popular and independent film and visual culture. Burnett's first film, *Killer of Sheep* (1973), is set in Watts not long after the Watts riots of 1965 but is focused on urban life rather than urban violence. *The Horse* (1973) revolves around a horse that needs to be put down, but the shooting is brief and off-screen and disrupts the lyrical quality of the film. *The Glass Shield* (1994) concerns police brutality, and its violence is depicted as institutional and systemic rather than spectacularized in the manner of Hollywood. The recent revival of strategies of hyperviolence in arthouse cinema and the controversy it has provoked draw attention to violence as an aesthetic and political choice. My exploration of the refusal of violence in the work of Charles Burnett necessarily begins in two very different symbolic and geographic territories, with the opening sequence from the 1977 Haile Gerima film *Bush Mama* and a quote from the 1999 Virginie Despentes novel *Baise-Moi*, in order to explore the notions that govern the display of violence as well as some of the presumptions that govern its use as a tool of political subversion.

The opening sequence of *Bush Mama* is legendary for the story behind the story it tells. The film opens as the main character (Barbara O. Jones) walks down a busy urban street in the Watts section of Los Angeles. The chaos of the street is heightened by the camera's quick cutting between the action of the street and the main character's obvious preoccupation with other things. In the background of this chaotic street scene that sets the stage for the telling of the film's main story, the police stop a group of African American men and forcefully search them and their car. This group of young men is none other than the film crew stopped by policemen who thought it "suspicious" that such a group of young African American men would possess expensive camera equipment. The intrepid cinematographer and cameraman Charles Burnett captured the entire incident on film as it unfolded as if to substantiate Haile Gerima's claim that African American cinema "must be umbilically linked to the community from which it comes."[2] Thus the film documents in reality the degradation of humiliation that it claims to represent fictionally through the story of a young Black family caught in the throes of Black urban despair.

Bush Mama is subsequently dependent on a mix of real-time police violence and the fictionalized abstract violence of the narrative so that rather than just represent Black life, the images of the film begin to exist as history made evident through the image of violence. The film, whose crew included not only Burnett but also Larry Clark (*Passing Through*) and Barbara O. Jones (*Daughters of the Dust*), remaps the urban streets recently made visible by the Watts riots in 1965 and a general crisis in urbanity that saw the city's shift from the site of progressive modernity to the site of violent disorder, decay, and racial strife as emblematized by the phenomenon of the urban riot. The Watts Riots, the largest urban uprising of their kind in the United States up to that point, signified back on Black urban populations so much so that, in the words of Mark Reid, "destruction and the destructive came to define the black community."[3] In *The Aesthetics of Hunger*, the 1965 manifesto of the Brazilian Cinema Novo movement, Glauber Rocha writes: "The moment of violence is the moment in which the colonizer becomes aware of the existence of the colonized," and "the most noble cultural manifestation of hunger is violence."[4] The moment of the Watts Riots created a new visibility for African American urban populations and for their frustrations with mainstream culture as well as a new visual language of violence and its possibilities in the wake of the perceived failures of the civil rights movement. This accounts at least partly for the Black film boom of the late sixties and seventies now known as blaxploitation, which set new standards for the depiction of violence on screen. But Glauber Rocha's provocative claim and its implications for the visual culture of the dispossessed raises important questions: What does "the moment of violence" do or make visible for the colonized? And what does it hide?

The recent controversial French novel by Virginie Despentes, *Baise-Moi*, which is translated in the English edition as *Rape Me*, was made into an equally controversial film that employed a strategy of hyper-visible violence as a means to challenge dominant representation and empower the disenfranchised. One passage of the novel is striking in its ability to succinctly collapse the narrative conventions around people of color, violence, possibility, and expectation.

> Fatima will go with her brother, with the money from the rocks. She's not happy about it. She knows that it will catch up with them. Not necessarily the law, but her own logic. She'll die like a dog; sure she can struggle like a fury but she'll die like a dog. It's in her blood, she's made to suffer. End up in a pool of her own blood and every story will end badly.[5]

Charles Burnett's work presents an opportunity to meditate on the status of violence and the refusal of an aesthetic of violence in the work as an evolutionary aesthetic coming first out of and as a reaction to the forces of production that created the Third Cinema movement and blaxploitation films in the sixties and seventies, as well as the ghetto/hood film boom of the 1990s, out of which came films such as *Boyz n the Hood* (1991) and *New Jack City* (1991). The representational trajectories coming out of the blaxploitation and "hood" film booms have become emblematic of a certain strand of representation within popular culture that reduces the cultural experience of Black urbanity to a base level—vulgar, violent selfexpression, stories in which characters are, in the words of Virginie Despentes, literally "made to suffer" and "end up in a pool of her own blood and every story will end badly."[6] I want to posit that the refusal of violence in Burnett's work, particularly his early film *Killer of Sheep*, provides a challenge to the representational space allocated to people of color around narratives of violence not only coming from dominant cinema that gives us films like *Boyz n the Hood* and *Juice* (1992), but also from radical attempts to challenge popular aesthetics, such as the Third Cinema movement or the hyper-violence strategies of films like *Baise-Moi*.

Baise-Moi is a narrative and visual experiment with ever-escalating forms of violence and pornographic sex that is meant, through its strategy of hyper-visibility, to critique gendered representations that tie together women, eroticism, and violence. The controversial novel, described by a review on its dust jacket as "pure payback," rotates around the killing spree of two young disenfranchised and completely apolitical French women. It was made independently by the author and Coralie Trinh Thi into an equally controversial film that took the strategy of making the pornography of violence hyper-visible to its farthest extremes by not only not shying away from representing the extreme scenarios of sexual violence found in the novel but also by casting two well-known French porn stars to perform the acts depicted in the novel. Because of this representational strategy, the film was banned not only in France but also in Australia, New Zealand, and the United Kingdom.

The forward march of the narrative's everescalating violence gives new meaning to "an orgy of violence" for the way in which it insists on linking pornography, eroticism, and violence narratively through the visual. The only respite from the random collage of purposeless violence and sex occurs when the young women rescue a young Frenchwoman of Arab descent from a police assault and arrest. The two killers have decided without explanation early in the novel that the only ethic they follow in their killing spree is a promise to not kill people of Arab descent. In this way the novel importantly completes its strategy of reversal, in which women enact violence by being both the sexual aggressors and killers of men by willfully insisting on leaving people of color out of its symbolic field of violence. Fatima, the young woman who has been rescued, has the opportunity to join the two killers in their killing spree but refuses. The text seems to suggest that her fate is already sealed by narrative conventions that demand for characters of color that "all stories will end badly." The book's radical strategy is thus to alter the contours and context for representing people of color in relationship to visual and narrative violence, but insomuch as it is unable to create visual or textual narratives in which every story will not end badly, it is unable to fundamentally alter the conventions governing representational norms of Black people and thus to open up space for new stories.

Charles Burnett and other Black filmmakers who came out of UCLA and formed the first important contemporary wave of Black independent filmmakers consciously worked against the visual culture of Hollywood that created hyperviolence as the definitional norm in relationship to Black urban culture, especially through the genre of blaxploitation, a genre that married Black masculine screen violence to the Black transformative identity called for through the popular rhetoric of the Black Power movement.[7] Of this group, which includes Burnett, Billy Woodberry, Larry Clark, Sharon Larkin, Haile Gerima, and, in a later phase, Julie Dash, Burnett's work most embodies a refusal of cinematic violence as a representational strategy. But while his work refuses to visually represent violence, it is almost situated squarely at the geographic and symbolic site and scene of violation of Black people and therefore of the violence it cinematically seeks to disavow.

The powerfully meditative *Killer of Sheep*, made in 1973 and released in 1977, is set in South Central Los Angeles—a geographic locale made mythic by the "hood" film genre—in the decade immediately following the Watts riots. Of the Black urban uprisings of the sixties and seventies, the Watts riots were particularly symbolically significant in the United States because their televisual representation set the tone for popular culture's representational collapse of urbanism and violence. Both the 1990 film *To Sleep with Anger* and Burnett's 1995 film *The Glass Shield* are set in Black Los Angeles in the years immediately preceding and following the second most significant Black urban uprising in US history, which occurred in Los Angeles in 1992. The urban uprising in Los Angeles in 1992 set the climate for intensified police repression and the attendant attempt to both counteract and explain the violent nature of that repression through the "hood" film genre throughout the nineties. *The Glass Shield* also significantly featured so-called "gangster rapper" Ice Cube, whose 1991 album, *Death Certificate*, used the drama of urban violence to forewarn a world that wasn't really listening of the approaching apocalypse of the 1992 Los Angeles rebellion.

Burnett's most recent film, *Nat Turner: A Troublesome Property* (2003), takes Black violence from the historical site and ground zero of its symbolic and representational core in the bloody but failed 1831 slave rebellion of Nat Turner. This film, rather than exploring Turner's legacy as a legacy of violence, essentially situates Turner as a historical enigma continually created and recreated by the politics of the moment. *Nat Turner: A Troublesome Property* significantly calls us to question the representational strategy that would have us creating visual pleasure through the representation of cinematic violence as a visual political strategy. The film reworks an audience's desire to witness the aborted carnage of the Nat Turner rebellion and transcends this desire in a way that speaks to Frantz Fanon's famous invective that "every spectator is a Coward or Traitor." The film calls into question what motivates a desire for filmic violence on screen and what is betrayed by a desire to see the violence of post-coloniality represented on screen.

The mandate that Black film make visible as evidence in a documentary fashion the history of Black oppression in the United States often obscures the aesthetic choices made in the representation of violence as well as its political implications. Certainly African American filmmaking has been charged—more so than other modes of American filmmaking—with the mandate to not only represent but also to provide documentary evidence of Black life in a society so much constituted by racial and economic segregation that many Americans are far more likely to be comfortable with images of Black people than Black people themselves. Both Haile Gerima's *Bush Mama* and Burnett's early film *Killer of Sheep* come out of a Third Cinema aesthetic that championed the "long war with the camera as a rifle . . . and expropriator of imageweapons" and the projector as a gun that can shoot twenty-four frames per second, as Fernando Solanos and Octavio Getino describe what they label "guerilla cinema" in the important Third Cinema manifesto "Towards a Third Cinema."[8] Following Julio García Espinosa's claim in "For an Imperfect Cinema" that "nowadays perfect cinema—technically and artistically masterful—is almost always reactionary cinema," the movement championed the use of techniques that could "show the process that generates the problems" through the use of handheld cameras, amateur actors, and an emphasis on transforming the spectator into what Solanos and Getino label "the participant comrade."[9] Julio García Espinosa concludes "For an Imperfect Cinema" with the following polemical command:

> An imperfect cinema is no longer interested in quality or technique. It can be created equally well with a Mitchell or with an 8mm camera, in a studio or in a guerrilla camp in the middle of the jungle. Imperfect cinema is no longer interested in predetermined taste, and much less in "good taste." It is not quality it seeks in an artist's work. The only thing it is interested in is how an artist responds to the following question: What are you doing in order to overcome the barrier of the "cultured" elite audience which up to now has conditioned the form of your work?[10]

The Aesthetics of Hunger is premised on the notion that the collapse of a rhetoric of revolution into a rhetoric of violence is necessitated by the fact that though the colonizer "can't sleep for fear of the hungry," the colonized, in fact, only becomes visible to the colonizer in the moment of violence. But what of the psychic life of the colonized? What strategies do we employ to make the oppressed visible to themselves? Does violence serve the same function of making the colonized visible to themselves as it serves to make the colonized visible to the colonizer?

Though *The Aesthetics of Hunger* speaks of those in power who "can't sleep for fear of the hungry," in both *Bush Mama* and *Killer of Sheep* it is significantly the oppressed who are haunted by their inability to sleep, whose inner lives are disturbed by the things that they cannot control in their waking lives. But while *Bush Mama* literalizes a cathartic violence not only in the killing of a police officer that constitutes the film's climax but also in the almost mundane acts of brutality throughout the movie, *Killer of Sheep* refuses overt displays of violence beyond the ritualized killing of sheep that the lead character enacts in his role as a slaughterhouse butcher and the warlike games the movie's children play. Violence is importantly never postulated as a solution in *Killer of Sheep*, either thematically for the characters or as catharsis for the audience. "Can't nothing ever make you smile?" the wife of the film's troubled main character chides him. When he doesn't answer, she offers, "You just need to get some sleep," suggesting that the answer to his deep discontent lies in a psychic rather than violent revolution. I want to suggest that ultimately there is something highly revolutionary about staging the ghetto as the site of a beauty that is precious but not simplistically so and that lies far beyond its prototypical presentations as the terrain of violence.

In one hauntingly beautiful sequence, a little girl sings along to what she understands as the words to Earth, Wind & Fire's "Reasons" as her mother lovingly looks on. The film manages to visualize the mundane moments of beauty occurring in the life of the ghetto in such a way that it rescripts the urban terrain into the site of beauty while not compromising the social deprivation that it also depicts and documents. I would argue that this sequence has more in common with modernist visions of the city, in terms of its formal interest in experimentation in light, form, and a specific investment in the power and beauty of the built environment of the city, than it does with films celebrated by Third Cinema, such as Luis Bunuel's *Los Olivdados* or even *Bush Mama*, films whose goals and documentary aims are more toward a critique of the city as both a psychic and physical space. The sequence encodes a formal and thematic investment in the transformative utopian aspects of the aesthetic, which for modernist visual artists such as Lászlo Moholy-Nagy and Lyonel Feininger came through as an absolute belief in the transformative power of functionalist aesthetics. For *Killer of Sheep* and Burnett's work generally, this interest in aesthetics comes through as an absolute belief in the power and beauty of Black culture.

Saidiya V. Hartman comments on what she labels the "obscene theatricality of the slave trade" as enslaved Africans were meant to perform against their obvious degradation through ritual sacred music and dance in staged performances of song, dance, and smiles. She chooses as emblematic of "the obscene theatricality of the slave trade" the moment in which Black slaves are made to "step it up lively," sing, and smile as they process shackled to the auction block in what is known as "the coffle."[11] Hartman notes the ease in which the "hideous" and "disgusting" mixed with "merriment" and "the entertaining" to "create the profane association of song and suffering" in a spectacle of blackness.[12] I wonder about the rare moments in the history of Black representation in United States that are able to imagine a space beyond the mix of "the hideous" and "the entertaining" as emblematized by the coffle.[13] *Killer of Sheep* encodes in its representation of the structures of urbanity a subtle but almost uncontainable joy. Because of this, *Killer of Sheep* creates a visual politics that both testifies to and aestheticizes the beauty of Black life in an unprecedented manner. Clear linkages could be drawn between functionalist modernist practices and the functionalist politics of manifestos such as "Towards Third Cinema" and *The Aesthetics of Hunger* that emphasized a sparse communication between aesthetics and action that is both functional and direct. Solanos and Getino argue: "Real alternatives . . . are only possible" in "making films that the system cannot assimilate" or "in making films that directly and explicitly set out to fight the system."[14] This mirrors the bare functionalism of the modernist architect Minoru Yamasaki's motto, "The purpose of architecture is to create an atmosphere in which man can live, work, and enjoy." What is most interesting about Burnett's work is precisely its refusal to participate in the easy functionalist equation of Third Cinema that reduces revolutionary political action to political violence. On an episode of the *Chappelle Show*, Dave Chappelle explained that a certain skit set on a slave plantation was cut because studio executives deemed the ending, which has him pull out a gun and shoot the slave master in the heart in repeated slow motion, "not funny." "Now I might be the only one," Chappelle quipped, "but I think that's funny and I would do it every episode if you could." There is a certain obvious visual pleasure for oppressed people in enacting or witnessing the enactment of the reordering of social power through symbolic acts of violence that I would argue extends beyond a simplistic desire for visual payback. Frantz Fanon's famous polemic "Concerning Violence" speaks on the dream life of the native.

> The dreams of the native are always of muscular prowess; his dreams are of action and aggression . . . During the period of colonization, the native never stops achieving his freedom from nine in the evening until six in the morning . . . The native is an oppressed person whose permanent dream is to become the persecutor.[15]

We need to take seriously Fanon's claim that the fantasy life of the oppressed is governed strictly by a desire for violent actions. What are the implications of this configuration if it is indeed true? Furthermore, if cinema exists as a fantasy projection of the lyrical possibilities of Black life, does the prevalent association of blackness with images of violence speak to an imaginative failure in relationship to dreaming Black possibility? Or does it simply bear out Glauber Rocha's claim in *The Aesthetics of Hunger* that "only through the dialectic of violence will we reach lyricism"?

I would argue that films like *Killer of Sheep*, *To Sleep with Anger*, and *The Glass Shield* work against the notion that "only through the dialectic of violence will we reach lyricism." Consequently, I would suggest that what is important and interesting about Burnett's work is precisely that it opens up a space for Black people that denies the necessity that "every story will end badly." Furthermore, it is precisely able to examine the aesthetics of political violence without representing actual violence, and this opens up a different sort of psychic space for the exploration of Black cultural life. In films like *Killer of Sleep* and *To Sleep with Anger*, Black characters reinhabit the space of urbanity in a manner that does not deny the poverty and the pain of the history of Black urbanism but also significantly gestures toward possibilities that are not imaginable within the existing conventions of visual violence. It is in this space that I want to end.

Notes

1. Elizabeth Alexander, "Can You Be BLACK and Look at This?: Reading the Rodney King Video(s)," in *Black Male: Representations of Masculinity in Contemporary American Art* (New York: Harry N. Abrams, 1995), 95.

2. Haile Gerima, "Triangular Cinema, Breaking Toys, and Dinknesh vs. Lucy," in *Questions of Third Cinema*, Paul Willeman and Jim Pines, eds. (London: British Film Institute, 1990), 86.

3. Mark Reid, *Redefining Black Film* (Berkeley: University of California Press, 1993), 271.

4. Glauba Rocha, "The Aesthetics of Hunger," in *Twenty-Five Years of the New Latin American Cinema*, Michael Chanan, ed. (London: British Film Institute, 1983), 13.

5. Virginie Despentes, *Baise-Moi* (New York: Grove Press, 2003), 241.

6. Ibid., 241.

7. For an account of the emergence of this group of filmmakers, see Ntongela Masilela, "The Los Angeles School of Black Filmmakers," in *Black American Cinema*, Manthia Diawara, ed. (New York: Routledge, 1993).

8. Fernando Solanas and Octavio Getino, "Towards a Third Cinema," in *Twenty-Five Years of the New Latin American Cinema*, Michael Chanan, ed. (London: British Film Institute, 1983), 24.

9. Julio Garcia Espinosa, "For an Imperfect Cinema," in *Twenty-Five Years of the New Latin American Cinema* (1983), 28, 32; Solanas and Getino 1983, 26.

10. Espinosa 1983, 33.

11. Saidiya V. Hartman, *Scenes of Subjection: Terror, Slavery, and Self-Making in Nineteenth-Century America* (New York: Oxford University Press, 1997), 17.

12. Ibid., 33.

13. Ibid., 17.

14. Solanas and Getino 1983, 21.

15. Masilela 1993, 241.

4

CHARLES BURNETT

Consummate Cineaste

Michael T. Martin

Note: This interview was conducted on the campus of Indiana University, Bloomington, at the Indiana University Cinema in front of a live audience in April 2011.

MICHAEL T. MARTIN: Mr. Burnett, I thought that we would begin this conversation about your formation as a filmmaker attending UCLA film school. What lessons, if any, did you learn while attending UCLA—lessons about filmmaking, about your craft?

CHARLES BURNETT: One of the things about UCLA then was that it was sort of, that there was a structure, but it was left up to the students to really sort of take the initiative to sort of learn on their own to some extent. After you today take all the preliminary courses, like film history and things like that, and some other classes; I don't know, I can't remember exactly. But to get into the production department, you had to do Project One and you had to be successful. Project One was a class where you made a little film—a silent film, but you added music later or something like that. It was your first film, and if you did very well—and out of seventy students, if they only took ten—and then after that, if you were successful, they gave you a camera basically and said, "Here, go out and make a film, and come back with something we haven't seen before." So that was a good thing about UCLA. The important thing was that you counted on your fellow students to sort of of get through the day because you had the sort of, you learned basically by working with other students' films. So we formed groups and worked on everyone's film. So it was learning to work with different—it was a very diverse group at the time. It was learning to sort of work with everybody, because later on it became so important in becoming a filmmaker is knowing how to work with other talented people.

MM: Did you discover in that process, in that experience, things about yourself that informed your work?

CB: I think because of the political times—it was during the civil rights movement and things like that—you became political. I think that's what happened to me when I went to UCLA or when I was going to college at that time. You were either a part of the problem or a part of the solution, as the phrase went. So you were sort of put in corners, so to speak, and something that we chose in a sense because we thought we were doing something, a part of the movement. But in terms of learning, I don't know. I was aware of the kind of films that I wanted to make, but it was a constant debate or a discussion about what is a Black film and what you should be doing as a filmmaker and what is your responsibility. In that sense, I was sort of forming what I wanted to be in that sense.

MM: There is considerable, in fact, there is unending debate around these designations by [Clyde] Taylor and by [Toni Cade] Bambara. Do you agree with them, all these brandings that are very provocative and suggestive of a level of political awareness and sophistication and commitment? Is that the tenor of the mood in your group?

CB: It was, in a sense. We were constantly asking ourselves and challenging each other about what is a Black film. We had discussions way into the night. That was one of the good things about UCLA, because the campus was open virtually twenty-four hours, at least the film department was. We were in many times really violent discussions about what we should be doing as filmmakers or potential filmmakers. But we never thought of ourselves beyond just that small group. We never thought of our place in history or anything like that. We were just trying to survive. We knew that after school, after you did your whatever it is, what was going to be out there was nothing if we didn't sort of try to form some sort of organization and try to aid one another after. At the time there wasn't Sundance or anything. There wasn't any sort of distribution of independent films as such. They had education films like Churchill Films, I think it was, and maybe there was a company in San Francisco that I think Clyde Taylor was associated with because he knew them. And there were some brothers who were—I mean actual brothers—who actually, and I can't think of the name of it, and they were the only ones. Like I mentioned, there wasn't a Sundance, there wasn't any means to get into Hollywood; unless you have cousins that worked there or something like that, you weren't getting in. I started off wanting to be a cameraman, even though I knew that you had to wait fifteen years just to work your way up to just become a loader and a first camera assistant and things like that. But we were prepared for that.

MM: So is it fair to say that it's an accurate description in hindsight?

CB: The thing that we have problems with is the name of the LA Rebellion or whatever else. We never thought of that in that sense. But I know there are arguments about it now.

MM: And there will be next week in LA.

CB: Yes, so Haile, I think, and I don't want to speak for him, but I think, because he just spoke the other day at the event.

MM: Haile Gerima?

CB: Yes. He was sort of hesitant about calling it a LA rebellion. I don't feel that we really accomplished what we thought we were going to do or should have done and missed an opportunity because of that. So I have these feelings about that because of that.

MM: Were you guys, were the group of men and women filmmakers at UCLA in conversation with your counterparts in New York City, the Stan Lathans, the St. Clair Bournes, Greaves is a little earlier generation or half a generation early. Were you in conversation with them during this period?

CB: No, not really. St. Clair Bourne was different because I think he came toward the end and taught at UCLA or something or another. That was the only connection. The others, there was a lady in New York who had a little screening room in her basement apartment, and I'm trying to think of her name, who was another connection we had. But other than that, no, it wasn't until much later that people were looking for independent films. I think it was because of that connection between New York and LA and all of the rest of the filmmakers around the country started to exist and we became very much aware of each other.

MM: What about in Chicago with the Black Arts Movement? Larry Neal is trying to make films, experimenting. Were you in conversation with that group?

CB: That was after. That came after. I don't know exactly what year it was. It was sometime in the eighties or something, late eighties. But it was only after for me, and we had already left school by that time, that it became apparent. The later filmmakers had that relationship more than we did.

MM: Let's turn to your film practice. Are there working principles of storytelling that you adhere to?

CB: For me it's like trying to represent people in a true fashion in a way, in a respectful way. I think a lot of our concerns when we were going to UCLA was this failure of Hollywood to see us as real people. So we always had that area to try, even if it was a comedy, whatever it is, a surreal or whatever it was to show a different narrative and to try to share our experiences and things like that basically.

MM: Are there aesthetic principles and considerations also that are featured, are a part of your toolkit?

CB: We always had that debate about what are Black aesthetics and things like that. We never really resolved those things, so I'm always hesitant to talk about how it applies to me in a sense. I just know that there are stories that I like to tell, and it comes from I guess just being around an environment where—I come from Mississippi, and there is a lot of storytelling. The area I lived in, everyone, was Texas, Arkansas, Louisiana, and all of those different Southern states. There was this sense of a community and people telling stories about the place they left, about home. One of the things, because of that the South has always been like a mystery to me. It's always been something that dealt with the memory of the past. I was always excited about it because these storytellers made it seem like it was this magical place on one hand, but yet still it was this other side to it, which they didn't want to go back to. My mother said she would never go back to Mississippi, and she gave me reasons why and things like that. So you had this little sort of dual kind of mixed feelings about it. But part of it was magical, and I always wanted to capture that sort of storytelling element about it.

MM: Are there particulars that stand out in the telling of the story?

CB: I think that's one of the things that I was hoping expressed it, but it was trying to give this people a voice in a sense, and because I thought the world that they created needed to be shared and I didn't see it on television or the movies or things like that. So there was this really strong, it was all of us in terms of our stories. I don't know.

MM: You said in a publication, and I don't remember which one, that the organizing motif of your films is, and I quote here, "the power to endure." What do you mean by that?

CB: The people I grew up with worked and worked and worked. They would complain or whatever, but still it was this sense that they didn't give up. Like the South, they moved here, we survived and that, and you look over, and it was all about survival. I wouldn't be here today if some distant relative hadn't jumped over the boat or something like that between a little passage or something like that. I look at those pictures of those slave boats, and

I'm claustrophobic to a certain extent, and I couldn't see myself lying in chains like that on top of each other like that. Just that alone I pay homage and tribute, because I don't think I could endure that. But the fact of the matter is, it's people I lived with that they held their family together. They were churchgoing and things like that, and they provided and they shared whatever they had with other people who didn't have. I really admired that. I wanted to—a winning lesson, that's the one thing I wanted to sort of share with everybody is that these people are real human beings and they worked in spite of the harshness, but they endured.

MM: Many of your films, among them *Killer of Sheep*, *To Sleep in Anger*, and *My Brother's Wedding*, are narratives about families, their travails but also their resilience in the face of crisis. Does the family serve as a sort of a trope in your films to address larger issues of social inequality, injustice, racism?

CB: In a way, but I keep it so simple about the family in a sense because everything sort of starts in the family. I read this whole thing with John Branshaw. He did this thing on the family. That was much later, but it reaffirmed what I had believed and suspected that if you have come from a good foundation, it really is such a positive thing. If it's all scattered, you really have to be strong to overcome that, but I understood that a lot of violence started within the family. So that's what I sort of focused on in cinema in a sense, because most of the kids in my neighborhood—because I grew up in an area where, I was very lucky anyway that there were a lot of sort of gang members. This was before all of the drug things became so deadly.

MM: We're talking LA now.

CB: Yes, [before LA] became so deadly, and so I was really lucky because I knew these guys, and so I was able to get along and learn a lot of things from them and things I didn't particularly pick up. But anyway, I got to know them in a sense that I saw that they really didn't want to be this sort of image that they were projecting in a sense. It was a matter of survival. They just were, they just had this perverse notion that sort of generated from just being in that environment. For example, like when I was there, I didn't think I was going to live to be twenty-one. Most of us felt like that. I remember when I got twenty-one, I was quite shocked and surprised. Literally, it was a total surprise when you say, oh, it's your birthday, and I'm twenty-one. It was like I began to live that. If I would have known or felt differently that I had all of these opportunities, that I was going to live to no particular date, I would have taken life differently or seriously more so. I saw most of the kids doing that because they didn't think, like this was it for them, that there was no future. It was only then that I started taking education seriously and things like that.

MM: Suggested in your comments is the notion that people, in order to survive in that kind of environment apart from what they do, they wear a mask. Did you wear a mask, and what was it if you did?

CB: I don't know if I wore a mask because I was sort of in-between. Something sort of held me back from going all the way with these characters. In a way, I was sort of a listener, I think maybe because I had this speech problem. So I always felt an outsider in a way. So that was a plus and a minus in a sense, just because I always had this distance because of that. I don't know if I wore a mask as such. I was really conscious of, I think, right and wrong in many ways, and I've always, I had this real extreme case of shyness. So I didn't have to wear a mask. I just avoided people. You would say it was sick in a sense, because I would see people and I would just turn and go down the alley or whatever it is and that sort of thing. It took me forever to realize why am I doing this and something like that. So I didn't have to wear a mask. I was just invisible. That was my case.

MM: You mentioned Hollywood on one or two occasions. Let's talk about Hollywood. You said to me in New Orleans that in the past, I quote here, "Hollywood wasn't assessible to Black independent filmmakers or to films about people of color unless they were blaxploitation films." That apparently has changed somewhat—like Julie Dash, Spike Lee, and others, you have successfully, and I'm going to be careful and condition that, crossed the Hollywood divide. How have you negotiated the demands and conventions of the studio system both in television and film, and are they different?

CB: I don't think I'm successful in it at all. I don't make films that often, and the people I know are in the same boat and don't make films. In fact, a lot of them have gone on to do other things and quit film altogether. It's very difficult. It's very difficult. I did a film, I think the last feature I did was in the summer about two or three years ago. It's a film, I won't mention the name and I don't want to hear about it on my résumé or anything it was so bad. Seriously, I thought I was going to have a heart attack or something.

MM: I hope someone asks you during the question and answer period about this.

CB: I'm in denial. Literally, I thought every day I went to this job I knew what I was going to do and plan and everything, but as soon as I got on the set, a total blank. I would be aware of the fact that I couldn't move. Everything that can go wrong on film could go wrong. The producer wanted to, I don't know why he hired me. One thing is because he wanted to direct the film.

He cast the film, and he had a producer on the set that said no, he wanted it shot this way. Literally every shot was planned. It was just a nightmare. It really didn't have anything to do with the movie basically, just made my appearance that day and that was it. So that was one of the worst experiences I had on a production. Plus I had an actor who wanted to direct the film. When you have those combinations and a particular actor who is a star, you can't do anything.

MM: Whom you won't name?

CB: I won't name. I should, but it may be someone's best friend here. I don't know. And so you light the scene, and the script says when he comes in the door. So the camera people would light for the door coming in, for him to come in. But he would come in and say, "No, I want to come in the back door." We had already lit for him to come in this way here, and it takes hours to do that sort of thing. He would do that constantly. You would set up something, and he wants to do the other thing. It would drive me crazy because working in films is very intense. So this went on and on, and you couldn't do anything. He would come in and he would say, "I'm not going to say these lines." It was no negotiation at all. But then there are some really nice moments you can have, but not on that film. All of them were bad. But in terms of other productions, when it works. it can be a very nice experience. Actors who are really actors and want to create, and you have camera people, you have all of the crewmembers working, and everyone wants to do something really good. That's when it works.

MM: But at the end of the day, your style and mode of directing is not done by consensus.

CB: No. No, you can't. There's no point in being a director, a filmmaker if you, it's not democratic. There has to be someone who has a focus and vision and has a sense of the whole story. If you have a script and you give it to anyone here, I mean each one would look at it differently and think it's about something else. I know this producer I had who did this film before he did *Sleep with Anger*. He was really mad at the director, and he said—it was the first time I directed, and he didn't know that the film was a love story until the end of the movie. But you can have people working on the film that you really have to tell, "This is what the story is about." You have to make sure everyone is on the same page, because even though you're reading the same thing, everyone has different ideas. So with that in mind, someone has to know what the story is and direct it in that sense.

MM: You also said to me in New Orleans that, I'm quoting here again, "Hollywood is the only game in town." Is it still the only game in town, and if that's the case, what's the future for Black independent filmmaking?

CB: There is an example if people are very successful, like Tyler Perry and people like that and some other folks. But it's so hard to make an independent film for anybody. It takes, when it was very successful in a sense, and that was like in the early nineties. I think there was a cutoff point after that. It took before that like maybe five or ten years to get a film financed independently, and that was about the average. That's what was said about it, and we accepted that. Now we're trying to get, when I did, what's that movie called, *Annihilation of Fish*, Paul Heller who is an Academy Award—

MM: James Earl Jones and Vanessa Redgrave?

CB: Yes. It took him over ten years to get the financing to make that film. Here's a guy who was a very successful producer and got an Academy Award for *My Left Foot* and things like that. He couldn't get the movie made until finally he was on a board of this company, and one of the board members is a very wealthy man, and his wife wanted to get involved in movie making. He wrote him a check that said yes, we'll do that movie as a producer.

MM: Three years ago, you told me you were still trying to get that film shown.

CB: Yes, we were and we are still. It's a comedy, and it was written by a Jamaican film writer, Tony Winkler. He's a very imaginative person. It's about these two people who are sort of eccentric, and they sort of get together because of loneliness and things like that. They're sort of made for each other. Earlier they show signs of senility or something or something not quite balanced. So we made the film, and I must say those were some great actors to work with. James Earl Jones is wonderful, and Lynn Redgrave was just an amazing person in every respect. Anyway, we finished the film, and we screened the film in Toronto. Todd McCarthy, I mentioned his name, Todd McCarthy didn't like the film. He wrote one of the worst reviews in the history of journalism about the film. We had a distributor wanting to distribute the film, and he pulled out because the review was such a bad review. So we lost our distribution because of that, and we've been trying to get it released ever since. But other people have seen the film and couldn't find out what was wrong. Todd McCarthy thought we were making fun of elderly people and the mentally ill. But it goes back further than that, because Todd McCarthy is a friend; I'll tell you how this whole thing is damaging in many ways. If you make enemies with people, you have problems, you have problems. Todd McCarthy is a good friend of Pierre Andrieux, and Pierre funded—helped to get financing for—a film that was called *The Glass Shield*. We had arguments with Pierre. That's the second big argument I had with Pierre, and he is the kind of person who, if you make enemies, you've made an enemy. He is one of these guys that sort of operates in Cannes. He sort of helps films in Cannes. He's retired now. We didn't do what he wanted us to do because he didn't like the particular actor we had, and he wanted to cut her out altogether before we made the movie. We said, no, no, no, we already made a deal with her, and she's a good actress, and that's it. So he never really had a good relationship after that. Then, after we finished the film, he wanted us to take every, all of her scenes out. She's the principal in the movie.

MM: Lori Petty?

CB: Yes. So to accommodate him and the French production company, CiBy 2000, just to show it wouldn't work, we made the cuts, took all of her scenes out. So the head of CiBy 2000, "Oh, it's great." I said no, I took it out and I showed you I would do that. Now it's all going back in. It doesn't make any sense. They're going to sabotage this film. So Pierre was going to attack one of the producers on the film, who was Carolyn Schroeder; he was going to, he almost did a somersault. And so anyway, Pierre and Todd McCarthy are great friends. That's the only reason we can think of anyone writing such a bad review is because Pierre being his friend and sort of dictated or whatever. That's what we think. It could be the opposite; it could be a bad film, but we don't think that. If you see the film, I don't know. We actually, the interesting thing was we screened it on the day of 9/11 in La Jolla or someplace near San Diego. The screening was already set before 9/11, but 9/11 happened the same day. We were supposed to be there and show the film. We weren't sure if it was going to happen or not because of 9/11. So we called the theater, and they weren't there. So finally we're still going on, we're still going to screen it. So we reluctantly went down there, hesitantly went, and they had the film. It was going to be in two theaters, and it was packed. So I asked the audience, we didn't know if we were going to be here because of what happened. Someone said something very interesting, and they said that they needed to be with somebody, and so they all came.

MM: That's the back story of it.

CB: Yes.

MM: One or two more questions, and then I think there are people here very eager to interact with you. Among your most recent features, Mr. Burnett, *Namibia: The Struggle for Liberation*, marks a significant departure from your previous work topically, aesthetically and in terms of scale. What attracted you to take on this project so distant from home, from everything you know and have lived?

CB: Well, it was a chance to do a number of things. One, when I was at UCLA, all of that stuff was going on and before, and so there were a lot of African students at UCLA. So I was very much aware of SWAPO but not fully, but it was rather superficial at the time. So when this project came, it was an opportunity to sort of do something and contribute. So I thought it was a very interesting story, a very good story, and so that was one of the reasons why I got involved in it.

MM: Did it challenge your way of making movies as you have in the past, your use of camera work, which is distinct from your other work, the fact that you are no longer working within a confined space like in *Killer of Sheep*, urban settings but on the savannahs of Namibia, where the cast of characters are in the thousands?

CB: The problem was language. I was very much aware that I didn't want to make a Hollywood film or an American film, but I wanted to make a Namibian film as close as possible—not about Charles Burnett, but about the Namibian struggle—and try to see it how they saw it. That was my main concern. Culturally, of course, it was different and things like that. There were many issues that I had to overcome, but the biggest one was—I think was—starting off it was individual things that happened, and you overcome them and overcome them. One of the biggest problems was, I mentioned language and names, because in Namibia, first of all, they speak a number of languages—Afrikaans, German, and their own tribal language, and then several other tribal languages. They are very multilingual. We would cast, and we would have a number—I forget how many, many hundreds of people literally in the film. We're in casting, and you bring people by for several other parts. The first problem was that the lady who was training them to be actors in the part was a stage actress, and she had trained them badly for the casting session. They were all overacting, and I thought, my God, I don't have any actors here. What am I going to do? Then the names were so difficult for me to remember. So I ended up casting the same guy for three or four roles, because I couldn't remember his name or anything, and I wanted the same thing. It was only until we got on the set that I realized that the lady had trained them badly. They were perfect actors—they were great in many ways, as far as I was concerned. But I hadn't, like I said, I had cast so many people for the same role because I couldn't remember them. It was a nightmare trying to untangle all of that stuff just because I couldn't remember their names. The other thing was that it was initially based on the book called *Where Others Wavered* [by Sam Nujoma], and he became the head of SWAPO and became the first president of Namibia. He was like a god to the Namibians, but he had made a lot of mistakes at being head of SWAPO and then the presidency and everything like that in the presidency. His popularity was just beginning to dip a bit, but his book told the story from his eyes, and he didn't give too many people credit. So the people wanted a film about not only him but others that contributed, important people in the movement. So it became this big expansive drama that included everyone's story. I listened to, I did a lot of reading, and then I interviewed a lot of people and listened to their story and then integrated all of that stuff together. It became this big canvas where everyone wanted their story told. You couldn't, we tried to make composite characters, like Danny Glover's character—it represents a number of priests—but mostly it was all individual people, and we had to tell their story. So it became difficult in that sense, but it's a beautiful place to shoot. Everywhere you look, it's a great place for composition and scenery and stuff. That was a good thing about it, plus we had the use of the military and everything. You're out there with wild animals. One of the things I want to say, people do really stupid things when they get the opportunity. Something about, particularly Americans, anyway. Because there were wild elephants coming through our set and stuff like that, and this is honest. We were traveling. They said leave the elephants alone. So we were traveling across this place and some elephants eighty meters away. There's this big rogue elephant over to the side, and John Demps, the cameraman, and I, stopped and sort of whistled at it. It was eating peacefully and then it turned and walked away, and then we started shouting more and more, trying to get his attention. It came back to where it was and then it came toward us. Those things move deceptively fast. I mean, you think they, you do this double take, and it's like it's dissolving closer and closer, like jump cuts, and just walking, and the next thing you know, it's on you like that. We had to jump in the car and take off. We have pictures of that. We did a lot of stupid things like that. But that was the fun part. That was one of the things that made it worth it. We slept right next to the Zambezi River. Our lodge was about, or cabin, was up above, and the water was, I don't know, from where that wall is there, right there, and the water down below. You could hear the hippos and stuff. So when you come out of your cabin at night, you had to look around. You just couldn't walk like you come in here and walk into the lobby or whatever it is. You had to look under everything. Gators or crocodiles in Africa, and hippos and things like that, and snakes. It was interesting to be in that kind of environment.

MM: What's in the can? What's in development?

CB: You always have something. We have about five or six projects trying to get off the ground and moving them out. There are several projects that we have been working on for a number of years, and that's the bad thing. It's sort of like you can't concentrate on one thing. You have to be scattered all over the place, so it makes it very difficult to be creative in a sense.

MM: Is that just to beat the odds?

CB: Yes, like I mentioned Paul Heller earlier. He just had that one film to do, and ten years go by, and you just, so you have to have a dozen of those things waiting in the wings so something may go. It's like, what's that expression, something like "throw a number of things against the wall, and something might stick." It's that sort of attitude, and you spend all of your time running from one project to another, trying to get it developed. I took this job at Cal Arts because nothing was happening. That's the irony of this business. I didn't want to take the job at Cal Arts because this might happen, and then it didn't, and so I took a job at Cal Arts, and the moment I signed the contract with them, then all of these other projects came back again. It's like it's either feast or famine. Now it looks like they're not happening now again. It's just madness. It's not a job for sane people.

MM: Any filmmakers in the audience? I see two. Any advice to a would-be filmmaker?

CB: First of all, I wouldn't encourage anyone. I would give them all sorts of warning. There are people who make it, but I swear to you, all of my friends are out of work now and have gone to other things. They're getting kicked out of their apartments. But I would say if you are going to be a filmmaker, you have to be very passionate about it and really work hard at it. Just improve on your skills and talent and things like that. But the thing I would say is that if you are going to be one, make sure you make a lot of films now and where you feel that you can make any film, that you walk on a set and you can make it work.

MM: I remember I asked you the same question three years ago. One of the things that struck me is you said to this would-be filmmaker, "Never lie to yourself." What did you mean by that?

CB: There's a number of things. For example, there are some films I can't do. There are some films I don't want to do. This last one that I told you about that I had this awful experience with I kind of wanted to do it, but then after I found out, I should have quit. It would have saved me a lot of gray hairs and stuff and all sorts of madness. There was one film I didn't want to do, but I tried to get out of it in a sort of strange way by being too critical initially when they asked me about the script. I read it, and I said well it needs this, and then I gave them a whole bunch of notes about this thick, and thinking that I would be able to get out of it gracefully. I was surprised when they came back and said yes, we like what you said, and we'll, and I was like, oh God, no. That was one of the worst experiences I had before this other one. It was madness on that one too. I think you have to really know what you can do and can't do. But the way things are now is that you'd better take anything. If you can't, you better say you can because of the way the job situation is, but no, you really have to be honest with yourself.

MM: Let's take some questions from the audience. Sir?

Q1: Can you talk a bit about your choice of scripts? Are the films we're seeing scripted by you? Did you choose them? What is the process, and can you talk about the whole process?

CB: I think my early work was from scripts that I did, but later ones, because it takes a while to write a script. At least it takes me a while to write a script. That keeps one off the playing field a long time. The agent says you should just get people who write scripts and find scripts you like and do it that way; it's a lot faster and so forth, which is somewhat true. It's really hard to find work that you like. You find things that are very close to what you like, and you find writers that have the same sensibilities, and you try to work like that, and you guys share the same kinds of feelings. It's hard for me because the things I like to write about is kind of hard to sell. So it's a problematic thing for me. No one seems to be interested in writing, in my material. They don't want to and run away from it if anything. *The Glass Shield* was. I had rewritten that from like a page one rewrite. In the first script, there's nothing in it, which is good—you can do something like that and find something that it can grow into something else. That was like a TV script in the beginning, and then it was very limited in a way, so I just took it and expanded it into something that made it where I was pleased with it and things like that. But I have to be careful what I do and work with other people, other writers' material, because you don't want to just arrogantly take over and just destroy their concept and ideas, because it's just as valid as yours. If you're a director, you want to make it work when you want to be able to make it work for you because it's going to be your vision in a sense. It's only through your eyes in a way that it could work. I did a film, I won't mention the name of it, but there was a writer, and I liked the idea, but there were some things that I had to—I knew there was going to be a war at each level of having to take things out of it because I was unhappy with it. But the basic idea I liked, and I managed to get a lot of the stuff out. There was a scene, and I couldn't get this writer to redo, and I couldn't understand the scene. I asked him, "Well, what does it mean?" And he said, "Well, you know, it means this is the answer, it means . . ." OK. So I knew at some point the actors are going to ask me about this scene, and sure enough, the day we were going to do this scene, the two actors came up to me and said, "Charles, can you just tell me about this scene?" You have to come up with something reasonable and logical for them to understand what it's about to work with. I came up with some logic that they were satisfied with, and I thought, God, but you get a lot of that sometimes. You don't understand it, but you have a writer that has a lot of control or something like that. So I try to avoid things, certain kinds of scripts if I can. And TV, there is no question the writer's, that's what happens, it's gone and things like that. You can't make any changes. It's a writer's medium. But in terms of independent film, it's best of you get material that you are really, really passionate about, not just for a job. The last couple of films I did, it was for jobs, and I really hate that, really hate that.

MM: Is *To Sleep with Anger* is your own script?

CB: Yes, *Sleep with Anger* is my own, yes. That was a difficult script because it was funded by—well, it was initially going to be funded by—CPB, Corporation for Public Broadcasting, and I had developed another script with them based on the true story of a murder that took place in my neighborhood of a young girl who witnessed a crime. She was asked to come forward and testify, and she did, but the police didn't protect her. The lawyer, the guy who was the defendant, lawyer gave her name out, and she was killed. I thought that was awful. She went to the same dentist I went to. I didn't know her, but it was just through that connection, but I thought it was just awful. So I developed that, and CPB wanted to change it to more of a Hollywood kind of thing. I said no, it's based on reality, true story. So I said, why don't we do another film I could develop that had nothing to do with reality, but if you wanted to make any changes, I wouldn't feel too bad about it. So I started *Sleep with Anger*. They started making these really strange demands on changing all this stuff. I said no, this is taking the heart of the movie away. So we parted company, and they wrote this awful letter to me saying I'm never going to be a writer and things like that, it was awful working with me, and so forth. But the funny thing is there was a scene in the movie that they wanted me to take out, and I said no. I just saw Horton Foote, and he had a movie on television that had this long scene that people were recounting the past on the veranda. So this person said to me, yeah, but you're not Horton Foote. OK. And of course it was very painful, but she said a lot of painful things. Anyway, so what happened was—and this was like eighty-nine or ninety or something like that. So I'm in Africa making this African film, *Namibia*. No, I had finished shooting, but I'm in post over there. So I get this call from the States asking me we would like for you to attend our event we're having. I said yes, but I'm in Mississippi, so what is it? Well, we're going to give out an award. Yes, but I'm in Namibia. Do I have to be there? They said yes, you have to be there to get the award. But coming back from Africa, and so I was going to say no but be cool, be polite. So I said what is the award, may I ask? The lady said it's a Horton Foote Award for screenwriters. I said I'll be right there. No problem; I'll be right there. So it's like validating this sort of thing, plus I got some awards afterwards. But it was very difficult. It was just like they wanted to take what was particular about it out, the folklore and stuff, and take out the whole thing with the grandparents. So you get those crazy, I don't know, situations.

Q2: I have two questions. The first one is about when you wrote most of your scripts, so when you were thinking and writing who were your audience? I mean just the Black movie audience, since these movies were talking to them only, or to the whole society? The second question is about, you said that these movies were at the civil rights movement time and that you felt you had to do something and speak and stuff like this. One of the movies, *Killer of Sheep*, there were so many long scenes and repetitions. You wanted to convey a message. Weren't you afraid that someone who is watching the movie would get bored or something so your message would be like so sophisticated that they won't get it at the end?

CB: No. I think what it was, was that *Killer of Sheep* was an experiment in many ways because it was a reaction against studios and what they were making. The film wasn't made for like a wide audience. It wasn't made for theatrical release. It was made, we were making films that we were trying to get people in the neighborhood to see the films, the sort to start a dialogue discussion on where we are and where they're going and sort of images that we like to promote. So that was it. It was more or less a tool for social change, a tool to create a dialogue, and it was also for the Black community on one hand, but it was for everybody. We grew up in this community, where it was very diverse and in terms of art films. When I was going to school, like if it was, you know, a French or German, whatever it is, film, it was like our films, because those films were speaking to us. We wanted to make films very similar in a certain way, not the sort of box office success and things like that of what was going on but the films that to sort of convey some message or idea or enlightened people to some extent. We didn't care about trying to entertain people. Entertain was the last thing that was on my mind. It was trying to not necessarily discover new language but, in a sense, yes, one that appealed to people who are in need of a different sort of image and story.

Q2: Was all of the community aware of this? I mean, I felt that there are some scenes nobody would recognize but the people that are living in this society.

CB: Basically we wanted that particularity and to share whatever else with everyone else. The language was supposed to speak to people who are, the film was supposed to speak to the community. Basically, that's what we were doing at UCLA at the time, actually trying to tell our stories. We didn't get a chance to have it shown in different Black communities that had this touring film festival thing that showed in different communities and things like that. So it did get a limited amount of airing and showing.

Q3: Unfortunately, I haven't seen your films yet, but I'll watch as many as I can this week. I read this paragraph comparing your work and its importance to Italian neorealism. I was wondering—and you were just saying that you studied art films from France and Germany, when you were in school—was there anything about, specific things about, Italian neorealism that struck you when you started watching those films?

CB: I think one of the things was it was a sense of honesty. It really gave you the impression that you were looking at reality in a way and there was distrust for the media in a way. But what affected me more than I think neorealism was I used to like, well I did like, still do, documentary films. One of the filmmakers, Basil Wright, who taught at UCLA was very important. He did *Song of Ceylon* and things like that. It was really instrumental.

Q3: One of the things that I really like about your work is the acting performances in them and the fact that you use amateur actors along with professional actors. Can you talk about the difference in working with amateur actors and professional actors?

CB: There's a big difference. If you have the time, amateur actors would be very good. If you don't, it gets difficult and more or less typecasting in many ways, and even that is problematic. I think they know what it's all about. When I was doing *Killer of Sheep*, it was to bring filmmaking to the community and have people work on it and friends and things like that. We had kids doing sound and whatever. The actors didn't quite get the concept. You see TV and movies, and that you probably know what it's about. For example, we had a scene where one of the actors in it couldn't make it. He was sick and he told me could he get his friend to come in and sit in for him. At that point, it's not like football, where you can change quarterbacks seamlessly and it doesn't matter. But he was very good in many ways because he was a friend of mine and took all his time. So I knew that then it wasn't clear to them what was going on. But when you get another actor who is really good and has presence, he would be really good. But working with professional actors, I mean, and particularly when you have time as an issue and things like that and needed to get something done, you can't really beat them unless you have months to work with a nonactor and things like that, unless he's someone very special. Other than that, an actor and what he brings to the screen—I mean a real good actor. There are a lot of actors acting, but the ones that are very good, those are the ones you look for, and they are the ones who carry the most, the largest, and then you can do anything.

Q2: I just wanted to thank you for keeping Lori Petty in *Glass Shield* because I love her performance in that. I think she is such an authentic actress. I just wanted to tell you. Loved that performance.

MM: The gentleman in the back?

Q4: Have you ever thought about making a film of the greatest story about South Central LA, which is Chester Himes's novel *If He Hollers Let Him Go*, which would make an incredible film? And I'd love to see you do that. The story is tailor-made for you.

CB: We had a Chester Himes story and we came close getting it made.

Q4: That particular book?

CB: No, not that one. We have *Crazy Kill*, which we changed the name of it.

Q4: But this one is about a detective—*If He Hollers Let Him Go*—in the shipyards in LA in the forties.

CB: Yes, he started writing in LA. I'd love to and just can't get studios interested. I don't know.

MM: I thought in *Killer of Sheep* that the use of music was very interesting. What I found even more tactile was the use of silence. I was wondering if you could talk about the use of silent space in your work.

CB: I'm trying to remember. I remember *Killer of Sheep* being almost like wall-to-wall music almost in a sense. But one of the things with the music was I wanted to preserve a lot of those old records. I was part of it, because a lot of the music I listened to as a kid, it created images. I remember talking to August Wilson, and he had the same kind of sort of way of working, because the blues created this sort of context and images for him to work. So I had sort of the same kind of thing going on. But silence, I don't recall too much. I don't think I was aware of having silence as being conscious of it in a sense. I'm just trying to remember where was it in the movie.

MM: When he was in the kitchen cutting the rug and then moving the chair. There were these moments of just silence with background noise that where almost you could feel the antagonism, the antagonism inside the carriers and sort of gave them an extra depth.

CB: I was aware of the sound in the neighborhood and that, but it was silence of a naturalistic kind of thing, which was just clearly there in a sense but not really consciously because it wanted to be silence conveying something. I wasn't aware of that.

MM: The young man in the back.

Q5: The question I had is a different one about acting. I'm curious about your take on somebody. How important do you think somebody like Danny Glover is to the very sense of Black cinema in the US?

CB: Very important. Danny is one of the unsung heroes in many ways as an actor and as a political person. A lot of these actors don't get a chance to really show who they are and their talent. But he was a tremendous advantage to us when we were making the film because it wasn't until he got involved that they thought it was a film, that there was a script that was commercial.

MM: It's almost like there isn't a category that we talk about filmmakers and screenwriters, and it's almost the actor/producer/quasi producer or almost on the end of being a producer putting deals together, participating in projects, that allow them to be made in the first place. It's fascinating.

CB: Yes. I say it again, he's just a tremendous humanitarian as an actor. He just brings so much to, and he brought, in fact, what was interesting is that I had it for one of the brothers in *To Sleep with Anger*, because I knew that he didn't want to do this things on older men. So he came to me and he said, you know, I really like the brother thing, but I would really like to write or read for the older guy. I said yeah, you can read for anyone you want to at that stage. He did, and he was really wonderful.

MM: In *Killer of Sheep*, there is this one scene in which you had three boys riding on a bicycle, and these dogs started chasing after them, and they kind of wrecked a little bit on the bicycle, and all three ran away. During this time, it's showing that the economy is rough and money is scarce. It seems as though they just kind of leave the bike behind and didn't even seem to care about it.

CB: No, the dog is after them.

MM: Right, when they were laughing and everything, I'm just wondering about that.

CB: This is embarrassing. I've got to go to the bathroom. Excuse me. All of that water is not working well.

MM: Let me escort you. It's right out here. We'll take your question and maybe one or two others and eventually we'll call it a day.

CB: Sounds good.

MM: Greg [Waller], do you want to speak a little more about Danny Glover?

GW: No. I think it will be interesting when the IU cinema has an actor here for the filmmaking. It's not just the performance on screen. I mean my sense is in the world of post-1950s Hollywood, actors are what gets movies. They get movies made, and they can have an enormous influence on bringing a project like *To Sleep with Anger* to the screen, I would guess. That's what struck me.

CB: Glover also did *Bamako* years ago. I think he was responsible for that.

GW: He also had this terrific role in a film about South Africa that Morgan Freeman did, where Glover plays a Black policeman and someone that is collaborating with apartheid, and he does a beautiful job of it. It's a very, very interesting film. Morgan Freeman was the director as well as the lead. It was great.

CB: Perhaps many of you already know, but Danny Glover has his own production company. The project that he has been working on for about six or seven years is on Toussaint Louverture. I heard just recently he dropped it for reasons of which I don't know. Anyone have any information to add to that?

GW: He talked about the economy being tight and films not being made, and that has made him want to just forget about the studio system and turn to documentary, as many filmmakers have, if you're trying to appeal to a larger audience, one, and two, to finance it. In fact, many documentaries are through the studio system. You go to the television companies. Is that right?

MM: When you stepped out for a moment, Professor Waller added something very different and very important to the discussion—the role of the actor in really getting films made. Do you consider in your casting decisions who will give you the best shot to get the film funded?

CB: It's important because a lot of times we are asked who is in the movie, and they won't consider it unless you have a list of stars or three or four names as principals. That's how they sell the film. It's easier to sell with a name than with no name. Almost every time we find someone who is the star in the film.

MM: Does it affect the money?

CB: It affects the money. It's basically the studio and how we are going to distribute the film. It's a commercial thing, so they're looking to put all of those elements together. When I did *The Wedding* for Oprah Winfrey, it was already a presold thing. They wanted all A-list names on there. A lot of actors aren't working, a lot of really good actors, and those who are working are fighting for these really small roles and things like that and people I haven't seen in there. It's important. A lot of good actors aren't working and need to work.

CB: Thank you, Mr. Burnett.

PART 2.
READING *KILLER OF SHEEP*

5

TOWARD A GEO-CINEMATIC HERMENEUTICS

*Representations of Los Angeles in Non-Industrial Cinema—*Killer of Sheep *and* Water and Power

David E. James

> The cultural landscape is fashioned from a natural landscape by a culture group. Culture is the agent, the natural area is the medium, the cultural landscape is the result.
>
> *Carl Ortwin Sauer*

IT IS COMMONLY RECOGNIZED THAT THE LOSS OF authority in the great paradigms of modernist culture was accompanied by a shift from time to space as the more fundamental category for cognition.[1] John Berger's novel, *G*, for example, both instanced and articulated the sense that the narrative line of the traditional novel was no longer adequate to the complex synchronic patterns that make up contemporary experience. "Prophecy," the narrative voice declared, "now involves a geographical rather than a historical projection; it is space, not time, that hides consequences from us." Foucault reached similar conclusions, arguing that history had been the nineteenth century's "great obsession," so the "present epoch will perhaps be above all the epoch of space;" and his proposal that our present experience of the world was one "of a network that connects points and intersects with its own skein" inspired a generation of postmodern geographers.[2] As a consequence of the *historical* shifts these reorientations manifest—and among them the closing of all spaces outside the global consolidation of capital must be reckoned as primary—the discipline of geography acquired a new importance and generated new projects for cultural studies, notably questions about the relations between the local and the national, and then, as the international restructuring of capital transformed the status of the national itself, questions about the local and the global. In film studies, the response has been primarily a reinvestment in the national as a fundamental historiographical concept, a somewhat paradoxical development since the worldwide hegemony of the American corporate entertainment industries leaves the concept of any other national cinema with little more than a heuristic value—a fact that is often the very point from which these studies begin.[3]

Commonly approaching cinema as essentially representation (rather than material production, which will be the particular concern of the present essay), projects of this kind have comfortably intersected with both postmodernist assumptions of the collapse of all reality into media spectacle and poststructuralist conceptualizations of reality as textuality. So, for example, the introduction to a recent collection of geographical considerations of cinema takes as its point of departure Baudrillard's conflation of the city and the cinema, a conflation that understands the cityscape as itself a screenscape: "Where is the cinema? It is all around you outside, all over the city, that marvelous, continuous performance of films and scenarios." From such a standpoint, David Harvey's attempt to retain an ontological difference between film and reality, one that obliges him to affirm that film is "in the final analysis, a spectacle projected within an enclosed space on a depthless screen," appears to be a distinctly *uncinematic* foreboding and is therefore to be discredited.[4]

Whatever the overall status of readings of contemporary social reality as intrinsically cinematic, their claims are nowhere more pressing than in Los Angeles, where, for the century of its existence as a major city, cinema has been central to its economic, social, and cultural developments. All have been shaped in the magnetic field of cinema; and cinema, as it has imitated urban growth in metastasizing at points increasingly remote from the original downtown center, in Silver Lake, Hollywood, Culver City, the San Fernando Valley, and (as the mutual imbrication of the electronics and the entertainment industries bridges the north/south division of the state) now in Silicon Valley, has preoccupied the entire region. As Reyner Banham observed, "Hollywood . . . the movies found Los Angeles a diffuse fruit-growing super-village of some eight hundred thousand souls, and handed it over to the infant television industry in 1950 a world metropolis of over four million."[5] More scrupulous historians have recognized the formative role of other industries, though from real estate through aerospace to crack cocaine, they have exhibited a Hollywood-like combination of spectacle and speculation—they have all been imaginary signifiers. But wherever the industry's actual geographic location, for three-quarters of the century, Hollywood has been recognized nationally and internationally as the tertium quid between Los Angeles and the movies, the proper synecdoche for each simultaneously.

More categorical even than Chicago's hegemony in meat-packing, the city's unique appropriation of an entire medium is reciprocated by that medium's similarly unique influence on the city, on its industrial base, its architecture, and its overall cultural tenor. The Hollywood sign remains the city's trademark and stamps its influence on other arts in the city, enriching them or depleting them, financing their experimentation or drawing them into its own aesthetic and entrepreneurial orbits. From the urban facades satirized by thirties' novelists to the more extravagant forms of hyperspace epitomized initially by Disneyland and more recently by the fabricated urban environment of Universal's City Walk, the continually reconstructed identification has been architecturally embodied, if not in concrete then at least in stucco, with a renewed cross-fertilization evident in the work of Frank Israel and other contemporary architects. In other cultural forms, the incorporation has been no less integral. Until relatively recent innovation by ethnic writers, the Hollywood novel was taken as the Los Angeles novel, while the city's other significant literature has been the screenplay. Local theater is sustained by film actors, and even the most avant-garde forms of music—from the severe atonality of longtime resident Arnold Schoenberg to the similarly severe amelodicity of Orange County hardcore or South Central rap—have eventually found themselves recruited to the soundtrack and other modes of incorporation into the now-totalized intermedia entertainment/advertising packages of corporate culture.

The attenuation of any real outside the media in Los Angeles has been reciprocated by a parallel tautological reflexivity in the way the city has been drawn into Hollywood films. Even in those that exploit local topography, its features are essentially mobile and nonspecific with the demand that they be internationally readable, prohibiting any comprehensive or accurate mapping of the city's spatiality and social structure.[6] The topographical variety, abundant light, availability of space, and other local conditions that sustained the industry have been deracinated, displaced from the actual geography of the region to the nonrestrictive, diegetic geography of "the movies." Two main processes may be distinguished. First, in eras when location shooting has been common and so the city has represented the narratives of all other places, its own specificity has been concealed. Even films that mobilize a thematic polarization of Los Angeles against some geographical alternative often use the city as the site of both itself and its other. Most of the "Berkeley" scenes in *The Graduate* (Mike Nichols, 1967),[7] for example, were shot at the University of Southern California (USC), while such films as *Godzilla* and the Arnold Schwarzenegger actioner *End of Days* (1999), which trade on the authenticity of their take on New York life, were actually shot here. The syndrome is longstanding. As early as 1911, it was recognized that the growth of the film industry in the region was substantially attributable to the topographical and architectural diversity that facilitated location shooting.[8] And a map of Southern California produced at Paramount Studio in the twenties shows the entire region overwritten as other places: the area north of Malibu is designated Coast of Spain; the Palos Verdes peninsula is Wales; Catalina is South Sea Islands; the channel between it and Long Beach is both the Malay Coast and Long Island Sound; the Salton Sea is the Red Sea; and south of it lies the Sahara Desert.[9] In Foucault's terms, while the Los Angeles area is then effectively a heterotopia, a site "capable of juxtaposing in a single real place several spaces, several sites that are in themselves incompatible,"[10] in any given film, perception of that plurality is sacrificed in the simulation of a single diegesis and a unitary, self-identical space.

On the other hand, when the topography of the area is used to represent narratives supposed actually to take place there—when, to appropriate the title of a film to which we shall return, *L.A. Plays Itself*—the specific spatial conditions are similarly elided. The number of feature films set in Los Angeles is by now so immense that any generalizations are hazardous; but, despite conspicuous exceptions like *Chinatown* (Roman Polanski, 1974), Hollywood films set in Los Angeles have rarely explored its real historical and geographical specificity.[11] Instead, the city is replaced by a handful of metonymic images: sunset at the beach, Beverly Hills streets lined with high palm trees, aerial shots of layered freeway intersections, the Hollywood sign itself. Like the picture cards in a deck, these have a greater resonance than other, nondescript images of the city, and they can appear in various combinations, but they always signify the same, a general sense of Los Angeles, but only as it has been coded in previous media incarnations. Or, when taken as a whole, the city is recruited to the fantasies of the national and global imaginaries and made the site of utopian or dystopian spectacles that may be justified by invoking real Los Angeles events—earthquakes, immigration, race riots, and life in Hollywood and Beverly Hills are among the most prominent—but which transform these according to the needs of the genre, ideology, or the entertainment function itself.[12] Again heterotopia is replaced by utopia; again Foucault: "Utopias are sites with no real place. They are sites that have a general relation of direct or inverted analogy with the real space of Society. They present society itself in a perfected form, or else society turned upside down, but in any case these utopias are fundamentally unreal spaces."[13]

So in both usages, representations of Los Angeles in mainstream film and television have overlapped with and been overdetermined by the requirements of the media itself. Whether the actual heterotopic diversity of the region that facilities the media industry is repressed in each film's selection of the one component its particular diegesis requires, or whether the city is presented in an idealized or inverted perfect form, Los Angeles has been an everywhere or a nowhere, but never itself. Media images of Los Angeles refer essentially to the media; in them the city's spatiality becomes the space of the cinema industry. Hollywood's overall inability to map the space of its own operation in any but the broadest and most sensationalized forms is probably no worse than its abrogation of any other social responsibility and certainly no worse than its misrepresentation of the social geography of other spaces—of the American West, for example, or of Vietnam. But the failure in respect to Los Angeles is particularly distinctive in that it has concealed the other extraordinary, if not unique, property of the city that supplies its postmodern prototypicality—the urban structure itself.

While to the entertainment industry Los Angeles was "fundamentally unreal," it became an all-too-real prototype of the postmodern conurbations now developing in many parts of the world, especially the Third World. Reflecting the human development of the topography, climate, and biota of the land and water masses, for the past century spatiality in Los Angeles has been most determined by hydrology, the automobile, and immigration. The first supplied the successive booms of suburban real estate development, and the second consolidated the rail and road networks into the most extensive freeway system in the world, one that simultaneously linked and segregated the local communities. The resulting voracious peripheral growth, horizontal rather than vertical development, produced a dispersed urban poly-nucleation, successively the "six suburbs in search of a city" of twenties' witticisms; the "nineteen suburbs in search of a city" of the 1939 WPA guide; and Edward Soja's "Sixty-Mile Circle" of "at least 132 incorporated cities." Through immigration these turned into "the most differentiated of all cities," "a combination of enclaves with high identity, and multiclaves with mixed identity ... perhaps the most heterogeneous city in the world."[14] The successive waves of immigration—Anglos from the Midwest and South, Blacks and Mexicans, and most recently East Asians and refugees, from US imperial adventures in Mesoamerica—precipitated not the radial, homogenous modern city, but a cosmopolitan megalopolis, more diverse than any city since Shanghai in the thirties, inhabited by people from all over the world—a microcosm of global diaspora. The unreal places of the Paramount Studio map have all been occupied, and now a corner at a mini-mall, with shop signs in Chinese and Tagalog as well as English, leads from Mexico to Korea.

Together with the long history of anti-labor politics that inhibited trans-ethnic working-class consciousness, this social dispersal precluded full urban integration; but it also had the advantage of allowing minority social groups, especially those that arrived in distinct waves of immigration, to settle in relatively homogenous and autonomous clusters. There, as well as infiltrating into Los Angeles aspects of distant spatialities, they have better sustained their original identity. Historically, these communities have become visible to the hegemony mostly at moments of racial or cultural strife: the anti-Chinese riots of the 1870s, for example, or zoot-suiters in the forties and Blacks in the sixties and nineties. At other times, within themselves they have nurtured and sustained local colors and traditions. The barrios of East Los Angeles, for example, or the African Americans' preservation of the culture of the rural South and more recently the "little" Asian cities of Tokyo, Manila, Taipei, Saigon, and so on are distinct cultural formations, some of which have flourished bountifully in relative obscurity, even as components of them were assimilated into the uniformity of mass media and advertising. These local places are structured between two primary vectors: a centripetal pull toward the downtown area, which has always been and remains the focus of the civic, economic, and transport networks of the basin, and a centrifugal pull generated by the semiautonomous industrial and residential clusters.[15]

The structural tensions that shape the city geographically generate parallel tensions that shape its arts. Minority cultures in Los Angeles are created in the tension between the centrifugal pull of the local communities and their indigenous practices and the centripetal pull of the entertainment industry. As over time and at different rates for different groups the balance between these pulls has shifted, the mediums they have used to sustain themselves culturally have similarly matured and declined. But, reflecting the extent to which film has been the city's medium in dominance, independent filmmaking in Los Angeles has been a crucial site of alternative cultural activity. Either unrepresented or misrepresented by the film industry, the city's local communities have had to develop modes of film production alternative to and counter to the studios' capitalist mode of production; and in the alternative cinemas they have pioneered, both the discursive structures of their films and their visions of the city and of their own relation to it have been quite unlike Hollywood's. These alternative cinemas have been intermittently recurrent since the beginning of the industry. In 1914, for example, Frank E. Wolfe and a Socialist collective produced a feature film, *From Dusk to Dawn*, to counter anti-working-class propaganda from the Trust films, and in it they rewrote the bungled explosion at the *Los Angeles Times* in 1911 and the subsequent Darrow trial as the beginning of a progressive labor movement in the city that led to the election of a socialist governor. *Conditions in Los Angeles, Calif.* (1934), the Los Angeles Film and Photo League's twenty-minute documentary on the effects of the Depression, was a parallel montage of the rich and poor sections of the city; the out-of-work people standing in lines outside employment agencies or sifting through refuse for food contrasted with golfers arriving in Rolls Royces at a resort hotel. *Hollywood Lockout! 1946*, produced by the Conference of Studio Unions (CSU) during that year's strike, showed pickets outside the studios being beaten and arrested by the police, who were protecting scabs on behalf of the owners. *The Exiles* (Kent MacKenzie, 1961), a 35mm documentary made by a group of USC students, celebrated the working-class Native Americans around the old Bunker Hill before both the architecture and the community were destroyed in capital restructuring. *Requiem 29* (David Garcia, 1970) documented the 1970 anti-war Chicano Moratorium in East Los Angeles, where police rioted, beating many people and killing

L.A. Times journalist Ruben Salazar. *L.A. Plays Itself* (Fred Halstead, 1972), a *Songs of Innocence and Experience* of homosexuality in Los Angeles, began with scenes of idyllic sex in the Santa Monica Mountains that, when interrupted by the sprawl of urban development, cut to a second half of ecstatic sadomasochistic sex on Santa Monica Boulevard. *Water Ritual #1: An Urban Rite of Purification* (Barbara McCullough, 1979), a four-minute film, opened on the skeleton of a ruined building in a cityscape so devastated that it looks like an impoverished area in the Third World; a young African American woman enters, sits down on the ground, blows sand through her fist, and then, hitching her skirts round her hips, she urinates. These communities and the Los Angeles they occupy have no place in the corporate cinema, except in caricature.[16]

The dispersed, poly-nucleated but nevertheless ultimately centered structure of the Los Angeles megalopolis and the broadly homologous conditions determining the alternative minority cinemas it sustains allow the question of the geographical relation of film to the city to be posed in a new and properly materialist way. When the issue is formulated exclusively as a question of representation, revolving on the relations between a given film's iconography and diegetic space to the architectural and social spaces of the city, the forces and materials that generate the representation are ignored—an idealism akin to poststructuralist assimilations of the city to other forms of sheer textuality. For studio films, the industrial mode of production and the commodity social relations it sustains are relatively uniform, and so only a concern with the overall implications of capitalist production of culture can prompt consideration of its effect on the textual properties of the films it produces and hence consideration of spatial factors affecting production. But for films produced outside the studio system, the geography of production is inscribed in the film itself.[17] In these cases, *a geo-cinematic hermeneutic* will investigate the relation between a given film's representation of the city and the actual urban resources that supply and govern its manufacture—the cinematic registers of social and material production. The different cities lived by Los Angeles's various local communities provide them with different topographical, architectural, social, and economic resources, and the visions of Los Angeles they produce reflect both the architectural and social appearance of the spatiality they inhabit and also the resources it allows them: the different formal means of cultural production—different stories, situations, images, rhythms, and points of view—and the different material means of cultural production. Since any given film is the point at which cultural work transforms a specific set of human and natural resources into a representation of and intervention in life in the city, the particular image of the city it presents will always reflect the resources from which it was made. The cultural means of production mediates between the reality of the city and its appearance in film. In order to develop a hermeneutic that can reveal these relations between cinema and geography, we must take one last detour through the *mediating apparatuses*, the actual institutions that have allowed marginal communities to develop autonomous or quasi-autonomous cinemas.

In Los Angeles, these mediating apparatuses typically grew on the edges of or in the interstices of the industrial cinema itself. They fall into three groups: production (e.g., equipment sales and rental houses, laboratories, and cooperatives that make equipment available to beginning filmmakers, media arts centers, and community-outreach workshops); consumption (e.g., distribution organizations, promotional mechanisms, and screening organizations, including specialty art theaters and groups formed specifically for this purpose); and suffusing these, ideological apparatuses (e.g., museums, archives, and libraries; journals, magazines, and lectures). Of these mediating apparatuses and performing all these functions, college and university film programs have been especially important, sustaining an interface and intercourse between industrial and independent production in Los Angeles. The city has historically been rich in those resources that also feed directly into the industry but relatively poor in those independent of it. Hollywood has sustained many para-industrial workshops, personnel marginally or partially employed in the studios, and film schools, while cultural resources oriented toward entirely independent cinemas have been correspondingly sparse. But though facilities for independent distribution and exhibition have been meager and attenuated, especially in comparison to equivalent institutions in New York and San Francisco, Los Angeles has—sporadically, but persistently—sustained the institutions of an independent film culture.[18]

Below, rather than considering the relation between the highly specific representations of Los Angeles in the marginal films mentioned above and the specific conditions that allowed them to be produced and the non-commodity functions they sustain, we will consider two films that more directly negotiate with the apparatuses of commercial production and that partially overlap with the industrial cinema. Their tendencies to autonomy and opposition are interwoven with tendencies toward collaboration, and in this, they foreground the combination of centrifugal and centripetal impulses that characterize the overall cultural situation in the city. To frame this broader project, I will invoke Reyner Banham's similarly broad and provisional answer to the question of whether Los Angeles was one city or 132; he said its architectural originality and multiplicity could be schematized into four "ecologies": the beaches (surfurbia), the foothills, the central flatlands, and the freeways.[19] Combining Sauer's term *cultural landscape* with Banham's *ecologies*, we can then think of the spatialities in which non-studio film is produced—including the different mediating cinematic apparatuses to which they permit access—as *cultural ecologies* and so propose a geographical allegory; just as every film silently tells the story of the social relations and the material functions it serves, so too does it tell the story of the cultural ecology in which it was produced. The way the city is figured in a film made outside the studio system reflects the way the city figured in the filmmaking.

The possibilities of such a *geo-cinematic hermeneutic* may be sketched by a comparison of Charles Burnett's *Killer of Sheep* (1977) and Pat O'Neill's *Water and Power* (1988), in which the relation between each film's very different pictures of Los Angeles and the cultural ecology that produced it is especially pointed. Both resemble more traditional avant-gardes in being intensely personal, for though both involved extensive collaboration, they were each conceived, photographed, and edited essentially by one person; and both were undertaken as self-justifying projects with comparatively little attention to the possibilities of financial return, certainly not to the valorization of invested capital. But both are more specifically prototypical of the Los Angeles avant-garde in being alternative to yet in clear negotiation with Hollywood; despite stunning formal originality, both approach industrial norms in that one is a feature-length narrative, while the other is close to feature-length, and both were shot and distributed in 35mm. Though in these respects they are similar, their styles are so diametrically different as to constitute a virtual case study in what introductory film aesthetics terms the *Bazin-Eisenstein debate*, a textbook contrast between "faith in reality" and "faith in the image." And while one is overtly political, the other is overtly aesthetic. These two film languages and their envisioning of Los Angeles reflect equally different spatialities in terms of both representation and production.

Killer of Sheep

The Los Angeles of *Killer of Sheep* is almost entirely the African American working-class neighborhoods of South Central. Architecturally, the ghetto differs from its counterparts in other cities in the predominance of single-family dwellings and small apartment buildings. The cityscape is flat, monotonous, dilapidated, of limited imageability, and with no conspicuous internal differentiation. There are no signs of commerce except a single liquor store or of industry except the slaughterhouse where the hero works (and it is generally seen only from the inside, so that its articulation with the community is unspecified). And there are no signs of connections with other parts of the city except, briefly, the Southern Pacific railroad that appears to share the area's defunct lethargy; its tracks are children's playgrounds and its engines mostly immobile. No trace of any other Los Angeles may be seen; no business districts, no supermarkets, no luxurious high-rise apartment or office buildings, no technicolor sunsets, no homes of the stars—not even the Watts Towers. Most remarkable of all, there are no freeways. Indeed, there are almost no cars, and the few that are not so permanently disabled that they have been reinvented as street furniture are at best unreliable. And so nothing can happen. Life here is entirely constrained within only one of Banham's ecologies, the central flatlands. The beaches, the hills, and the freeways are all unavailable, and the only narrative event of any substance is the protagonist's attempt to secure a car to take his family outside the ghetto, if only for a day trip. But hardly is an outside glimpsed before the car breaks down, forcing a return to a stultifying carceral stasis. Here, lack of geographic mobility is a figure above all for the lack of social mobility, and in presenting poverty as simultaneously an economic and spatial condition, the film foregrounds the racial and class apartheid that constitutes the Los Angeles of South Central: that lack of access to work, to communications networks, to self-governance, or to any of the other resources of the city proper, commonly proposed as the immediate cause of the 1965 uprising and which has only deteriorated since.

The image of African American family life and the quasi-documentary verisimilitude of the representation both categorically differ, not only from mainstream Hollywood (for which the area is essentially unrepresentable and known only as a lair from which emerge the predators who prey on bourgeois society), but also from the two eras of para-studio African American filmmaking that frame it—the early seventies blaxploitation that followed *Sweet Sweetback's Baadasssss Song* (Melvin Van Peebles, 1971) and its recent revival in films like *Boyz n the Hood* (John Singleton, 1991), *South Central* (Steve Anderson, 1992), and *Menace II Society* (Albert and Allen Hughes 1993). In general contrast to the generic conventions of both eras, in *Killer of Sheep*, the family is whole. It consists of Stan, the father, who is present, regularly employed, and proudly independent; and, however precariously, he supports his wife and children. He disdains petty crime and the petty criminals of the community; alongside fellow working-class Whites, he continues in backbreaking labor in the slaughterhouse. Coffee is his drug of choice, and while the grind of his life has its toll, it doesn't provoke promiscuity but rather destroys sexual desire—the "impotence" of "a dream deferred," as Langston Hughes's poem "Same in Blues" puts it. Since his principal relation remains with his wife, the film's action is mostly the melodrama of domestic space, rather than the violence of exterior, public spaces. And though the film's overall vision is bleak, it ends on a note of humanist optimism as a crippled young woman announces that she is pregnant. The film's portrayal of an African American working-class family stands as a heroic demystification of the industrial media's combination of neglect and exploitation, not only of Black but of all working-class life, and an exemplary premonition of a community-inspired alternative cinema. But its production was not a case of spontaneous community self-expression, so much as a historically and geographically specific negotiation between the community in which Burnett had lived since coming to Los Angeles from Mississippi as a child and the cinematic apparatuses mediating between that community and the film industry. In this case, the principal agency was the film school at the University of California at Los Angles (UCLA), where Burnett was the leading figure in a generation of young Black filmmakers who used its resources to produce industry calling cards.

One of the only four Blacks in the film school proper,[20] Burnett was eventually joined at UCLA in the early seventies by Billy Woodberry, Haile Gerima, and Ben Caldwell; in the same period, Julie Dash was at the American Film Institute, an organization even more thoroughly aligned with Hollywood than UCLA. All of their student projects were realistic narratives, oriented toward the production of populist feature films for mass distribution inside and outside the African American community, and they all worked on each other's projects. Burnett, for example, wrote and photographed Woodberry's *Bless Their Little Hearts* (1983) and photographed

Dash's *Illusions* (1982), Gerima's *Bush Mama* (1976), and parts of Larry Clark's *Passing Through* (1977). For these filmmakers, the academy made the combination of three things available: production equipment and a semiprofessional filmmaking community; a degree of access to the industry; and models of alternative film languages compatible with low-budget feature production.

By the early seventies, the international hegemony of the Hollywood film industry had been challenged by two modes of film production alternative to the corporate-controlled film industry, each allowing different mobilizations of political aspirations: on the one hand, the attempt to create non- or even anti-commodity cinemas, and on the other the commodity production of films by other industrial centers. The most strongly politicized versions of these two productive possibilities were respectively the militant "impoverished" and "imperfect" cinemas of Latin America and Vietnam and the sequence of "New Wave" art cinemas subsequent to Italian neorealism that reached a culmination in the work of Jean-Luc Godard and the Groupe Dziga Vertov. In the United States, the former tendency produced the Newsreels, while the latter, the American political art film, was essentially stillborn and would remain so apart from the briefly conspicuous exception of *Speaking Directly* (1974) and other works by Jon Jost (some of which were made in Los Angeles). Generally in Los Angeles, however—where the blacklist and the HUAC investigations had extirpated virtually all traces of progressive film culture, where the police and judiciary were notoriously racist, and where spatial segregation made any class-based, transracial political cooperation extremely difficult—neither was a real possibility. There was, in fact, an LA branch of the Newsreel, and it worked very closely with the Black Panther Party on a film intended to clarify the Panthers' class-based analysis of American racism in an attempt to counter the Black Nationalism of Ron Karenga's US organization, also based in the city. But on December 8, 1969, two days after the Illinois police murdered Deputy Chairman Fred Hampton, the LAPD, in collaboration with the FBI, destroyed the LA Panther headquarters, effectively ending Panther leadership of the Black community in Los Angeles and opening the road for the recrudescence of the gangs. And though Los Angeles Newsreel had included well-equipped, experienced filmmakers and sophisticated Marxist intellectuals, it failed to bring a single film of its own to distribution.[21] Refracted through Hollywood's insistent presence, the impossibility of an agitational cinema in Los Angeles in the early seventies thus left only the option of populist narratives, made with a view toward dissemination via the festival circuit and liberal public institutions; that is, the art film, and specifically neorealism, "a revolutionary cinema in a non-revolutionary society."[22]

The determining effect of these specific community and institutional resources is everywhere apparent in *Killer of Sheep*. They produce its thematics, its liberal humanist appeal for sympathy and understanding—if not sheer pity—from the hegemony, rather than a historical analysis or a militant call to contestation directed to the community itself. As a result, the film has been primarily distributed not in the Black community it depicts, but in the White institutions of liberal humanism, in festivals, schools, and museums.[23] And they produce its form: the combination of narrative strategies and economic imperatives that prompt the use of deep-focus long takes; the nonprofessional actors playing roles close to themselves; the emphasis on an organic connection between people and the environment; the documentary feel of grainy black and white; and especially the attenuation of narrative, its replacement as a site of meaning by studied takes of human faces permitting the observation of what Roberto Rossellini called "the movements of the soul." In these respects, the film is an audaciously ambitious accommodation of impoverishment in resources and an accommodation to the politics of the liberal institutions that, in the absence of a militant Black cinema, allowed it to be made. But in one other respect, the film is wealthy. Immediately available to it was the most bountiful resource of African American culture—music—and Burnett uses it to enrich and extend the visual track of *Killer of Sheep*.

Used intra-diegetically, recorded songs affirm music's special role as a means of spiritual sustenance and imaginative expression for African American people. But Burnett's use of non-diegetic music in elaboration of that role allows him metonymically to expand early-seventies South Central into the whole history of African American resistance. His visual mapping of the environment may be constrained by the empiricism of realist photography, as well as by the poverty of the community and by the poverty of the resources for which he, as a UCLA student, was only partially able to compensate; but in the soundtrack, he loosened the realism and used music to access other times and spaces, introducing a historical dimension and a sense of continuity whose destruction he regarded as primarily responsible for the degradation of the Black community.[24]

Both framing eras of blaxploitation were fueled by contemporary Black music—soul and gangsta rap, respectively—and indeed were essentially attempts to reproduce in cinema the music's cultural intervention and its enormous financial return. In both eras, the films' overall ideological postures were derived from and amplified by their soundtracks, which were also marketed as commodities in the way that has typified the integrated entertainment industry, especially since *Saturday Night Fever*. Positioned outside even the compromises of independent commercial feature production, *Killer of Sheep* lost the marketing platform of such corporate-controlled music, but it also escaped determination by commercial priorities. Not obliged to identify with a single, simultaneously marketed genre, it referenced a much wider library and used music in much more complex ways.

Indeed, if the visuals alone resemble the verisimilitude of neorealism, the image-music relations create a variety of highly artificial montage effects in which classical Black music—blues from the thirties and forties—add resonance and counterpoint to themes the attenuated narrative itself holds suspended: Paul Robeson singing "Ballad for Americans"[25] as youngsters play on ruined lots, for example, and Dinah Washington singing "This Bitter Earth" as Stan and his wife embrace each other in their misery and slowly dance.

In some instances, the play of song lyrics across the visuals is very complex. The scene where it first becomes clear that Stan's anomie is destroying his relation with his wife, for example, is accompanied by Earth, Wind & Fire's mid-seventies megahit, "Reasons." The tension between the timbre of Philip Bailey's ecstatic falsetto that affirms erotic passion and the lyrics that broach the inevitability of its fading over time perfectly encompasses the tensions in the woman's life. But since the sequence begins with their baby daughter singing along to the record, the questioning of love is initially redirected from husband/wife to daughter/mother, with the child placed as the objective correlative of the erotic passion that once existed but that has been drained away by the grind of poverty, with she herself already in the process of being constituted as a subject by the mass media. "I don't want to feel," the child sings, groping to follow the record. "I'm in the wrong place to be real." Contextualized in this specific narrative, these lyrics suddenly transcend their banality, and the moment becomes a summary index of the history of a people.

Water and Power

If Burnett's Los Angeles appears as an oppressive enclosure that thwarts all attempts to escape, O'Neill's is a shimmering vision through which disembodied figures are transported by magic. No prison this, but rather a plethora of radically dissimilar spatialities that, linked by the restless trajectories of camera movement, all incessantly dissolve one into another. Their multiple superimpositions and constant interpenetration create a composite space, for implicit in any one topography are an unlimited number of others. For Burnett, the ontology of the neighborhood and its boundaries are undeniable; for O'Neill, any one place is only a pocket in another, not even a momentary rest in the ceaseless twining of heterotopias. None of these ever stabilizes sufficiently to become normative, but instead a relation among them emerges as a kind of deep structure to most of the film's sequences and its overall theme. This consists of a dissolve from one or more shots of desert scenes into one or more shots of the city, not necessarily authorized by some visual resemblance, with the transition bridged by an interior showing traces of human creativity and craft—a workshop, for example, or an abandoned industrial space turned into an artist's loft.

Fundamentally, then, the film is an extended parallel montage, and though it is one premised on continuity rather than collision, on Pudovkin rather than Eisenstein, nevertheless it marks a radical development for O'Neill. His earliest works had been each mobilized around a single formal and thematic principle, but his immediately previous films, such as *Saugus Series* (1974) and *Sidewinder's Delta* (1976), had been rather dossier-like compilations of discrete sections, each mobilizing a different formal procedure in optical printing and linked to the others by only the loosest thematic continuity; they were generally scenes of everyday events and wilderness landscapes all transformed by art.[26] These were essentially late underground films, even though the theoretical and institutional infrastructure supporting such short films had collapsed by the late seventies under the combined assaults of structural film, the politicization of the avant-garde by feminism and other identity groups, and the catastrophic increase in film costs. The avant-garde's consequent turn to feature-length works designed for commercial distribution was not an inimical direction for O'Neill, except that the compositional principle of his entire oeuvre to date had been montage. *Water and Power* marks the beginning of an extremely tentative engagement with narrative.

In published notes, O'Neill has sketched a narrative underlay to the film.[27] Its main character is Aaron Haskell, who commits suicide by plunging from the bridge in the movie's opening shot, just before the title. (Perhaps the film is what he sees in the moment of his death, parallel to the expanded moment of consciousness of the man in Robert Enrico's *An Occurrence at Owl Creek Bridge* [*La Rivière du hibou*, 1962], who also falls from a bridge as he is hanged, or of Stan Brakhage, whose suicide by hanging frames his visionary 1958 film, *Anticipation of the Night*). At any rate, according to the notes, Jack, a detective investigating Haskell's death, visits his wife, who lives in a trailer in the desert near their mine, and her lover, Rudy, who tells stories about corruption in the Russian army. Scenes from various Westerns follow, which in turn lead the story back to The Studio, where shooting is underway on the crowd scenes for *The Biggest Picture of All*; the movie is sponsored by four multinational corporations led by Seoul businessman, Kim Chong, who is actually Haskell, "very much alive and . . . deeply involved in the picture business."[28] Many of these incidents do appear in the film—the corruption in the Russian army, for example, is illustrated by scenes from *The Lost Command* that are floated in over time-lapse photography of a desert lake bed—and others are spoken or presented as text accompanied by black leader, with the visual equivalents appearing elsewhere. But such a narrative substrate is certainly not recoverable from the film, nor does the film imply narrative as a compositional principle, except insofar that subtitles satirize it by generating contradictory continuities in the manner of the intertitles of *Un Chien Andalou*. As remote as the motive of a dream, narrative is dispelled by the immediacy and intricacy of the optical printing and by the insistence of the montage.

Knitting together a skein of Los Angeles associations, O'Neill's deconstruction of the opposition between city and desert recalls the metaphors of local lore: "The World is a Suburb of Los Angeles," "Los Angeles is a cultural desert," "The World is a Ghetto," and so on.[29] And the visual trope may be read literally in several ways: human industry has turned the desert into a city, or the artist's vision is capable of seeing through the urban fabric to the landform below. It also has a very specific historical basis in the Owens Valley Project, a visionary undertaking that brought the water that allowed the city's expansion, even as it turned the previously fertile valley into a desert. This was in fact the beginning of the city's department of water and power, and the pipelines bringing the water through the desert to the city are a leitmotif in the film. But O'Neill's historical retrospection is intertwined with a more contemporary attention to the rhetoric that matured in the period of the film's production, proposing the city's historical representativeness. Overnight and from several different directions simultaneously, it was transformed from a more or less hideous anomaly, a kind of late-capitalist Philadelphia, into "a *protopos,* a paradigmatic place . . . a *mesocosm,* an ordered world in which the micro and the macro, the idiographic and the nomothetic, the concrete and the abstract, can be seen simultaneously in an articulated and interactive combination"—the representative postmodern city invoked above.[30] Within the many different agendas at stake in such promotions, two are especially important: first, the post-Fordist economics of the Pacific Rim, and second, a putatively new mode of subjectivity, usually correlated with the post-structural theory promoted in Orange County by the "Parisian fakirs"[31] who flocked to the University of California at Irvine in the seventies and eighties. Traces of the city's role in Pacific Rim finance capital and the massive importation of both Third World workers and Third World labor relations are glimpsed in *Water and Power*—in the juxtapositions of the different downtown skylines, for example, and in the fragments of a history of capital restructuring stretching from Sir Francis Drake to Kim Chong, the Korean businessman involved in shady corporate transactions in the picture business. But implications of this kind are subordinate to those of second area, postmodern subjectivity, specifically to a formal structure that disassembles the filmic vocabularies of the classic narrative and the humanist subject.

In *Water and Power,* stable narrative subjects are replaced by fragmentary and evanescent protagonists, what Paul Arthur has called "a set of vagabond voices and images connected briefly by theme or proximity," and narrative continuity itself is replaced by the "intricate semi-coherence" of the montage.[32] Consequently, the medium's unique capacity to redeem reality by simulating unified, continuous space and time is abandoned in the film's two most fundamental strategies, collage superimpositions of multiple registers of the former and time-lapse photography condensations of the latter. These technical effects are persuasive as allegorical figurations of the conditions of postmodernity, of its putative time-space compression and the continued dissolution of one place into another that constitutes the Foucauldian heterotopic space, "capable of juxtaposing in a single real place several sites that are in themselves incompatible."[33] Such resonances may be pushed even further since, in so forcefully making material space and time subject to the medium itself, these filmic techniques lead all but inevitably to the superimposition of found footage over the landscapes and so to the discovery that the topographies of Southern California are all already inhabited by old Hollywood movies.[34] The difference between natural and filmic space is confounded, and diegeses photographed elsewhere and often long ago for other films are discovered within O'Neill's own photography of the local landscapes—an inverse recapitulation of the process that historically allowed Hollywood to find all other places in its backyard.

In respect to these multiple figurations of media-dependent hyperreality, O'Neill's chief industrial intertext is then the essential Hollywood film, not of the seventies, but of the eighties: not *Chinatown* (which is usually cited as the correlative to his investigation of the Owens Valley Project), but *Blade Runner*. But rather than choosing between the nostalgic modernist film and the dystopian postmodernist vision that has replaced it as the key representation of the Los Angeles of all our futures, it is probably more fruitful to see *Water and Power* as superimposing these too, for its take on hyperreality and the trappings of postmodernism is deeply ambivalent. Explaining this and so explaining the film's unique visual appearance again involves a geographical detour, for though like *Killer of Sheep*, *Water and Power* occupies an interzone between the industry proper and the disaffiliated avant-garde, its liminality is one of quite different contexts.

In Banham's terms, O'Neill's ecology is that of the foothills, the space where several modes of cultural production intersect and nurture each other. Predominantly it is the social space of Hollywood and para-Hollywood workers; Hollywood Boulevard is its "main street,"[35] and its main activity is the manufacture of commodity entertainment. This Hollywood also sustains the host of para-industrial enterprises of the kind that, from the mid-sixties until computer imaging became the industry norm, allowed O'Neill to make a living and subsidized his independent projects; his special effects work on commercials and features, such as *Return of the Jedi* and *Poltergeist*, continues, then, the tradition of avant-garde interpolations in Hollywood films that began with Slavko Vorkapich's experimental montage interludes in thirties' features. But the foothills also sustain art that is not so oriented to or completely dependent on the interests of capital. For O'Neill himself, its significant institutions were UCLA, where he was formally educated (not in the film school, whose industry orientation was so fruitful for Burnett, but in art and design), and two of Los Angeles's long-standing art theaters, the Coronet and the Cinema Theater, where in the seventies he informally educated himself in the classic European and contemporary

US avant-gardes.³⁶ And they sustain the other institutions of the avant-garde: art galleries, cafés and bars, bookstores, and screening organizations, most notably Oasis Cinema. For a number of years in the late seventies, Oasis was one of two independent screening organizations in the city. Collectively organized by avant-garde filmmakers, it became the focus of a distinct era in avant-garde production; O'Neill was a founding member, and he premiered the most consummate of his fourteen shorts there.³⁷

Located in the middle of this mixed cultural ecology is Lookout Mountain Films, the most recent of the several independent production companies O'Neill has headed. From this aerie on Lookout Mountain Avenue, high in the Hollywood Hills off the Cahuenga Pass, O'Neill does indeed look out over some of the chief geographical and historical divides of the city and the industry, all of which structure *Water and Power*. He is midway between Los Angeles proper to the south, and to the north the San Fernando Valley, the area added to the city to meet the terms of the Owens River bond issue. He is also midway between the pre- and postwar locations of the industry, between Hollywood itself and Studio and Universal cities. Further to the north lies the Owens Valley itself (where most of the desert footage was shot), while closer is the town of Saugus and California Institute of the Arts, where he taught for the first half of the seventies, with several of his ex-students returning to him to work on *Water and Power* in a team that also included three animators, along with specialists in audio design, mechanical design and construction, and optical printing.

These geographies and the schizophrenic combination of industrial and artisanal potentials in this cultural ecology ubiquitously inform *Water and Power*'s production. A homemade film, only partially funded by the National Endowment for the Humanities, it nevertheless cost $90,000. It uses a very sophisticated motion-controlled time-lapse camera, but the images were shot spontaneously. Though the image processing is beyond the industrial standards, it was ordered intuitively; it contains fragments from O'Neill's commercial jobs and also from his dreams. This interpenetration of avant-garde and industrial proclivities and the combination of imaginative and arcane manual skills are also historically specific, the former instancing the switch from shorts to feature-length projects that a generation of avant-garde filmmakers made in the eighties and the latter a not-unconnected tension between technological nostalgia and prolepsis. Occurring on the threshold of a totalized electronic environment and electronic image processing, the implications of the film's elaborate fabrication nevertheless shy away from the aesthetics of postmodernism to reclaim a thick, modernist materiality and invoke a homespun pride in hands-on craftsmanship and authenticity figured in the images of artisanal environments that bridge the city and the desert in the film.

These tensions trace an individual and a general crisis for avant-garde film. The pull between a modern past and a postmodern future, both of which (though in quite different ways) were in the mid-eighties *not really here*, was a specific historical and geographical moment, for the effects of which O'Neill is a virtuoso master in film were all becoming routinely possible, but as computer generated using digital technology. At this point, the yearnings of avant-garde film to be autonomous practice, independent of the now-international industrial culture, give up the ghost. Antipathy to rationalized, corporate electronic media will be expressed as a radical conservatism that privileges earlier phases of Hollywood itself—a response that has been endemic in the avant-garde at least since Kenneth Anger. To work today, as O'Neill does, photochemically and in film bespeaks a longing for a world of mechanical reproduction, of simple apparatuses like optical printers that can be domestically assembled from World War II cameras (as O'Neill himself did), and so it is a nostalgia for visual precision, for full visual sensuousness, for vision itself. As we are absorbed by television, a medium which makes vision redundant, *Water and Power* appears as an attempt to reclaim Los Angeles for film and to reclaim the medium in which Los Angeles lived. One of the last machine's last master craftsmen, O'Neill made what inevitably looks more and more like the last Hollywood *film*.

Notes

1. My thanks to Clark Arnwine and Jesse Lerner for their reading of an earlier draft of this essay. I have silently incorporated a number of their insights.

2. John Berger, *G* (New York: Pantheon, 1972), 40, and Michel Foucault, "Of Other Spaces," Jay Miskowiec, trans., *Diacritics* 16, no. 1 (spring 1986), 22. Foucault's essay provided the point of departure for Edward W. Soja's *Postmodern Geographies: The Reassertion of Space in Critical Social Theory* (New York: Verso, 1989), a text to which the present essay will return.

3. The scant geographical approaches to cinema include one ambitious attempt to rethink cinema in global terms, a couple of collections of essays, and an earlier issue of this journal, respectively, Fredric Jameson, *The Geopolitical Aesthetic: Cinema and Space in the World System* (London: BFI Publishing, 1992); Stuart C. Aitken and Leo E. Zonn, eds., *Place, Power, Situation, and Spectacle: A Geography of Film* (Lanham, MD: Rowman and Littlefield,

1994); David B. Clarke, ed., *The Cinematic City* (New York: Routledge, 1997); and Clark Arnwine and Jesse Lerner, eds., "Cityscapes I," *Wide Angle* 19, no. 4 (October 1997).

4. Clarke 1997, 3. The Baudrillard quote is from *America* (London: Verso, 1988), 56; the Harvey quote is from *The Condition of Postmodernity: An Enquiry into the Origins of Cultural Change* (Oxford: Blackwell, 1989), 308.

5. Reyner Banham, *Los Angeles: The Architecture of Four Ecologies* (London: Penguin, 1971), 35.

6. *Spatiality* is Edward Soja's summary term for the "created space of social organization and production," mediating between space as a topographical given and the social relations constructed in it. "The structure of organized space is not a separate structure with its own autonomous laws of construction and transformation, nor is it simply an expression of the class structure emerging from social (and thus aspatial?) relations of production. It represents, instead, a dialectically defined component of the general relations of production which are simultaneously social and *spatial*" (Soja 1989, 78–79).

7. See Robert Carringer, "Designing Los Angeles: An Interview with Richard Sylbert," *Wide Angle* 20, no. 3: 97–131.

8. Richard V. Spencer, "Los Angeles as a Producing Center," *Moving Picture World*, April 8, 1911. Excerpts from the article are reprinted in Eileen Bowser, *The Transformation of Cinema, 1907–1915* (Berkeley: University of California Press, 1990), 160–61.

9. The map was reprinted in a prospectus produced by Halsey, Stuart & Co., "The Motion Picture Industry as a Basis for Bond Financing," dated May 27, 1927; the prospectus including the map was published in Tino Balio, ed., *The American Film Industry*, rev. ed. (Madison: University of Wisconsin Press, 1985), 195–217.

10. Foucault 1986, 25.

11. Exceptions to this are often the industry's most transparently ideological projects. In his walk from one side of the city to the other, the protagonist of *Falling Down* (Joel Schumacher, 1993), for example, passes through a cross section of the city's ethnic and class divisions, mostly fairly accurate in their geographical placing, while *Rising Sun* (Philip Kaufman, 1993) can sketch the penetration of Pacific Rim capital into the city and even envision its relations with the "boyz in the hood," the African American working-class communities of South Central that have otherwise been almost entirely unrepresented by Hollywood.

12. See Mike Davis's summary conclusion: "No city, in fiction or film, has been more likely to figure as the icon of a really bad future (or present, for that matter). Postapocalyptic Los Angeles, overrun by terminators, androids, and gangs, has become as much a cliché as Marlowe's mean streets or Gidget's beach party. The decay of the city's old glamor has been inverted by the entertainment industry into a new glamor of decay." *Ecology of Fear: Los Angeles and the Imagination of Disaster* (New York: Henry Holt, 1998), 278.

13. Foucault 1986, 24.

14. These are drawn respectively from Kevin Starr, *Material Dreams: Southern California Through the 1920s* (New York: Oxford University Press, 1990), 84; the *WPA Guide to California* (New York: Pantheon Books, 1984), 208; Soja 1989, 224; and Charles Jencks, *Heteropolis* (London: Academy Editions, 1993), 17 and 32.

15. As Kevin Starr points out, it is "simply a myth to state that twentieth-century Los Angeles had no downtown." Starr 1990, 78. Starr's mapping of the emergence of the Los Angeles basin, and indeed Southern California in general, around the focus of downtown recapitulates Soja's geography, which envisages downtown as "a strategic vantage point, an

urban panopticon counterpoised to the encirclement of watchful military ramparts and defensive outer cities" (Soja 1989, 236).

16. Mike Davis, *Ecology of Fear* (1998), makes a very strong case that the disaster genre that so completely dominates Hollywood films about Los Angeles are allegorical expressions of White, middle-class fear of these working-class, ethnic peoples.

17. So, the filmic cities of Vertov, Ruttmann, Rossellini, Godard, or Mekas are so extraordinary that the spatialities of their production are foregrounded, and in some of them—Vertov and Mekas, for example—the social relationships constructed in the filmmaking are proposed as propaedeutic to those surrounding it, as a metonymy or even a blueprint for the city's ideal form, a trope of the commonality it might allow.

18. The University of Southern California (USC) and the University of California at Los Angeles (UCLA) both have very substantial film schools dating back to the twenties and forties respectively, with more recent programs being instituted at the California Institute of the Arts (Cal Arts) and Occidental College. With the exceptions noted below, the first two are essentially tributary to the industry and dominated by industry values, while the other two have stronger commitments to alternative film. Providing instruction and access to equipment for young artists and employment for independent filmmakers, since World War II film schools have constituted a specific mode of film production in intersection with various avant-garde practices. In Los Angeles, the most important of such intersections was USC's Department of Cinema in the late forties, where the presence of Curtis Harrington and Gregory Markopoulos (who became seminally important—though quite antithetical—figures in the evolution of the fifties avant-garde and its position in relation to Hollywood) and of montage and special effects maestro Slavko Vorkapich (who chaired the department from 1949 to 1951) made it the global center of avant-garde filmmaking of the time. Also important have been the generation of ethnic filmmakers in UCLA's EthnoCommunications Program in the early seventies and an ongoing experimental tradition at Cal Arts, distinguishable from the Disney orientation of the character animation department. Academic/avant-garde filmmaking has been increasingly important since the late sixties; especially when consolidated with tenure, the economic stability of college teaching for filmmakers transformed the avant-garde's social position, producing in the seventies the academic iconography and themes of structural film and then the identity politics of feminist, ethnic, and queer academic filmmaking. Los Angeles has also had a string of independent screening organizations that has been virtually continuous since the mid-forties. The independent distribution of avant-garde films also began in Los Angeles with Kenneth Anger and Curtis Harrington's Creative Film Associates in the late forties; it was followed by the Creative Film Society (founded by Robert Pike in 1957, it emphasized locally produced films, including many UCLA student films), the Los Angeles Filmmakers' Cooperative (which distributed mostly Los Angeles films, 1970–75), and Visual Communications (which distributed Asian American work after the seventies), though USC has also distributed its own student films. But, in contrast to those of other American cities, the major museums have been despicably servile to the industry and unsupportive of alternatives.

19. Despite its off-the-cuff casualness, Banham's attention to the social discontinuity underneath Los Angeles's architectural heterogeneity should be contrasted with the giddy facility of Charles Jencks's proposal that the pastiche architecture of the Frank Gehry school is "clearly intended to represent the different voices that make up the city" (Jencks 1993, 75). All the instances of this hetero-architecture he cites are from the information industries'

elite, privileged sectors (mostly the beaches) "and not at all from the aerospace and garment industries of the central flatlands and the San Fernando Valley which, despite huge areas of poverty, still employ more people than Hollywood."

20. Overall, the chief crucible for the independent Black, Latino, and Asian American film cultures in Los Angeles of the seventies and since was not UCLA's film school, but an EthnoCommunications Program in the anthropology department, founded in 1968 in the wake of the 1965 Watts Rebellion and the civil rights movements and in immediate response to student complaints about the racial exclusivity of the film school itself.

21. Bill Nichols's account of what he considered "the most politically advanced Newsreel center" cites the effect of geographical dispersion of the city, the isolation of its people, and the relative weakness of labor unions, all of which combined to "promote a climate of sectarianism and dogmatism, and the worst kinds of unprincipled conflict between various Movement groups." See his *Newsreel: Film and Revolution* (MA Thesis, University of California at Los Angeles, 1972), 241 and 243.

22. Penelope Houston, *The Contemporary Cinema* (London: Penguin, 1963), 29. Burnett has described his own disapproval of the Los Angeles Panthers in an interview with Monona Wali, "Life Drawings: Charles Burnett's Realism," *The Independent* (October 1988), 19. Despite this, he did tape LA Panther Geronimo Pratt in San Quentin (when he was incarcerated after being framed by law enforcement for murder), but the project never came to fruition; see Lynell George, *No Crystal Stair: African-Americans in the City of Angels* (New York: Anchor Books, 1994), 140.

23. *Killer of Sheep* won First Prize at the United States Film Festival and the Critics' Prize at the Berlin International Film Festival in 1981; in 1990, it was selected by the Library of Congress as one of twenty-five films chosen for preservation. Burnett has received a Rockefeller Grant and a Guggenheim Fellowship, and in 1988, he was awarded a MacArthur Foundation Fellowship.

24. In terms which directly address the narrative of *Killer of Sheep*, Burnett has linked the loss of this historical sense to attacks on African American social structures: "'There has always been the attempt to destroy our consciousness of who we were, to deny the past, and to destroy the family structure; and since for us each day has not a yesterday or a tomorrow, to make the use of experience a lost art"; see his "Inner City Blues" in *Questions of Third Cinema*, Jim Pines and Paul Willemen, eds. (London: British Film Institute, 1989), 225.

25. Written by Earl Robinson of the Workers Laboratory Theatre, "Ballad for Americans" has, as Michael Denning pointed out, "come to stand for the aesthetic forms and ideologies of the Popular Front," with Robeson's recording of it the "unofficial anthem of the movement." It also became a prime target of postwar attacks on Front culture. As well as sustaining a terrible irony in the film, the use of the song signals Burnett's commitment to a non-racist, working-class populism that the combination of corporate postmodernism and Balkanized identity politics has otherwise extinguished as cultural possibility. See Denning's *The Cultural Front: The Laboring of American Culture in the Twentieth Century* (New York: Verso, 1996), 115.

26. P. Adams Sitney observed, "One strains in vain to find a unity to the 'series' aside from the obvious invention of the imagery," and proposed that the systematic disjuncture was linked to Los Angeles, "which is so overwhelmed by fragmentation and gerrybuilt perspectives." See his *"Saugus Series," Millennium Film Journal*, no. 16/17/18 (fall/winter 1986): 158 and 160.

27. Pat O'Neill, "*Water and Power*, A Fragmentary Synopsis," *Motion Picture* 3, no. 1–2 (winter 1989): 19–20. A selection of his working notes for the film, "Notes for *Water and Power*," was published in *Millennium Film Journal*, no. 25 (1991): 42–49.

28. O'Neill 1989, 20.

29. Respectively the title of a collection by local poet Michael Ford; a mass-media cliché; and a best-selling record album by War, a seminal interracial Los Angeles band of the seventies.

30. Soja 1989, 191.

31. The phrase is Mike Davis's; see his *City of Quartz: Excavating the Future in Los Angeles* (London: Verso, 1990), 70.

32. "In Two Dimensions: Lewis Klahr's *In the Month of Crickets*, Pat O'Neill's *Water and Power*," *Motion Picture* 3, no. 1–2 (1989): 23. Paul Arthur has consistently been O'Neill's best commentator, and my reading is indebted to his, even though he rejects the postmodernist associations. I take the phrase "intricate semicoherence" from Peter Plagens's account of San Francisco collagist Jess in his *Sunshine Muse: Contemporary Art on the West Coast* (New York: Praeger, 1974), 94.

33. Foucault 1986, 25.

34. Arthur lists these interpolations: *Detour, The Last Command, The Docks of New York,* and *The Ten Commandments*, as well as references to Kenneth Anger's *Fireworks* ("In Two Dimensions," 1989, 21).

35. Banham 1971, 101.

36. See Pat O'Neill, "Transcript of a Discussion," *Cantril's Filmnotes*, no. 59/60 (1989): 24–8, for his account of his youth "in the shadow of the Paramount water tower" and for production details for *Water and Power*.

37. At various times Oasis members also included Paul Arthur, Morgan Fisher, Robena Friedman, Amy Halpern, Beverly O'Neill, Susan Rosenfeld, Grahame Weinbren, and David and Diana Wilson. For an account of Oasis, see Terry Cannon, "Through the Sands of Time: A Tribute to the L.A. Independent Film Oasis, 1976–81" in *Scratching the Belly of the Beast: Cutting-Edge Media in Los Angeles, 1922–94*, Holly Willis, ed., (Los Angeles: Filmforum, 1994), 60–61.

6

AN AESTHETIC APPROPRIATE TO CONDITIONS

Killer of Sheep, (Neo)Realism, and the Documentary Impulse

Paula J. Massood

> Scooter: You can be a man if you can, Stan.
> *Killer of Sheep* (Charles Burnett, 1977)

ON AUGUST 11, 1965, VIOLENCE BROKE OUT IN the Watts section of Los Angeles, the result of an incident between officers from the LAPD and an African American man named Marquette Frye. Faced with another instance of police brutality, the predominantly Black community rebelled against the police presence, the prevailing poverty, and the government disinterest that had long defined and limited life in South Central Los Angeles. Watts burned over the next six days as the nation and the world viewed televised coverage of the rebellion while hearing reports of rioters "run[ing] loose, looting, burning, and rampaging."[1] Following the Watts Rebellion, urban insurrections occurred again in 1967 and 1968 in cities including Newark, Detroit, and Chicago. Unlike earlier racially motivated uprisings—from the teens or the forties, for example—the urban rebellions from the sixties were nationally televised. They acted as a warp in the United States' racial repressed by bringing to the surface White America's deeply buried fears of African American aggression with footage remarkably resembling *Birth of a Nation*'s (D. W. Griffith, 1915) infamous images of Reconstruction-era looting and rampaging. For White suburbia, these images defined the Black ghetto.[2] The broadcasts sensed a different purpose, however, for many African American spectators who saw resistance to the specific wrongs, such as poverty, decay, and unchecked police brutality, faced by residents of the inner city.[3] In contrast to earlier problem picture depictions of race relations that graced movie screens in the fifties and early sixties or news coverage of civil rights protests, the newscasts redefined the images of African Americans on screen for both Blacks and Whites.

By the end of the sixties, televisual images of inner-city anger and despair were supplemented by new representations of African American city space introduced into mainstream cinematic discourse in the form of the short-lived, though influential, blaxploitation, or Black action, genre. Serving as the precursor to the genre, Melvin Van Peebles's independent feature, *Sweet Sweetback's Baadasssss Song* (1971), introduced many of blaxploitation's conventions, such as an empowered Black masculinity, on-location shooting in recognizable city spaces, and a sense of temporal immediacy aided by costume, dialogue, and musical soundtrack. More "mainstream" blaxploitation vehicles, such as *Shaft* (Gordon Parks, 1971), quickly appropriated these features into their narratives. Inspired by the financial success of *Sweetback,* the Shafts, Superflies, and Dolemites that followed became box office hits, especially with an audience that was primarily (though not limited to) young, urban, African American men. At the same time, however, their images, like *Sweetback*'s before them, were highly contested, as both Black and White critics opposed the films' glorification of criminal life. Soon, religious and political groups such as the Coalition Against Blaxploitation (CAB) were demanding more "realistic" representations of Black life in film, and the pressure exerted on the industry by these groups (as well as an industrial shift toward blockbuster and crossover films) resulted in the eventual disappearance of blaxploitation productions.

Emerging on the periphery of both Hollywood and blaxploitation was a group of filmmakers working under the auspices of the film program in the Theater Arts Department at UCLA. This group, variously referred to as the "LA Rebellion" and the "LA School of Filmmakers," was made up of African and African American graduate film students and included Haile Gerima, Ntongela Masilela, Larry Clark, Billy Woodberry, Alile Sharon Larkin, Julie Dash, Zeinabu irene Davis, and Charles Burnett, among others. Unlike many of the African American filmmakers working within the mainstream, members of the LA School expressed an explicitly political agenda that extended beyond profit making and the superficial interrogation of representation; instead, they were concerned with what they saw as the internal colonization of African Americans and film's role in the construction of subjectivity and self-respect. To this end, they were interested in deconstructing Hollywood's ideological prison house, "recoding black skin on screen and in the public realm by revising the contexts and concepts with which it had long been associated."[4] Rather than replicating Hollywood's classical realism and linear narrative structure, members of the LA School drew from a diverse cross section of filmmaking styles in order to formulate "an aesthetic . . . appropriate to [their] conditions."[5] They were concerned with finding a film form that was, according to Ntongela Masilela, "unique to their historical situation and cultural experience, a form that could not be appropriated by Hollywood."[6]

Charles Burnett enrolled at UCLA in 1967 and was one of the "first wave" members of the LA School. The films Burnett worked on while at UCLA, especially his directorial debut, *Killer of Sheep* (1977), Haile Gerima's *Bush Mama* (1976), and Billy Woodberry's *Bless Their Little Hearts* (1984), provide us with an interesting example of the intersecting influences coming to bear not only on Burnett, but also on most of the filmmakers working within the university's film program. Furthermore, they illustrate the way in which a filmmaker's political and cultural context can directly affect his or her aesthetic choices. This fact resonates once we examine Burnett's *Killer of Sheep*, a film about a family man (Stan) who works at a slaughterhouse during the day and who spends sleepless nights, desensitized and distanced from everything surrounding him. The film combines both documentary and fictional filmmaking techniques—products of the many political and aesthetic discourses that influenced the LA School group—in an attempt to formulate an aesthetic that spoke to a post–civil rights, post-rebellion context. *Killer of Sheep* and other LA School films are examples of situation-specific African American filmmaking: works that are simultaneously positioned on the geographic and industrial margins of Hollywood and which self-consciously reject the concerns and conceits of blaxploitation.

In "The Los Angeles School of Filmmakers," Masilela provides a firsthand account of the groups' diverse, yet interconnected, influences: The Black Arts Movement and its concern with identifying a Black aesthetic; the revolutionary politics of the Black Panthers; the writings of Amílcar Cabral and Franz Fanon on the effects and aftereffects of colonization; Oscar

Micheaux's independent filmmaking practices, reworked for a "working class milieu"; and the revolutionary Third Cinemas emerging from Latin American and African countries, particularly Cuban Cinema and Brazil's Cinema Novo. Masilela notes that "cinema from the Third World . . . was to have a lasting influence on the Los Angeles school" and even resulted in the formation of a Third World Film Club, which screened many of the films emerging from Latin America and Africa at that time.[7] Many of the filmmakers associated with the LA School adapted Third Cinema's revolutionary and reflexive filmmaking techniques, along with its proponents' concern with the effects of internalized colonialism, for an American context. Burnett and others were attempting to free their audience "from the mental colonization that Hollywood tries to impose on its audiences, black and white."[8]

A similar rhetoric of revolution and resistance was echoed by Van Peebles with *Sweetback*. He too had an interest in "de-colonizing" his audience's minds.[9] Sweetback's mythic qualities, his virility, and his agency were Van Peebles's attempt to rewrite Hollywood representations of a disempowered or tamed Black masculinity, the most recent being those linked with Sidney Poitier and his roles in problem pictures like *Guess Who's Coming to Dinner* (Stanley Kramer, 1967). Notwithstanding *Sweetback*'s experimental form, inspired by cinema verité, the French New Wave, and Soviet filmmaking practices, members of the LA School were not drawn to the film as a model because while "some of *Sweetback*'s techniques and procedures were acceptable to the insurgents . . . its politics were not." Instead, films made by members of the LA School, especially those by Burnett and Gerima, focused on "family, women, history, and folklore."[10] The concern with family, in particular, determines *Killer of Sheep*'s narrative and helps define Burnett's vision of Black urban space, one that is, unlike *Sweetback*'s, enabled by communities working together in various forms rather than by individuals working alone.

Burnett's particular version of what has been called "Black urban realism," "poetic realism," "subtle realism," and" "neorealism" has direct antecedents in the political and aesthetic practices of Third Cinema, as was the case with many filmmakers working within the environment engendered by UCLA at this time. The political impulse of many Third Cinema filmmakers was a desire to break with a colonial past by rejecting dominant cinematic codes in favor of articulating a film form that was appropriate to its own national context—Cuban, Brazilian, Senegalese, for example. In formulating their aesthetics, filmmakers like Tomás Gutiérrez Alea and Carlos Diegues looked to disparate cinematic forms and national cinemas, such as Soviet Cinema, Italian Neorealism, and the French New Wave, as models. Third Cinema filmmakers, especially those in Latin America, also drew from the documentary filmmaking practices of John Grierson, the founder of the British documentary movement in the thirties.[11] British social documentaries from this time presented a model of advocacy that provided its subjects with a voice and a focus on matters that were important to the working classes, a rubric first seen in Edgar Anstey and Arthur Elton's *Housing Problems* (1935). Additionally, both Neorealism and British documentary were models of low-budget filmmaking. They were "examples of an artisanal, relatively low-cost cinema working with a mixture of public and private funds, enabling directors to work in a different way and on a different economic scale from that required by Hollywood and its various national-industrial rivals."[12]

Like many filmmakers working within the environment engendered by UCLA at this time, Burnett's particular version of what has been called "Black urban realism," "poetic realism," "subtle realism," and "neo-realism" has direct antecedents in the political and aesthetic practices of Third Cinema. The political impulse of many Third Cinema filmmakers was a desire to break with a colonial past by rejecting dominant cinematic codes in favor of articulating a film form that was appropriate to its own national context: Cuban, Brazilian, Senegalese, for example. In formulating their aesthetics, filmmakers such as Tomas Gutierrez Alea and Carlos Diegues looked to disparate cinematic forms and national cinemas, such as Soviet Cinema, Italian Neorealism, and the French New Wave, as models. Third Cinema filmmakers, especially those in Latin America, also drew from the documentary filmmaking practices of John Grierson, the founder of the British documentary movement in the thirties.[13] British social documentaries from this time presented a model of advocacy that provided its subjects with a voice and a focus on matters that were important to the working classes—a rubric first seen in Edgar Anstey and Arthur Elton's *Housing Problems* (1935). Additionally, both Neorealism and British documentary were models of low-budget filmmaking. They were "examples of an artisanal, relatively low-cost cinema working with a mixture of public and private funds, enabling directors to work in a different way and on a different economic scale from that required by Hollywood and its various national-industrial rivals."[14]

While *Killer of Sheep* has been often associated with Neorealism, its debt to documentary has been just as often overlooked. Yet Burnett possessed a firsthand knowledge of Griersonian documentary principles through his association with Basil Wright, one of the original members of Grierson's film unit during the thirties and an instructor at UCLA while Burnett was enrolled in the program. In fact, Wright is credited with persuading Burnett to pursue film in the first place.[15] Burnett himself notes that Wright was a mentor who provided the initial impetus for his own filmmaking. According to Burnett, "Before I discovered Third World Cinema, Basil Wright's [documentary] class started things for me."[16] It wasn't only Grierson's and Wright's low-budget approach to filmmaking or their interest in working-class social problems that influenced Burnett; it was also their method of documentary observation. Whether or not it is possible to gauge the success of the films made under Grierson's supervision (because of their links to the films' sponsors), many combined advocacy with a notion of observation with minimal intervention. Burnett, with the additional influences of cinéma vérité and direct cinema documentary methodologies, reworked this approach to observation for his own specific and personal context, thus using global aesthetics for local ends.

Burnett's method of observation is distinct from that practiced by Grierson and Wright. Both filmmakers and other personnel associated with the Empire Marketing Board (and later the General Post Office) originally came from the British middle and upper classes and were not immediately familiar with the concerns or experiences of their subjects. Burnett, on the other hand, lived most of his life in the community, possessed a firsthand knowledge of the district's history as an African American neighborhood, and drew upon his experiences for his depiction of Watts. In interviews and writings, we get a sense that Burnett's subject matter is influenced by his own observations and experiences, in which "characters are definitely based on . . . a collection of things I have seen in people, in my community, in my family."[17] Yet, I want to caution against falling into the trap of assuming a false or oversimplified indexicality from Burnett's observations, since he never claims that his characters or settings are true or real. Instead, his characters and settings are influenced by what he's seen, and they provide us with some insight into his statement that *"Killer of Sheep is supposed* to look like a documentary."[18] They are not a reflection, but rather a refraction in the Bakhtinian sense; they dialogue with context, but they are not mimetic replacements for reality.

Burnett's approach to personal observation also is concordant with the Neorealist techniques to which he was exposed while at UCLA. Seemingly incompatible in terms of style and mode, Griersonian documentary and Italian Neorealism shared certain core attributes beyond their modest economies of scale. British documentary principles, such as location shooting, the use of everyday people, and an improvisational approach, influenced Neorealist filmmakers, especially Roberto Rossellini, who began his career making nonfiction films in Italy during World War II.[19] Just as documentaries such as Grierson's *Drifters* (1929) focused on the working man (albeit as a means of championing Britain's herring industry), Italian Neorealist films like Vittorio De Sica's *The Bicycle Thief* (1948) focused on the lives of everyday people in a fictional format. This was an important shift in focus from the more mainstream fascination with stories of the extraordinary practiced by Hollywood and Hollywood-influenced cinemas. Furthermore, both documentary and Neorealist practices emphasized site-specific location filmmaking, as is evidenced in the council housing in *Housing Problems* and the streets of Rome in *Open City* (Roberto Rossellini, 1945). In these examples, the space defines the film and serves as an example of what Grierson referred to as "the drama of the doorstep."[20]

Part of the Griersonian approach to documentary was an emphasis on providing the film's subjects with a voice, as when people in the films explain their jobs or their grievances. The sounds of the streets, particularly vernacular and slang, can also be found in Neorealist films, although it wasn't until the sixties that lightweight and affordable sound technologies allowed for reliable sync-sound recording. Direct sound became a characteristic of films in the sixties, and its use, especially when exploring African American language and stories, is an important facet of Burnett's films in particular and those of the LA School as a whole (especially Gerima's *Bush Mama*). The use of direct sound, combined with location shooting, provides the films produced by the LA School with a sense of documentary realism, establishing what seems to be "only the slightest, if any, departure from the contiguous offscreen reality."[21] Burnett takes firsthand observations of his environment and transposes them into a fictional narrative that is documentary in both look and sound. In this combination of fictional and documentary techniques, *Killer of Sheep* also exemplifies its Third Cinema roots in its formulation of an aesthetic that "make[s] use of the documentary or the fictional mode, or both" and uses "whatever genre, or all genres."[22] (This is not to suggest that blaxploitation films, or other films from the sixties and seventies—*Easy Rider* [Dennis Hopper, 1969], for instance—did not also incorporate vernacular into their soundtracks. The difference with Burnett is that his characters combine contemporary slang with words and phrases from a Southern, rural past, thus acknowledging the influence of African American history on Watts's present, a historical perspective that is rarer in blaxploitation films from the same time.)

In its emphasis on the everyday, *Killer of Sheep* also borrows closely from Neorealism, with *The Bicycle Thief* its closest precursor. Both films focus on family men and their struggles to support their families while maintaining some semblance of dignity and self-respect. Both films also situate their dilemmas in specific post-traumatic contexts: *The Bicycle Thief* in a post–World War II Rome recovering from bombardment and occupation and *Killer of Sheep* in a post-1965 Watts showing the scars (empty lots, abandoned buildings) of the rebellion. Finally, both suggest the ways in which their male leads' existential crises—sparked by global politics and economics—affect their families, as both men punish their loved ones for their own perceived personal failings. Yet, while Burnett borrows his approach to subject matter from Neorealism—so much so that *Killer of Sheep* has been described as a "masterpiece of American neorealism" and other similar observations[23]—he adapts his narrative structure for an African American cultural context. At the time they first appeared, Neorealist films were novel because of their focus on the everyday and for their aesthetics of immediacy. But they were not novel in terms of their narratives, which continued to be structured according to dominant (Western) cinematic approaches to story, especially in their plot-driven, linear narratives and in their reliance on the codes of melodrama.[24] The films' plots continued to involve some form of narrative advancement—climax, resolution, and closure—even if modest in comparison to Hollywood classical narrative.

Killer of Sheep, on the other hand, combines a series of dramatic narrative vignettes with documentary-like nonnarrative footage both of Stan's job in an abattoir (fig. 6.1) and of neighborhood children at play, a cyclical and episodic structure that has its roots in African oral traditions.[25] Manthia Diawara includes *Killer of Sheep* in a cross section of African American films that, as he says, "defamiliarize . . . classical film language" by containing "rhythmic and repetitious shots, going back and forth between past and present."[26] The film makes strange dominant film language by juxtaposing a number of seemingly disparate scenes, offering no clue to time frame and providing no sense of a linear progression. In other words, the structure disallows conventional narrative agency because the plot does not seem to progress, and the rising action of melodrama is substituted

Fig. 6.1

by a more permanent (or, at the least, recurring) cycle of pathos that provides a complex sense of the frustrating sameness of Stan's experiences. While the sections are distinct, each is distinguished by features that offer insight into Stan's existential dilemma because they connect different aspects of his life and suggest the effects of context on psyche.

Killer of Sheep's episodic structure intertwines three stylistically distinct sections that are loosely related through setting and character. The majority of the narrative is set in the domestic sphere and includes most of Stan's interactions with his family, as well as all of his contact with his friends, and provides a firsthand sense of the characters' personalities. Most of the domestic scenes are aimed at illustrating Stan's complex and contradictory frustrations. On the one hand, he has a demoralizing and desensitizing job that, for all his hard work, still impoverishes his family. Stan spends his time at home emotionally distanced from his wife and kids, and yet his malaise does not stop him from engaging in attempts to better their lives (through laying a new kitchen floor or trying to fix their car). While these activities suggest Stan's attempts at agency, the only way out

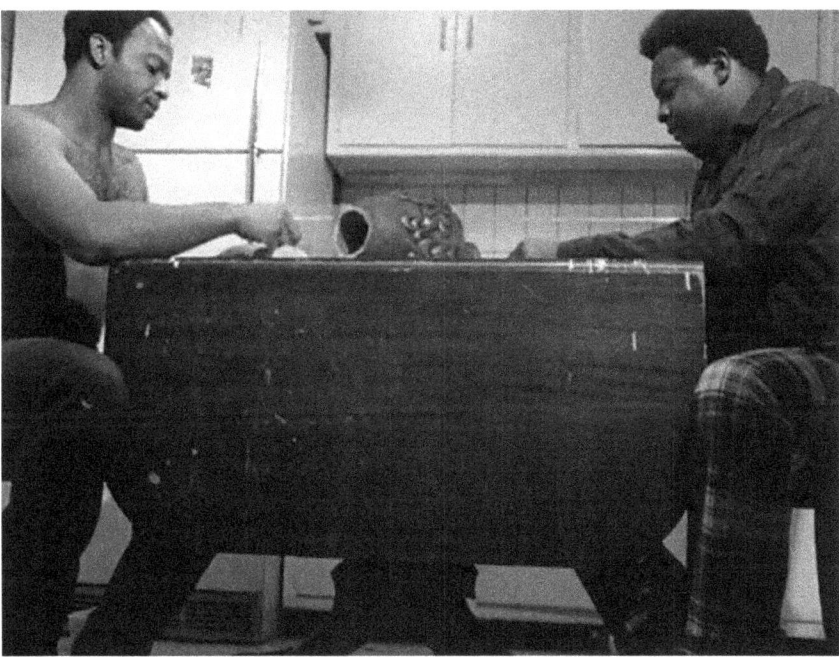

Fig. 6.2

of his situation—at least as presented by a number of the men surrounding him—is to turn to crime, an option he resists. Stan is trapped, and in many of the domestic scenes, Burnett uses tight framing, long takes, slowly paced editing, static camera, and stilted dialogue to illustrate the stagnation and claustrophobia of his situation. He is on a treadmill, and his inability to effect change indicates a lack of power—as a father, as a man, as a citizen—so profound that he can no longer envision a way to escape.

The narrative scenes are indebted to Neorealism in the use of location shooting and performances by nonprofessional actors, including Burnett's daughter, Angela (who also appeared in Woodberry's *Bless Their Little Hearts*). Most scenes are shot in interior domestic spaces—kitchens, bedrooms, living rooms—and the mise-en-scène, combined with shot composition, suggests both Stan's paralysis and his emotional distance from those around him. An example of this stagnation appears early in the film in a scene between Stan and his friend Bracy. Sitting in Stan's kitchen, the pair is framed in a two-shot, facing each other across the table as they drink coffee and play dominoes (fig. 6.2). The emotional distance between Stan and

Fig. 6.3

his friend is communicated by the physical expanse separating them, while the sense of limits, of a forced immobility, is suggested in the tightness of the frame (which presses in on the pair) and their lack of movement. Additionally, the gap between the men is apparent in their stilted dialogue and the long silences, indicating either that they don't have much to say to one another or that they lack the energy, the will, or the emotional vocabulary to communicate their thoughts and worries.

Moments between Stan and his wife (who is not named in the narrative), especially those set in the kitchen, are similarly claustrophobic and stilted, underlining the couple's almost complete emotional estrangement (an estrangement that is much more Stan's than his wife's). Most of their scenes in the first three-quarters of the film are shot in this manner; however, an interesting break from this pattern occurs in a scene of the couple dancing with one another (fig. 6.3). Rather than being separated by their usual physical distance within the frame, the couple embrace to the sounds of Dinah Washington's "This Bitter Earth." Framed in a medium shot, they engage in a long, slow dance while backlit by a window doubling as an additional framing device. In the static camera and the long take, this moment resembles most of the film's other domestic scenes, particularly scenes in which Stan's wife unsuccessfully attempts to connect with her husband. The difference in this scene is that both Stan's alienation from his wife and her frustration with him are nonverbally communicated through her facial expressions and body language, which register desire first, then desperation, and finally frustration and anger.

The slow dance scene is also illustrative of the film's complex sound design. It is unclear whether the sound is diegetic or non-diegetic; the song is meant to be diegetic, but no other noises are audible when it's playing. In most of the narrative sections, Burnett uses direct sound; however, there are times when non-diegetic music occurs on the soundtrack. In these moments, the music functions as a sound bridge leading either into or out of the more "documentary" sequences. Here Washington's song lasts for most of the scene, commenting ironically on the characters' actions, a strategy that Burnett uses more frequently in the documentary-like sequences in the slaughterhouse or of the children at play, the former of which are characterized by non-diegetic music. Like the less narrative scenes, the music here comments upon the couple's relationship, and as such it exemplifies "the impact of black music on the new black cinema" in its "broadening [of] the primary narrative statement" of the film.[27] The tightness of the frame may visually suggest the boundaries of the relationship, but Dinah Washington's voice truly captures the agony that the emotional and physical separation has wrought on both individuals.

While family and friends offer little opportunity for emotional release, Stan's lesser-known acquaintances present alternatives that are not much better. Near the beginning of the film, Stan is visited at home by two men, Smoke and Scooter, from the neighborhood. The pair are coded as street characters, their leather jackets and hats reminiscent of the clothing choices of blaxploitation's pimps and dealers. In the process of discussing their exploits, Smoke and Scooter try convincing Stan to participate in the murder of another neighborhood man named Buddy. Upon overhearing their conversation, Stan's wife first disagrees with them over their suggestion that Stan's participation would be proof of his manhood, then she chases them off. The scene is shot outside the house, which would suggest more freedom and openness than the claustrophobic interiors we have seen previously, but the overall shot composition and editing pattern bears a remarkable resemblance to earlier domestic scenes. It is shot with a static camera in a long take lasting from the moment the men reach the door of the house to a point just after Stan's wife's interjection. While Smoke

Fig. 6.4

and Scooter proposition Stan, he sits with his back to the house with the pair standing in the foreground, bracketing him. When Stan's wife first appears, she stands behind him, completing the triangle and further entrapping him (fig. 6.4). As she begins to disagree with Scooter, she moves in front of Stan, removing him from the conversation and literally erasing him from the on-screen action (she blocks our view of him). Stan's static and submissive position symbolizes his paralysis in the face of both Scooter's rather tautological demand that Stan "can be a man if [he] can" and his wife's definition of manliness.

This scene suggests that each component of Stan's environment—his job, his community, his family—attempts to define his masculinity for him. For Smoke and Scooter, manliness is related to economics and violence; as Smoke argues, "Look at what Stan got? He don't even have a decent pair of pants. All we trying to do is help, nigger. You can't live if you are afraid of dying."[28] For Stan's wife, masculinity is related to intelligence. Either way, Stan has little to say in the constructions of these definitions, even when his wife urges him to stand up for himself. The overwhelming suggestion is that Stan's struggle with self-definition is linked to a larger community dilemma of self-definition, as exemplified by the tension between the men and Stan's wife.

In its focus on the interrelated themes of masculinity, agency, and the family, *Killer of Sheep* is related to a group of independent "Black-subject" films from the sixties and most closely resembles Michael Roemer's *Nothing But a Man* (1964).[29] Roemer's film draws together themes of Black masculinity, its relationship to the family, and the prevailing social forces, such as poverty, racism, and governmental programs (welfare, for example), decimating African American communities. In *Nothing But a Man*, Duff, the main character, is forced to choose between quietly accepting abuse (in the form of union-busting or outright racism) in order to keep a job or standing up for his beliefs and hence failing to support his family. The film's central crisis revolves around the perceived incompatibility of the maintenance of a unified African American family and an empowered Black masculinity and suggests that doing what's right is a complicated venture when one take into account the specificities of context, especially poverty-line subsistence and a lack of jobs paying a living wage. Both films offer a more complex rendering of family life than the fatherless, welfare-dependent Black family demonized by the Moynihan Report of the sixties. The difference between *Killer of Sheep* and an earlier film like *Nothing But a Man*, however, is that the former's family dilemmas are situated in a post-rebellion, and thus a more pessimistic, Watts environment. The family has to fight against the dehumanizing combination of Stan's job, inner-city Los Angeles, *and* the lure of crime (which forms the subtext to many of Stan's relations with friends and acquaintances).

While the film's narrative episodes illustrate Stan's interactions with family and friends, his work experiences and urban environment are more clearly detailed in documentary-like vignettes interspersed between them. The slaughterhouse scenes provide detail about Stan's life as a wage earner. As if to indicate this change in focus from the family scenes, the film's style changes as well, and in this shift we can see most clearly the influence of documentary conventions on Burnett's filmmaking aesthetic. Rather than continuing with the static camera, the long takes, and the stilted dialogue, the slaughterhouse scenes are characterized by the shaky movements of a handheld camera and a looser framing style. This visual design allows the audience to witness Stan, the other workers, and the sheep freely move about the space of the slaughterhouse. In keeping with the observational impulse of Griersonian documentary, combined with the shaky camera work of cinéma vérité and the direct cinema movements, these scenes are more directly "documentary" in their exploration of the blood and gore of the abattoir, complete with footage of actual sheep being bled, skinned, and dismembered.

In addition to the rapid camerawork and editing strategies, the sound design in the slaughterhouse scenes also differs from that in the domestic scenes. Where the scenes in the home are mostly shot with direct sound and the occasional piece of music on the soundtrack, the slaughterhouse scenes are characterized by an absence of dialogue or any other diegetic sounds and the addition of an asynchronous musical soundtrack—comprised of vocal and musical blues, gospel, swing, and orchestral pieces—that often comments ironically on the images. In this use of sound, the scenes differ from the more observational strategies of their closest documentary antecedents with their reliance on sync-sound technologies. Instead, the juxtaposition of sound and image is an adaptation of a Soviet approach to filmmaking for an African American cultural context. For example, the first time the slaughterhouse appears on screen, the images are accompanied by swing music. This soon segues into a children's rendition of "This Old Man" as the interior vérité shots are replaced by long, static shots of the abattoir's exterior. The children's song is a sound bridge connecting the events occurring within the slaughterhouse to the following scene, a return to the domestic sphere introduced with shots of Stan's wife in the kitchen. The lullaby links the abattoir with the kitchen not only because both spaces are connected to Stan, but because the spaces affect his psychological state. In a larger sense, the sound bridge relates Stan's job to the themes that most define the family scenes—fatigue and malaise—thus suggesting that his condition has become a vicious cycle in which work effects home and vice versa.

The slaughterhouse scenes graphically detail Stan's job. We know, from earlier family scenes and his discussion with Bracy, that the job is a source of tension and disillusionment and that Stan would like to find another source of employment. The footage documenting actual blood and gore (the real slaughter of sheep), combined with Stan's criticisms of his job, has led most critics to focus solely on his job as the primary cause of his crisis. Nathan Grant is more accurate, however, when he argues that "it is not his job at the slaughterhouse that is responsible for his state of ennui. Lack of connection with all that is around him, a being out of touch, appears to have gained control."[30] Stan seems almost paralyzed in the family scenes.

He is either clearly immobile, as in the scene with his wife, or unsuccessful in his endeavors to change things (for instance, when he and his friend Gene buy an automobile engine, only to drop it—an ironic metaphor for the pair's lack of agency in Los Angeles's car culture). On the other hand, Stan is most active in the slaughterhouse scenes; he moves freely in and out of the frame, sure of his actions and movements, thus suggesting that he is neither incapable nor afraid of hard work. In the final slaughterhouse scene, Stan even manages a rare smile, an act he has problems completing in most of the family scenes and which is noted by one character earlier in the film. Thus, Stan's crisis should be understood as part of a combination of pressures: the slaughterhouse fails to satisfy him on both a personal and an economic level, but his family and friends, as we have seen, also complicate his life by demanding that he conform to a set of expectations that takes no account of who he is.

The third part of the film's triad of approaches further supports the suggestion that Stan's internal crisis is the result of external factors. The scenes of children at play appear first in *Killer of Sheep* and help introduce the film's setting by including footage shot on location in Watts's railyards, alleyways, empty lots, and streets. Most of the scenes use direct sound, combined with loose shot compositions, relatively slow-paced editing, and a variety of long or medium shots rather than close-ups. This style provides more of a feel for the children's spaces than the setting for other characters in the other sections of the film, and the view of Watts provided here is more graphic and despairing than what we see elsewhere in *Killer of Sheep*. The space itself resembles a war zone, with empty lots and abandoned buildings dotting the urbanscape. This metaphor is carried over into the children's activities: in almost all the scenes, the kids are engaged in some sort of combative play, ranging from rock-throwing battles to wrestling, hitting, and bullying each other (normally on the basis of gender). The family scenes also include examples of children at play, but with the exclusion of the sibling rivalries between Stan Jr. and Angie, these interactions are peaceful in comparison. Perhaps it is because of the bloody footage of dead sheep that the abattoir scenes have received more critical attention, but the children's scenes offer more compelling suggestions about context: in the streets, the interactions are violent, with the shots of kids throwing rocks eerily echoing the televised images of Watts from a decade before.

While the children's scenes are not directly related to Stan's narrative, they are connected to the overall story through the presence of Stan Jr. and

Angie in a few of the earlier episodes. The connections with Stan are much more allegorical and center on the suggestion that the community is in crisis. Watts, according to Burnett, was left with "a vacuum—moral, economic, political"; it was a "community without a center."[31] By linking Stan's crisis, as explicated in other parts of the film, with his immediate context (Watts of the past and present), *Killer of Sheep* expands what first appears as a sole focus on a singular hero and suggests that Stan's existential dilemma is undeniably linked to a larger community crisis. With this connection, Burnett shifts conventional narrative identification from the individual to the community, thus adapting the film's narrative for an African American collectivity by expanding the aesthetic influences of Neorealism and documentary and disputing blaxploitation's assertion that an empowered lone male figure leads to salvation.

The expansion from individual to community is made most clearly in one of the rare moments when the children's sections shift out of sync-sound. In an episode in which the kids play near an abandoned building, the direct sounds are joined by the non-diegetic sound of Paul Robeson singing "The House I Live In." As the song continues, the images of kids at play are replaced by footage of the interior abattoir. Again, there is the faint, synchronized noise of the space, now combined with Robeson's voice on the soundtrack. To Robeson's repeated refrain, "What is America to Me?," sheep are led to the slaughter. At this, the images segue to another narrative episode, the scene with Smoke and Scooter discussed earlier. The series of cuts, combined with the unifying sound bridge, expands the dilemma from a single focus on Stan to his entire community by linking playful violence (acted out in the empty lots left in the wake of the rebellion), literal capitalist violence (Stan's dehumanizing and bloody job), and the neighborhood's prevalence of violent crime (the result of a post-rebellion, postindustrial economy). According to Grant, in the combination of slaughterhouse images and the narrative scene focusing on murder, Stan "is witnessing not only the threat to his own survival as that is made evident by the actions of his friends, but he is also watching his community's self-destruction."[32] Grant's observation, while prescient, is limited to Stan's difficult job and Smoke and Scooter's plans for a murder; my assertion is that we also see the continuation of community self-destruction in the kids' activities and surroundings. In this context, the family not only contends against the specific forces Stan faces, but also against those awaiting the next generation, Stan Jr. and Angie. Stan Jr.'s budding nihilism is suggested by his repeated statements about needing money and his sullen demeanor. Moreover, he seems as distant from his family, especially his mother, as his father is. Stan Jr.'s emotional distance is much more malicious, however, as he misbehaves and, by the end of the film, refuses to come when his mother calls.

Burnett's concern for the community and its future welfare can be traced back to his firsthand knowledge of Watts. His observations regarding the area's loss of a center—a shared epistemology of sorts—remembers a pre-1965 period, when Watts *did* have a center (a center that was perhaps best captured in Carl Franklin's *Devil in a Blue Dress* in 1995). *Killer of Sheep* links the area's African American community base to its rural, Southern past—the "back home" that Stan mentions near the beginning of the film and in other subtle references to his and his wife's Southern roots—and the migration that resulted in the growth of a vibrant Black community in Los Angeles during the forties. This past is quoted in the vernacular spoken by some characters in the film and in the railroad yards and trains used by the children as a playground and toys. (It will be quoted fifteen years later in a similar scene in John Singleton's *Boyz n the Hood* in 1991.) The sounds and shots of the past reference a form of social and geographic mobility that, Burnett suggests, was disappearing for men of Stan's generation and is all but gone for Stan Jr. In the Los Angeles captured in *Killer of Sheep*, social mobility is curtailed by higher unemployment and a lack of job opportunities like the defense industry and porter jobs that had promised a move into the middle classes for many African Americans of Stan's father's generation. Stan's generation seems stuck in the wreckage of a postindustrial, postrebellion urban landscape. What remains are low-paying and demoralizing jobs, like Stan's (and what Bracy refers to as a "slave") that lead nowhere. He embodies a middle-class work ethic and ideology that are ultimately outmoded in the context of late-twentieth-century industrial practices. Stan labors, but he will never get ahead.

These historical and cultural references, as well as the film's episodic narrative structure, suggest the impossibility of considering *Killer of Sheep*'s Watts setting without a comparable consideration of its history. Such spatio-temporal relationships are connected to Mikhail Bakhtin's notion of the chronotope, or "materialized history," where temporal relationships are made literal by the objects, spaces, or persons with which they intersect.[33] While seemingly geared toward Western literary texts, the chronotope is a useful concept for analyzing Third Cinema texts that, according to Paul Willeman, organize "time and space in their own specific ways."[34] Elsewhere,

I've used the chronotope as a tool for analyzing African American cinematic constructions of the city and to argue that sections of the urbanscape associated with African American life are presented as truly material (whether contemporary, recent, or older), as the streets and buildings call up a multiplicity of pasts.[35] In a related way, Burnett's rendering of the abandoned lots and railroad yards of Watts illustrates both the history of an African American presence in the city and (possibly more importantly) provides a sense of the paradox presented by the city: migration was what enabled the settlement of Watts in the first place, but the mobility of the area's Black population became severely constrained over time. Stan's experiences are thus related to a larger historical and political context, and as such, his quiescence represents failed expectations and the lack of options on a much more global scale.

What is surprising, then, is that the film ends on a slightly uplifting, though definitely unresolved, note when Stan, his wife, and Angie return from an unsuccessful attempt to spend the day at the racetrack. For a brief moment there is an intimacy in the trio's interactions, as Stan answers Angie's query about the origins of thunder during a storm. As Stan provides Angie with an explanation, drawing upon a folktale about the devil beating his wife, the three exchange glances and smile at one another. In the course of the film, this is the first time that Stan has shown any sort of pleasure toward his wife and children, and it suggests the possibility of a continuing, if tentative, intimacy in the household in spite of the surrounding conditions. In using the folk references in one of the rare scenes of connection among family members, Burnett suggests that the welfare of Stan, of his family, and of the community as a whole is dependent upon the maintenance of an historical perspective that acknowledges a Southern, or rural, past.

In *Killer of Sheep*, Third Cinema, documentary, and Neorealist influences, combined with Burnett's personal knowledge of Watts, create a unique form of cinematic realism that marries techniques such as on-location shooting, long takes, and direct sound with the more disparate stylistics of moving camera, rapid editing, and the ironic juxtaposition of sound and image. On its most literal level, the film focuses on Stan and his interactions with his family and friends by providing vignettes of his day-to-day existence. On a more allegorical level, the film explores Stan's crisis of self-definition and its relationship to masculinity and the family, linking his experiences to a community-wide dilemma faced by, at the least, the African American residents of Watts. In its polyphonic combination of documentary and fictional modes, the film is an example of what Third

Cinema filmmakers and members of the LA School were striving for in their filmmaking in the sixties and seventies: the formulation of an aesthetic that dialogued with and refracted a unique set of cultural conditions. *Killer of Sheep* offers one example of what this might mean for a post–civil rights, post-1965 alternative filmmaking practice.

Notes

1. Robert Mayer, ed., *Los Angeles: A Chronological and Documentary History, 1542–1976* (Dobbs Ferry, NY: Oceana Publications, Inc., 1978), 136.
2. Mark A. Reid, *Redefining Black Film* (Berkeley: University of California Press, 1993), 74.
3. Thomas Cripps, "*Sweet Sweetback's Baadasssss Song* and the Changing Politics of Genre Film," in *Close Viewings: An Anthology of New Film Criticism*, Peter Lehman, ed. (Tallahassee: Florida State University Press, 1990), 240.
4. James A. Snead, "Images of Blacks in Black Independent Films: A Brief Survey," in *Blackframes: Critical Perspectives on Black Independent Cinema*, Mbye B. Cham and Claire Andrade-Watkins, eds. (Cambridge: The MIT Press, 1988), 22.
5. Paul Willeman, "The Third Cinema Question: Notes and Reflections," in *Questions of Third Cinema*, Jim Pines and Paul Willeman, eds. (London: BFI Publications, 1989), 4.
6. Willeman 1989, 108.
7. Ntongela Masilela, "The Los Angeles School of Black Filmmakers," in *Black American Cinema*, Manthia Diawara, ed. (New York: Routledge, 1993), 110.
8. Masilela 1993, 111.
9. Quoted in James P. Murray, "Running with *Sweetback*," *Black Creation* 3, no. 1 (fall 1971): 10.
10. Toni Cade Bambara, "Reading the Signs, Empowering the Eye: *Daughters of the Dust* and the Black Independent Cinema Movement," in *Black American Cinema*, Manthia Diawara, ed. (New York: Routledge, 1993), 119–20.
11. Willeman 1989, 5.
12. Ibid.
13. Ibid.
14. Ibid.
15. Masilela 1993, 112.
16. Quoted in Bérénice Reynaud, "An Interview with Charles Burnett," *Black American Literature Forum* 25, no. 2 (summer 1991): 328.
17. Reynaud 1991, 326.
18. Quoted in Morona Wali, "Life Drawings: Charles Burnett's Realism," *The Independent* 11, no. 8 (October 1988): 20. Emphasis added.
19. Roy Ames, *Patterns of Realism: A Study of Italian Neo-Realist Cinema* (Cranbury, NJ: A. S. Barnes, 1971), 19.
20. Quoted in Erik Barnouw, *Documentary: A History of the Non-Fiction Film*, rev. ed. (New York: Oxford University Press, 1983), 85.
21. Clyde Taylor, "Decolonizing the Image: New U.S. Black Cinema," in *Jump Cut: Hollywood, Politics, and Counter Cinema*, Peter Steven, ed. (New York: Praeger Publishing, 1985), 168.

22. Julio Garcia Espinosa, "For an Imperfect Cinema," in *New Latin American Cinema*, vol. 1, Michael T. Martin, ed. (Detroit: Wayne State University Press, 1997), 81.

23. Wali 1988, 16.

24. Andre Bazin, "An Aesthetic of Reality: Cinematic realism and the Italian School of the Liberation," in *What is Cinema?*, vol. II, Hugh Gray, trans. (Berkeley: University of California Press, 1971), 21.

25. Taylor 1985, 172.

26. Manthia Diawara, "Black American Cinema: The New Realism," in *Black American Cinema*, Manthia Diawara, ed. (New York: Routledge, 1993), 10.

27. Taylor 1985, 174–5.

28. Phyllis Rauch Klotman, ed., *Screenplays of the African American Experience* (Bloomington: Indiana University Press, 1991), 105.

29. Taylor 1985, 167.

30. Nathan Grant, "Innocence and Ambiguity in the Films of Charles Burnett," in *Representing Blackness: Issues in Film and Video*, Valerie Smith, ed. (New Brunswick, NJ: Rutgers University Press, 1997), 139.

31. Wali 1988, 17.

32. Grant 1997, 140.

33. M. M. Bakhtin, *The Dialogic Imagination*, Michael Holquist, ed., Caryl Emerson and Michael Holquist, trans. (Austin: University of Texas Press, 1981), 247.

34. Willeman 1989, 15.

35. Paula J. Massood, *Black City Cinema: African American Urban Experiences in Film* (Philadelphia, PA: Temple University Press, 2003), 4–9.

7

NEOREALISM MEETS THE BLUES IN CHARLES BURNETT'S *KILLER OF SHEEP*

Keith Mehlinger

> The very existence of the blues tradition is irrefutable evidence that those who evolved it respond to the vicissitudes of the human condition not with hysterics and desperation, but through the wisdom of poetry informed by pragmatic insight.[1]
>
> Albert Murray

ALTHOUGH LITTLE KNOWN OUTSIDE OF CRITICS' CIRCLES AND dedicated cineastes, Charles Burnett's *Killer of Sheep* (1977) "remains to this day a near mythic object, one of the first fifty films inducted into the Library of Congress's National Film Registry."[2] The film "tenderly recounts a few days in the life of a slaughterhouse worker, Stan (Henry G. Sanders), whose existence is as bounded by invisible threads of hopelessness as that of the sheep that he is forced to kill each day."[3] During its brief theatrical release in 1977, *New York Times* critic Janet Maslin dismissed *Killer of Sheep* as "amateurish" and "boring." Since then, the film has won awards at festivals and "acquired honorary protection by the National Film Registry accorded to a select few 'masterpieces' such as *Citizen Kane*, and aided its author in winning a prestigious John D. and Catherine T. MacArthur Fellowship," popularly known as the "genius award."[4] In addition to being selected as one of America's fifty most culturally significant films, the film was named one of the "100 Most Influential Films of All Time" by the National Society of Film and gained critical acclaim in Europe. Burnett told film critic

Terrence Rafferty in 2001, "It just takes an extraordinary effort to keep going when everybody's saying to you, 'No one wants to see that kind of movie' or 'there's no black audience.'"[5] The story of this film's thirty-year journey from cult classic to re-release by Milestone Films in theaters and on DVD in 2008 is the story of its music in many ways. To pull together the $150,000 for copyright licenses required for the film's re-release, the director Steve Soderbergh "providentially stepped forward with a generous gift" that enabled Milestone Films, a small distributor, to save the project.[6]

This article examines core elements of Charles Burnett's film *Killer of Sheep* as a "blues statement"[7] with shared aesthetics of neorealism and the blues including the visceral power of both modalities, their universal themes of human struggle, and their use of the "objective correlative" or adequate metaphor in the pursuit of truth and consciousness.[8] Burnett merges blues as a diviner of truth with a "state of mind" much like that of the Italian neorealists, which allowed them to "broaden, first of all, the cinema's spiritual horizon," to take moral positions with respect to the social, political, and economic issues facing the nation.[9] In the case of *Killer of Sheep*, Burnett's focus is the Black working class of Watts less than a decade after the 1965 riots, when over thirty people lost their lives in violence involving the Los Angeles Police Department, the National Guard, and private citizens. Burnett examines present conditions (circa the seventies) and frames circumstances that could easily call for the necessity of action, but like the Italian filmmakers, Burnett makes truth his advocate through cinematic techniques that appear more documentary than narrative and are in the spirit of what Luchino Visconti called an "anthropomorphic cinema," portraying people in their lived environment.[10]

Neorealism meets the blues in *Killer of Sheep* (1977) as Burnett brings a blues aesthetic to a style of filmmaking "associated with Roberto Rossellini, Luchino Visconti, Vittorio De Sica, and Giuseppe De Santis, among others, working with writers including Cesare Zavattini and Federico Fellini."[11] The films deal with the "ravages of fascism" that leave rifts in national identity and that cause the decay of communities. The films show Italians "suffering various forms of material and spiritual poverty and oppression that could not be blamed completely on the Black Shirts and the Nazis."[12] Neorealism also represents resistance by providing a "continuing critique of the conditions, institutions, and individual predilections that cause violence, poverty, isolation, and spiritual distress."[13]

Of the merged approach that Burnett takes with the blues and neorealism, it is the blues that is the least understood or valued as a powerful aesthetic envoy that can induce self-reflection and stir questions of identity with respect to a nation's past and future, as neorealism did at the end of World War II. Although there is a body of recorded work from the turn of the twentieth century forward, the blues was the province of Black artists and storytellers. The art form was marginalized because of cultural hegemony, though the blues were foundational to rhythm and blues and rock music. Burnett, a native of Vicksburg, Mississippi, brings his Delta blues values to bear in the film, while coincidentally practicing many of the "Ten Points of Neorealism," as described by screenwriter Cesare Zavattini in a 1952 film journal that stresses a stripped-down cinema verité emphasizing reality through documentary aesthetics, including location, production, and the use of nonprofessional actors.[14]

Burnett practices the neorealist aesthetic ever more powerfully because of the blues, for long before the advent of the cinema, the blues has been capable of generating cultural self- reflection by embracing humanity.[15] The blues is music that is older than the European literary movements of the early twentieth century in realism and naturalism that can be traced forward to neorealism in the cinema.[16] As early as 1550, English lexicographers found records of the phrase *to look blue* meaning "to suffer anxiety, fear, discomfort, and low spirits."[17] The term "*blue devils* to designate baleful demons has been traced back as far as 1616," so it is likely that African Americans "acquired both the word and its special connotation" from European Americans.[18]

Blues music has its beginnings in Africa just like the banjo but was fully evolved in America by slaves expressing their hope, pain, and desires through song that derived from their life experience in a form less choral than spirituals and not necessarily respectful of the church.[19] The blues, like the literary movements from which neorealism can be traced, was concerned with truth and stories of real life. The Deep South, especially Mississippi, is where the blues seeped out of swamps and hollers in a character that pilgrims in the 1960s described as "rough, spontaneous, crude and unfinished," dominated by "stark, unrelieved emotion," an intense distillation of the music of slavery "only a step from the wordless field cries and hollers of an older generation."[20]

Killer of Sheep, produced in 16mm black-and-white film, in some respects seems an artifact. With its primitive look and feel (adding to its sophistication), unconventional plotting, sparse dialogue, and use of episodic vignettes integrating a soundtrack that is dominantly blues based, I liken the experience of watching this film to that of listening to a vinyl LP with all the pops and scratches in the right places. It is this kind of raw experience that helps to authenticate the pain, the joy, and the sorrow of the blues as an art form less dependent on vocal precision than on musical precision and nuance that comes as the result of a *blues statement*.[21] Instead of the twelve-measure technicalities of the blues form—the "holy trinity" ("three harmonies like the beginning, the middle, and the end of things. Three sung statements and three instrumental responses").[22] I am focused on the look and feel of *Killer of Sheep* as a cinematic incantation of *the blues statement* to reflect "a sense of life that is affirmative," despite blues lyrics that include "the absurd, the unfortunate, and the catastrophic," and to "reflect the person making the confrontation, his self-control, his sense of structure and style" and the expression of, among other things, "his sense of humor as well as his sense of ambiguity and his sense of possibility."[23] These are all issues of portrayal and characterization for the filmmaker, as they are for the *blues balladeer*.[24]

In the case of *Killer of Sheep*, the soundtrack charts an unusual improvisational course throughout the film as more than accompaniment, but as a character (a balladeer) whose presence imbues the movie with an overall blues feel that underscores the poetic modes of its visual story. The result is a blues nuance that dominates the film despite its soundtrack blending jazz and blues with spiritual and folk music (Paul Robeson), R & B (Earth, Wind & Fire), and classical (including George Gershwin and Sergei Rachmaninoff). The film and its story have their *objective correlative* in the blues, and Burnett extends cinematic language into the repertoire of the blues where "the definitive blues statement is not verbal," as words, "however well chosen, are secondary to the music" because "what counts for most is not verbal precision (which is not to say vocal precision) but musical precision, or perhaps better still, musical nuance."[25]

Burnett's nuance comes through sight and sound, not unlike that of the purveyor of the blues—the storyteller who conjures a picture through music and verse laced with metaphor. Burnett is the extension of "how the story teller works with language, as a 'song and dance man' (a maker of *molpês*) whose fundamental objectives are extensions of those of the bard, the minstrel, and the ballad maker which, incidentally, are those of the contemporary American blues singer."[26] Ironically, the music that prevented the film's release for thirty years because of copyright issues combines with its mise-en-scène to make one of the most powerful blues evocations ever on screen. David Denby, of the *New Yorker*, was one of the few nationally known film critics to observe that "Burnett used many kinds of African-American music on the soundtrack, and the music itself has the bedraggled eloquence of an old blues record."[27] As in most blues music, violence, joy, and pain hang over *Killer of Sheep* because of what unfolds due to human circumstances, emotions, and matters of the heart that could at any moment careen to tragic dimensions or veer toward redemption and the recapitulation of love. The blues is the perfect vehicle for this film because "the blues is full of metaphor in words and music."[28] Like the blues, *Killer of Sheep* is ultimately concerned with "the most fundamental of all existential imperatives: affirmation, which is to say, reaffirmation and continuity in the face of adversity," or like Hamlet, "to be or not to be," or to ponder, as Burnett's main character does, "whether things are worth all the trouble and struggle of waking in your bed with the blues all in your head."[29]

Like a musical incantation, the soundtrack interlocking Burnett's story and images provides a feeling of sadness and joy—and most importantly, pain, something that the blues knows a lot about.[30] James Bell writes: "Rarely have songs and images been combined so resonantly and beautifully as in *Killer of Sheep*, whose soundtrack boasts Scott Joplin, Louis Armstrong, and blues singers like Little Walter, Elmore James, Faye Adams, and Dinah Washington." Burnett recalls, "The music was mainly pieces that my mother used to play." He "decided on them before filming and they helped me to think of certain images for the film. For example Luis Russell's 'Sad Lover Blues' inspired the scene of Stan and his wife dancing through the end. I broke the record so I didn't get to use it, and used Dinah Washington's 'This Bitter Earth' instead."[31]

Killer of Sheep was completed during the so-called blaxploitation period of Hollywood films anointed by a new kind of Black cinematic hero in Melvin Van Peebles's independent blockbuster, *Sweet Sweetback's Baadasssss Song* (1971). Burnett's stark documentary-like approach seems iconoclastic or an act of resistance, given the prevailing Hollywood trends to fund Black action films for the then-growing demand at the box office. Instead, Burnett's film evokes the black-and-white film work of Roberto Rossellini, Vittorio De Sica, and other filmmakers whose work defined Italian neorealism. The film also bravely stakes rare ground in its realistic portrayal of an African American working-class family trying to "preserve its meaningful relationships and sense of humanity in spite of the pressure and indignities of exploitation."[32] Bérénice Reynaud, the New York correspondent for *Cahiers du cinema*, pointed out that *Killer of Sheep* was one of the first films in which European audiences saw a sensitive, un-condescending portrayal of a Black family.[33] The main characters of the film represent generations of African Americans who found themselves on the crossroads between urban and rural life in the twentieth century after migration from the South to large cities. It is along these pathways that blues evolved from the Delta to cities in the East and in the Midwest. Stan's peril to keep his family out of the clutches of poverty and to be a loving husband and father places his "down home" values in an uncomfortable coexistence with life in Watts (and a new kind of blues). Stan's response is to remain focused, to take a steady course that takes a toll on his psyche and emotional state but does not deter his affirmation of life in the spirit of Murray's blues statement.[34] Burnett poetically portrays Stan's blues life by intercutting the ardors of adulthood and toil at the slaughterhouse with "long, real-time master shots of youths playing that suggest their carefree lives while also conveying the potential cruelty and danger of their games. Echoing cinema verité, Burnett often allows the action to unfold in front of the camera, capturing the results on grainy black and white 16 millimeter film; at times the film lumbers along, at other times it slides out to the edge of dissonance."[35]

The film is culled from Burnett's experiences growing up and living in Watts after his family moved there from Mississippi in the late 1940s. In *Killer of Sheep*, "dusty South Central alleyways evoke the roads of Mississippi, Alabama, Arkansas, which is where most of the neighbors of his youth came from."[36] Burnett threads Stan and his family though a series of vignettes suspended between the rituals of childhood and the rigors of adult life. His musical soundtrack forms the call-and-response of a blues incantation that serves as a layer of consciousness for the film. Just as the blues is informed more by its music than lyrics, because even a "strong verbal statement can be contradicted and in effect canceled by any musical counterstatement,"[37] so too is the result for Burnett's visual story (sad or not) that by virtue of musical counterstatement can bring hope to despair or reinforce sadness and alienation as portrayed. The result of Burnett's blues counterstatement as a contradiction comes as the result of juxtapositions like "impressionistic fragments from the lives of the working poor against Paul Robeson singing" the uplifting "What Is America to Me?," "Renoir-like" humanism through images and sequences that "are the scatterings of joy Burnett finds amid the gray gloom: fleeting moments—a junk strewn lot transformed into a playground by the power of a child's imagination, a husband and wife holding each other in a long-forgotten embrace—that are like mirages in a desert."[38]

Burnett heard most of the music used in the film "as a kid growing up," and the songs "conjured up images" as he was "thinking of each scene." When it came to Paul Robeson's song "What Is America to Me?," Burnett provided a visual contradiction to the "happy life" described that reminded him of a Norman Rockwell painting. Instead, "what you see on the screen is the opposite; kids living in places where things are torn down, yet still being kids and not really realizing it. It's a contrast between the lyrics and what's going on in the screen. This mean old world comes into play. You see the slaughterhouse and reflect on what's going . . . I was always interested in showing a slice of life and recording an experience that had a narrative inherent in it."[39] Burnett's visual contradiction to "What Is America to Me?" is also his blues counterstatement, for as the filmmaker, he is also the blues balladeer.[40]

Burnett's portrayal of working class African Americans remains unique and still garners critical acclaim to this day, for there "is nothing else in American movies quite like *Killer of Sheep*. Thematically the film is a reaction against the blaxpoitation films that were filling downtown theaters in the early seventies. There are no supercops or superpimps in Burnett's Watts."[41] Further evidence of Burnett's Hollywood counter-narrative as a blues statement (affirming life) comes from his remapping Watts as more than a physical space, but as a sociological one, as well, not inhabited "just by pimps, hookers, and OGs (Original Gangsters), but by poverty-line families eking out meager existences while hoping against hope for change to come."[42]

As the filmmaker of *Killer of Sheep* in a blues context, Burnett also serves as the balladeer making a blues statement about the nature of joy and pain for children and adults.[43] As Burnett says, "The very structure of the film comes from this preoccupation: how to represent life, the everyday crises"[44] The fate of the sheep "is in fact is a metaphor for Stan's own helplessness in the restricted world in which he lives. That impotence has made him withdraw from his family, especially his wife, to whom he denies the affection she craves."[45] At the Toronto Film Festival of Festivals (1981), David Overby called *Killer of Sheep* "a masterpiece" and "a positive demonstration that there are still filmmakers in the United States who care about film and, more importantly, about people."⁴⁶ Nowhere is this more apparent than in how Burnett captures the faces of his characters in rapturous close-ups that tap into consciousness. "The Renaissance painters like Leonardo inserted a glow—Charles Burnett does this when he looks at faces."⁴⁷ Burnett's kudos are as much for his skills as a filmmaker as they are for his skills as a balladeer with a commitment to his blues statement.⁴⁸

The improvised feel of *Killer of Sheep* adds to its bluesy feel through a raw cinema verité and lyrical mise-en-scène that is scripted and storyboarded. There is no mistaking that the film "owes an obvious cinematic debt to Italian neorealism and documentary, but with an inspired improvisatory feel that's unique in cinema—something closer to the feel of blues or jazz."⁴⁹ Burnett recalls ad-libbing in a few places but more purposely controlling the film's aesthetic to make it "look like a loosely shot film, where the narrative sort of evolves, but it was scripted. A lot of the images were drawn. I was looking for specific things in the scenes, but the idea was not to have perfect lighting and stuff like that."⁵⁰

The primitive look of the film shares a common aesthetic with the classics of neorealism and their documentary feel but also produces the cinematic equivalent of a blues statement. Burnett recalls, "I wanted the film to have a rough raw aspect, without light . . . I wanted the texture to be rough, as if the movie had been made by someone who didn't know how to make movies. I wanted this movie to seem like a work in which the filmmaker didn't try to manipulate things."⁵¹

Killer of Sheep takes a decidedly different approach to narrative form than that of Hollywood genre films and shares aesthetic and narrative characteristics of classic Italian neorealism. Films done after the classic period fall into a broader definition of neorealism as "a cinema of the Resistance, but it is a cinema of resistance interpreted broadly, linked not only specifically to the anti-fascist partisan movement—their practical struggle as well as their utopian dreams—but to a continuing critique of the conditions, institutions, and individual predilections that cause violence, poverty, isolation, and spiritual distress."⁵² *Killer of Sheep* ponders the same issues in a different time and place and represents resistance. Burnett can be further linked to "resistance" by virtue of creating a counter-narrative to Hollywood's stereotypes, much like Oscar Micheaux had done a half century earlier in opposition to D. W. Griffith's *Birth of a Nation* (1915).⁵³ Burnett is identified with a group of filmmakers identified by film scholars as the LA School, or alternatively the LA Rebellion, including Burnett, Julie Dash, Haile Gerima, and Billy Woodberry, all UCLA trained filmmakers.[54] Burnett recalls at the time that he was just trying to tell the story he wanted on film, as were the others. "But it wasn't a "school" of Black filmmakers, or a conscious effort. Things just happened. Of course, everybody was more or less rebellious at that time."[55] The student filmmakers "set out to tell stories that rejected Hollywood stereotypes that depicted the black community in strictly negative terms—drug infested, violent, malevolent and dysfunctional."[56]

Although he didn't study neorealism in film school prior to the genesis of *Killer of Sheep* in the late 1960s and "didn't really set out to create a film like the Italians," the look and feel of neorealism emanate from his artistic choices. His approach was an effort "to try to get at the truth," to confront "the whole issue of Hollywood and the misrepresentation of black people in film—with *Gone with the Wind* and Stepin Fetchit—well, the idea was to get at the truth of the representation. In that respect, it was neo-realist."[57] This suggests that Burnett's pursuit of truth made him one of the "fragile shoots" of American filmmaking that A. O. Scott finds stronger evidence for in other national cinemas as a "neorealist impulse that proved remarkably mobile and adaptable" long after the end of Italian neorealism. He includes *Killer of Sheep* among a handful of American films that "offer not only bracing, poetic views of real life, but also tantalizing glimpses of a cinematic tradition that might have been." As with Burnett's desire to tell a story of the Black working-class counter to the headwinds of exploitive Hollywood trends, Scott suggests that when neorealism pops up, "it might be thought of less as a style or genre than as an ethic that finds expression in various places at critical times."[58] Scott has been challenged for the misappropriation of the term *American neorealism* by another film critic, Richard Brody, of the *New Yorker*. Brody takes exception to *Killer of Sheep* as an example of neo-neorealism, taking the position that the neorealist-like approach was practiced widely to become America's dominant independent film trope in the fifties and sixties.[59] It is my view, however, that Burnett forges new ground by combining a blues aesthetic with the instincts and aspirations of neorealism, and the result seems the "fragile shoot" that A. O. Scott writes about, for there are few films that have answered the call of resistance so boldly at a critical moment in history as did *Killer of Sheep*. With the civil rights movement and the 1965 Watts riots still fresh in his mind, Burnett's gestation and production of *Killer of Sheep* came at one of those critical times. Ironically, it was at the same time that the Black action film was going strong, with films such as *Superfly* and

Shaft helping to anchor the blaxploitation era of Hollywood films. Burnett's contrary urges merged with his desires for an African American counter-narrative about the blue-collar people he cared about. His focus on African Americans in Watts shared thematic fluency with the universal plight of the poor to survive, whether in Italy at the end of World War II or in Los Angeles in the seventies. Though not the site of a declared war, the Watts area of Los Angeles was nevertheless a scarred terrain of urban unrest that pitted African Americans against police in a racially driven conflict. This landscape of impoverished and working-class people provided the backdrop of desolation and poverty for *Killer of Sheep*, and it would take decades for Los Angeles to recover from riots in the sixties, only for the riots to be repeated again (most notably) in the nineties following the acquittal of police in the infamous beating of Rodney King.

Burnett's artistic approach to *Killer of Sheep* was less the pursuit of Rossellini and De Sica and more the pursuit of truths about the lives of a working-class Black family in Watts in a period not long after the 1965 Los Angeles riots. It is his camera, however, "like that of De Sica and other masters of Italian neo-realism" that "captures love for his characters—not because they are good or beautiful but because—they are."[60] From dirt playgrounds to rooftops, the slaughterhouse, and the street, the black-and-white and silver images of *Killer of Sheep* play like lyrical moments from a dream that tap into our emotions and spark our consciousness. Burnett's camera is part of his "holy trinity" for the blues in the sense that it serves the cycle of verse and instrumentation that is foundational to the blues. *Killer of Sheep*'s most intimate moments are between Stan and his wife and bring to mind classic silent films that Burnett professes an appreciation for in his admiration for Charlie Chaplin and Buster Keaton.[61] As a skillful filmmaker, Burnett "is able to render the mundane lyrically: the little details move us. The camera on its own—separate from the narrative and the powerful music—is damp with meaning. In *Killer of Sheep* there are haunting shots of Judas goats at the head of a ramp, below them the dumb, sweet faces of future lamb chops now hesitant, now gullible, finally carcasses and parts lining the walls of the Solano Meat Company."[62] He draws metaphorical connections without being "self- pitying" between the helplessness of sheep, their inevitable march to the killing room, and the trapped quality of Stan's existence leading to his insomnia and insular sadness. *Killer of Sheep* is a blues manifestation as much for its music as for its images and their aesthetic look and feel, which confirms that neorealism shares the instincts of Murray's blues statement for "a sense of life that is affirmative" despite struggle and tragedy as obstacles to human dignity. This blues sentiment is shared in films such as *Paison, Open City, Bicycle Thief,* and *Umberto D*, all classics of Italian neorealism with the blues at their core.

Hopes and dreams are frequently dashed in the blues or remain just out of reach, and *Killer of Sheep* is no exception. Even when Stan and his friends plan an escape to the horse races, "their spare less car blows a tire," and they return home on a steel rim without ever having reached their destination. When Stan's friend Eugene (Eugene Cherry) buys a car engine with all the money he has plus the shirt off his back, we see the two men struggle precariously to move the hunk of metal down multiple levels of steps, heft it onto a truck, and drive off only to have it slide out and crack on the street. Each vignette is its own blues. "The audience empathizes with the character's frustration, and even sees ironic humor in it, but always senses a keen and sympathetic, un-condescending presence behind the camera. But this is not a film that discards the care of its characters because of their plight, nor does it deny them loving moments with their families, or meaningful friendships because of exploitation."[63] As Wynton Marsalis reminds us: "Sad or funny, factual or fantasized, raunchy, majestic, or even maudlin, the blues reassures us with the unpredictable inevitability of life itself. Bad as things may be, they will get better or they could have been worse, and no times are so bad they can't be turned into good times."[64]

Burnett the filmmaker—the blues balladeer—puts lives in motion like fragmented lyrics to a soundtrack that serves as reinforcement or counterstatement to vignettes that unfold around Stan and his family. As a skillful storyteller, he makes us worry for his people and care about them despite denying us absolute resolution in the way of a Hollywood ending. What holds firm throughout Stan's travails is the "warmth and tenderness" of his family, "especially his wife." Stan will return to work and move in a direction to repair his relationship with his wife, but things are left largely unresolved, as in real life.[65] We will not have the satisfaction of finding out if Stan can guide and protect his strong-willed teenage son from the streets or shield his daughter from her fears for her father's and mother's estrangement. But these are the universal problems that families live with, and there is hope in the spirit of the blues statement when a shy handicapped girl (obviously incapable of being prepared for motherhood) reveals she is pregnant and is embraced and supported by Stan's wife and other women. The nature of the blues is to seed hope, and Burnett, despite "the powerful undercurrent of fatigue and despair" in the film, provides the blues counterstatement as "an odd buoyancy" that recognizes that "although the people are poor, they haven't, most of them, altogether stopped living: the grown-ups get by somehow or other, and the kids find ways to play." Burnett, like the blues balladeer, provides the integrity of a blues statement that is more than "a drab, grinding chronicle of misery," because we can still sense Stan's affirmation of life through his loving moments with his wife and daughter and through his friendships.[66]

At dusk in the dusty playgrounds of undeveloped spaces in *Killer of Sheep*, the apparent ringleader of a group of boys tries to entice the others to visit the "Vicksburg" to watch the pimps and prostitutes. No doubt this is Burnett's nod to his birthplace and to the Mississippi Delta, arguably the home of the blues. Though Burnett intends no meeting (or blending) of neorealism and blues, it is inevitable. As Burnett reminds us, "I was raised with music, with blues." He recalls his mother's record collection that included "a lot of blues records that she was constantly playing and replaying. At that time rock 'n' roll was our big thing. In people's minds at the time, the blues were linked to alcohol, but I felt like I was forced to listen." The indelible impact of the blues leaves its mark on his search for truth in *Killer of Sheep* and on other of his major works, including *To Sleep with Anger*, which is consistent with his explorations of "the South's enduring and complex legacy in the American consciousness."[67]

When looking at *Killer of Sheep* in terms of its objective correlative or metaphorical debt to the blues, one must consider its combination of mise-en-scène, narrative form, pacing, characterization, dialogue, and of course music. In other words, the aggregate disposition of the elements that comprise the film and inform the film through its author's point of view have the "blues" on their mind or as a reference point. Burnett recalls, "It was only much later that I could listen to those blues records and discover that I loved the blues without knowing it, that I needed it. And when I made *Killer of Sheep* I wanted to preserve those old records that no one listened to anymore and put them in the movie."[68]

Burnett as a balladeer delivers a cinematic blues statement that provides "an indefinable poetry to many of the film's images, which display flashes of humor and beauty, underpinned by a deep sense of melancholy—much like the blues."[69] Images and music in the film serve as blues counterstatements that reinforce irony as a community on the margins of society goes about their lives to strains of orchestral music by Rachmaninoff, Gershwin, and the rollicking *African-American Symphony* by William Grant Still. From the majestic voice of Paul Robeson to the raw blues of Lowell Fulson, the soundtrack for *Killer of Sheep* expresses and complements the themes of the film and in its totality plays the role of a character in affirming this film's blues statement. This character knows the swamps and hollers, the juke joints, the country sermon, and the devil of a price to seek a better life in the city where promise brings peril to the family and the community at the cost of human dignity. This is the blues! And powerful things happen when neorealism meets the blues to aesthetically share an objective correlative, as is evidenced by the visceral power, consciousness, and nuance of *Killer of Sheep*.

"With the blues you have layers of meaning. The words say one thing, the way they're sung can say another, and the music always says something else. For all of the sorrow of some blues lyrics, the music is always grooving; a groove implies dance, and dance always brings joy. Dizzy Gillespie said it best: 'Dancing never made nobody cry.' That's the key to understanding the blues. The blues delivers both joy and sorrow."[70]

Notes

1. Albert Murray, *The Blue Devils of Nada: A Contemporary Approach to Aesthetic Statement* (New York: Pantheon Books, 1996), 208–209.
2. Scott Foundas, "Independent Lens: Charles Burnett," in *Charles Burnett: Interviews*, Robert Kapsis, ed. (Jackson: University Press of Mississippi, 2011), 138–140.
3. Aida A. Hozic, "The House I Live In: An Interview with Charles Burnett," in *Charles Burnett: Interviews*, Robert Kapsis, ed. (Jackson: University Press of Mississippi, 2011), 75–94.
4. Ibid., 75.
5. Robert Kapsis, "Introduction," in *Charles Burnett: Interviews*, Robert Kapsis, ed. (Jackson: University Press of Mississippi, 2011), ix.
6. Dave Kehr, "Shadow of Watts, in the Light," in *Charles Burnett: Interviews*, Robert Kapsis, ed. (Jackson: University Press of Mississippi, 2011), 141–145: 143.
7. Murray 1996, 208–209.
8. Ibid., 2.
9. Sergio Pacifici, *A Guide to Contemporary Italian Literature, From Futurism to Neorealism*, (Cleveland and New York: Meridian Books, 1962), 241.
10. Sidney Gottlieb, "Rossellini, Open City, and Neorealism," in *Roberto Rossellini's Rome, Open City*, Sidney Gottlieb, ed. (Cambridge: Cambridge University Press, 2004), 31–42.
11. Ibid., 32.
12. Ibid., 32.
13. Ibid., 32.
14. Cesare Zavattini, "Some Ideas on the Cinema," in *Film: A Montage of Theories*, Richard Dyer McCann, ed. (New York: Dutton, 1966).

15. Wynton Marsalis and Geoffrey C. Ward, *Moving to a Higher Ground: How Jazz Can Change Your Life* (New York: Random House, 2009), 61.
16. Albert Murray, *Stomping the Blues* (Cambridge: Da Capo Press, 1976), 63.
17. Ibid., 63.
18. Ibid., 64.
19. Francis Davis, *The History of the Blues* (New York: Hyperion, 1995), 36.
20. Marybeth Hamilton, *In Search of the Blues* (New York: Basic Books, 2008), 3–4.
21. Murray 1976, 79.
22. Marsalis and Ward, 49.
23. Murray 1996, 208–209.
24. Ibid., 21.
25. Murray 1976, 79.
26. Murray 1996, 21.
27. David Denby, "Watts Happening," *The New Yorker*, April 2, 2007.
28. Marsalis and Ward, 59.
29. Murray 1976, 6.
30. Marsalis and Ward, 60.
31. James Bell, "Blues People," in *Charles Burnett: Interviews*, Robert Kapsis, ed. (Jackson: University Press of Mississippi, 2011), 181–186.
32. Phyllis Rauch Klotman, *Screenplays of the African American Experience* (Bloomington: Indiana University Press, 1991), 1.
33. Lynell George, "The Long Distance Runner: Charles Burnett's Quiet Revolution," in *Charles Burnett: Interviews*, Robert Kapsis, ed. (Jackson: University Press of Mississippi, 2011), 28–37.
34. Murray 1996, 208–209.
35. Sojin Kim and R. Mark Livengood, "Talking with Charles Burnett," in *Charles Burnett: Interviews*, Robert Kapsis, ed. (Jackson: University Press of Mississippi, 2011), 109–117: 114.
36. Michel Ciutat and Michel Ciment, "Interview with Charles Burnett," in *Charles Burnett: Interviews*, Robert Kapsis, ed. (Jackson: University Press of Mississippi, 2011), 42–52.
37. Murray 1976, 82.
38. Foundas 2011, 139.
39. Susan Gerhard, "Charles Burnett Celebrates a Milestone," in *Charles Burnett: Interviews*, Robert Kapsis, ed. (Jackson: University Press of Mississippi, 2011), 174–180.
40. Murray 1996, 208–209.
41. Kehr 2011.
42. Foundas 2011, 139.
43. Murray 1976, 21–22.
44. Catherine Arnaud and Yann Lardau, "An Artisan of Daily Life: Charles Burnett," in *Charles Burnett: Interviews*, Robert Kapsis, ed. (Jackson: University Press of Mississippi, 2011), 5–9.
45. Ibid., 9.
46. Klotman 1991, 98.
47. George 2011, 35.
48. Murray 1996, 208–209.
49. Bell 2011, 181.
50. David Lowery, "A Conversation with Charles Burnett," in *Charles Burnett: Interviews*, Robert Kapsis, ed. (Jackson: University Press of Mississippi, 2011), 161–167: 163.

51. Arnaud and Lardau 2011, 9.
52. Gottlieb 2004, 32.
53. Ntongela Masilela, "The Los Angeles School of Black Filmmakers," in *Black American Cinema*, Manthia Diawara, ed. (New York: Routledge, 1993), 108.
54. Paula Massood, *Black City Cinema: African American Urban Experiences in Film* (Philadelphia, PA: Temple University Press, 2003), 107.
55. Bérénice Reynaud, "An Interview with Charles Burnett," in *Charles Burnett: Interviews*, Robert Kapsis, ed. (Jackson: University Press of Mississippi, 2011), 53–64.
56. Hozic 2011, 81.
57. Michael Jones, "An Interview with Charles Burnett," *James River Film Journal*, https://jamesriverfilm.wordpress.com/2016/06/25/an-interview-with-charles-burnett/.
58. A. O. Scott, *New York Times*, n.d.
59. Richard Brody, "About Neo-Neo Realism—The Front Row," *New Yorker Online*, http://www.newyorker.com/online/blogs/movies/2009/03/in-re-neoneorea.html.
60. Gilberto Perez, *The Material Ghost* (Baltimore, MD: Johns Hopkins University Press, 1998), 35.
61. Charles Burnett and Charles Lane, "One on One: Charles Burnett and Charles Lane," in *Charles Burnett: Interviews*, Robert Kapsis, ed. (Jackson: University Press of Mississippi, 2011), 65–74.
62. Lisa Kennedy, "Black Familiar," in *Charles Burnett: Interviews*, Robert Kapsis, ed. (Jackson: University Press of Mississippi, 2011), 38–41.
63. Klotman 1991, 97.
64. Marsalis and Ward, 52–53.
65. Masilela 1993, 112.
66. Terrence Rafferty, "Invisible Man," in *Charles Burnett: Interviews*, Robert Kapsis, ed. (Jackson: University Press of Mississippi, 2011), 118–125.
67. Bell 2011, 183.
68. Ciutat and Ciment 2011, 50.
69. Bell 2011, 182.
70. Marsalis and Ward, 68.

8

KILLER OF SHEEP

James Naremore

As the main title of *Killer of Sheep* appears over a black screen, a chorus of children's voices sings:

> Lull-a, lull-a, lull-a, lull-a by-by.
> Do you want the moon to play with?
> All the stars to run away with?
> They'll come if you don't cry.
> So, lull-a, lull-a, lull-a, lull-a by-by,
> In your mother's arms a creeping,
> And soon you'll be a sleeping.

Just before the song ends, we see a tight close-up of a preadolescent boy with tearful, frightened eyes. The song fades into a man's angry voice from off-screen: "You let anyone jump on your brother and you just stand and watch, I'll beat you to death!" A slow retreat of the camera reveals a father berating his son: "I don't care who started what . . . you pick up a stick or a god damn brick!" The father, wearing a wifebeater T-shirt, is ill, fatigued, or maybe drunk; his speech is slurred, and at one point in the harangue, he breaks into a coughing fit. Cut to a brief shot of a woman's torso as she stands in a kitchen doorway embracing a young child, his face buried in her perhaps pregnant stomach. A shot from behind the father shows the frightened son standing quiet, tense, trying to remain expressionless and accept humiliation. "Knock the shit out of whoever is fighting your brother," the father says, "because if something happens to me and your mother, you ain't got nobody in the world except your brother!" Cut to a thin old woman seated with her back to us in a poor but brightly lit kitchen, calmly leafing through a newspaper. Return to the father: "And if the son of a bitch is too big for you, come get me! Look, you're not a child anymore. You'll soon be a god damn *man*! So start learning what life is about *now,* son!" The heavy woman exits the kitchen, smiling slightly; behind her, seated in the kitchen, we glimpse a teenage boy. In a reverse angle, the woman walks up to the boy who is being chastised and slaps him in the face. The screen goes black, and the rich bass voice of Paul Robeson sings the same tune we heard at the beginning.

This sequence contains seven shots and five camera setups, most of them close-ups. There's no establishing shot, and viewers work a bit to determine spatial and temporal continuity. The only dialogue is the father's angry rant, and some of the shots (the woman holding her child to her belly, the old woman reading a newspaper, and the male teenager glimpsed in the kitchen) generate questions that aren't answered. Burnett leaves it to us to sort out details and decide how the scene and the people in it will relate to everything that follows. The characters don't reappear, although some of the players can be glimpsed later in different roles. There's no causal, spatial, or temporal connection between this and any later scene, and thus the opening of the film takes on thematic or poetic rather than narrative importance. The film deals with the themes it dramatizes: Black family life, the growth of Black children into adulthood, the problem of becoming a "man," the relationship between Black family and Black community, and the chances of Black survival in a dangerous world.

A great deal of the film centers on children, because, as Burnett has remarked:

> Without children, there is no survival . . . In my community, the most important thing is to survive above all else, and children are taught that they have to support their brother, or their family, no matter what they do . . . When you're growing up, it poses some moral problems. You become more and more insensitive: the only thing that matters is survival. This callousness gradually alienates you, distances you from other people and complicates relations in a peculiar way—survival implies a good deal of mistrust—particularly relations between men and women. That's why I show these children in *Killer of Sheep*, always there, attentive to what their parents are doing, witnesses of everyday drama.[1]

Throughout the film, music is as important as imagery. Burnett's eclectic compilation score ranges from King Oliver to Rachmaninoff but is chiefly associated with African American culture. The song that frames or bookends the opening sequence, called simply "Lullaby" in published credits for the film, is also known as "Ma Curly-Headed Baby," one of a series of faux "plantation songs" by the classically trained Australian and later British composer George H. Clutsam, who in the early twentieth century wrote light operas and a single movie score. Clutsam's song was intended to be performed as art music, but its lyrics were written in a crudely phonetic, naively racist, appallingly bad imitation of Southern Black dialect. Paul Robeson later recorded the song, dispensing with phony dialect and giving the words simple dignity. Burnett's choice of it is significant, not only because *Killer of Sheep* concerns Black families in Los Angeles who have ties to the Deep South, but also because of Robeson's historical importance as a Black artist, star, and advocate for social progress. (Burnett has long wanted to make a film about Robeson.)

Burnett's treatment of music differs from that of a typical Hollywood picture because he seldom mixes it with diegetic sound, thus giving it a degree of independence and allowing it to function as counterpoint or commentary. But if the song at the beginning is intended as some sort of comment on the action, exactly what does it say? Obviously there's an ironic relationship between the song, which evokes parental love, peace, and celestial beauty, and the scene, which deals with parental punishment, violence, and danger. The song is about a child falling asleep in its mother's arms, the scene about a boy awakening into the duties of manhood and the imperative of survival; the song is comforting, the scene shocking; the song is dreamlike, the scene harshly realistic. But there's also a sense in which the song is coterminous with the scene, so that music and image aren't in complete conflict and one doesn't take priority over the other. The song bleeds into the visual action in the form of a chorus of children's sweet voices and reemerges at the end in the form of a man's grave bass voice; it joins with and permeates the "plot" of the scene, lingering afterward like a poignant memory or yearning.

Killer of Sheep gradually develops a plot, of sorts, made up of a series of vignettes involving the problems of a married Black man with two children who works in a sheep slaughterhouse and suffers from depression. Burnett got the basic idea for the film from a man he often saw riding the bus in Los Angeles. "One day he happened to sit by me, and I had the opportunity to ask him what he did. He told me he worked at the slaughterhouse, and what he did was kill sheep. What they did then was they had a sledgehammer, and they would hit the animal in the head with the sledgehammer and crush the skull. And I just couldn't imagine someone doing that every day, day in and day out, without creating some nightmare effect."[2]

Burnett's central character and his wife have come to Los Angeles from the South and are trying to divest themselves of a "country" background, such as when the father tells his son to stop addressing his mother as "mot dear" (an old expression meaning "mother dear," made fun of in Tyler Perry's films about the character Madea) or when his wife admonishes their daughter for going barefoot. He's a proud man who at one point angrily claims he isn't poor: he's able to give a few things to the Salvation Army, he loans or gives small amounts of money to his friends, and unlike another man in the neighborhood, he doesn't have to survive by eating greens from vacant lots. Even so, he seems perpetually weary and dejected and is unable to make emotional contact with his family. During the film, he undergoes a very modest emotional change for the better, but he doesn't achieve true progress; his day-to-day projects—helping a friend repair an old car, a trip to a racetrack—usually end in frustration, and he keeps the same awful job at the end that he had at the beginning.

This is a film lacking a clear resolution or a strong cause-effect relationship between events, centering on a man whose personal crisis is both economic and psychological. Burnett's purpose, he has explained, was to depict a character who works in terrible conditions but whose "real problems are within the family, trying to make that work and be a human being. You don't necessarily win battles; you survive."[3] Hence, as Manthia Diawara has pointed out, *Killer of Sheep* almost completely rejects the forward momentum of classic Hollywood and the typical social problem picture, "with its quest for the formation of the family and individual freedom, and its teleological trajectory (beginning, middle, and end)."[4] Like certain other Black independent films, among them *Ganja & Hess* (Bill Gunn, 1973) and *Daughters of the Dust* (Julie Dash, 1991), its form is "rhythmic and repetitious" and its narrative style "symbolic." It has something in common with "Black expressive forms like jazz, and with novels by such writers as Toni Cade Bambara, Alice Walker, and Toni Morrison, which stop time to render visible Black voices and characters."[5]

In more specific terms, *Killer of Sheep* renders visible the 1970s Black community in Watts. Burnett doesn't show us the area's most famous landmark, the Watts Towers, a notable example of outsider art constructed by Italian emigrant Simon Rodia in the period between 1921 and 1954. During Burnett's interview/commentary with Richard Pena on the Milestone DVD of the film, he says he wanted to depict more of the local life in the schools but was unable to do so. He also doesn't show us churches; indeed, his central character remarks that he hasn't been to church since he was "back home" in the South. Burnett nevertheless gives us documentary evidence of the city streets and produces striking images, some disturbing, some beautiful, of a kind that had never been seen in theatrically distributed movies. Most of his large cast was made up of nonprofessionals, including many children, who lived in Watts; some of them had even participated in or been witnesses to the Watts riots. One of his purposes was to encourage local participation and "demystify filmmaking in the community," but he also dramatized aspects of daily life he had witnessed, creating a more personal sort of film than the Italian neorealists or the Brazilian Cinema Novo.[6] Like *Several Friends*, his earlier student film about Watts, *Killer of Sheep* has a scene that was shot directly behind the house where Burnett once lived (it involves the theft of a TV in broad daylight). He knew people who stored car parts inside their houses to keep them from being stolen, just as a character in this film does; in fact, he once walked into a house and saw the entire front end of a car sitting on the floor. The dangerous games played by young people in the film are the same games he played.

Scattered throughout *Killer of Sheep* are short scenes of kids playing in the streets and of sheep going to slaughter. Burnett traveled to San Francisco with his lead actor to find a factory that would allow him to document the killing of sheep, which he photographed without the aid of a crew. He shows us ghostlike crowds of snowy ewes; a Judas goat leading the innocent to their deaths; sheep carcasses strung up on hooks and moved down an assembly line for butchery; sheep heads stuck on pikes and stripped of flesh, eyes, and brains; and sheep blood washed from floors. More often, he shows children running and playing their dangerous games in Watts. Boys throw rocks at one another, jump gracefully from rooftop to rooftop, and race bikes down the street chased by angry dogs. Sometimes they torment girls; when a girl in a sunlit, blindingly white dress starts hanging her white laundry on a sagging wash line, boys throw dirt on her and her clean clothes. Occasionally the girls get back at the boys. In one scene, as a group of preteen girls dance in an alleyway, a boy on a bike enters from behind the camera, rides over to the group, and shoves one of them; the girls push him, kick him, and break his bike. In another scene, a boy on a porch watches a couple of girls walk down a sunny sidewalk. "Look at them ol' ugly girls," he says loudly; the girls shout back "Your daddy is ugly!" and stroll off. "Wanna come here and fight?" the boy half-heartedly yells. In still another scene, a rangy girl climbs onto a rooftop and leads a group of boys in a rock-throwing fight; as she aggressively tosses missiles at kids on the street below, one of the boys on the roof suffers an injured wrist and tries to make his way down, wincing and wiping away his tears.

When the kids aren't playing, they're silent, sometimes amused witnesses of rough adult behavior, as when a drunken man in an army uniform is forced out of an apartment by an angry woman bearing a gun. Burnett's treatment of them has a complex tone, often humorous and remarkably unjudgmental. He never sentimentalizes the children or looks away from their occasional cruelty; at the same time, he repeatedly shows their ingenuity, curiosity, and energy. Manohla Dargis has rightly compared some of his images of kids in Watts to the photos of legendary New York street photographer Helen Levitt, who specialized in still pictures of children's games. Levitt's sixteen-minute 16mm film *In the Street* (1945–1952), a straight documentary photographed in New York's Spanish Harlem in collaboration with James Agee and Janice Loeb, has almost no scenes of raw poverty and far less roughhouse play than *Killer of Sheep*, but it resembles Burnett in its humane respect for the anarchic spirit of children and its awareness of the beauty in their improvised amusements. In *Killer of Sheep*, children have very few things to improvise with—a few bikes, an old top, a string of unexploded cap-pistol caps, a gum wrapper, a rubber mask, a beat-up white doll—and they often make do with rocks and rubble. Burnett records the meanness of their life, but he observes them with tenderness and wit.

Killer of Sheep isn't a thesis film that overtly argues for solutions to social problems, but it implicitly compares the children in Watts with the sheep going to slaughter and makes viewers think about what could be done to give them a reasonably secure future. To solve that problem, one needs to confront a wide range of social, political, and economic issues. No doubt Burnett wanted audiences to discuss such things, but his immediate aim as an artist was to objectively dramatize the quotidian struggles of a working-class Black family, its attempts to reproduce itself and raise its children against almost impossible odds. Fittingly, he introduces us to the family—Stan (Henry Gale Sanders), Stan's unnamed wife (Kaycee Moore), Stan Jr. (Jack Drummond), and Stan's daughter, Angela (Angela Burnett, who is Charles Burnett's niece)—by way of neighborhood children playing daredevil war games in the decaying remains of the Watts rail yard.

The games are gritty and spontaneous looking, staged in a wasteland of dust, dirt, and rocks, but like nearly all the scenes in *Killer of Sheep*, they were scripted, storyboarded, and guided by Burnett's unobtrusively poetic feel for space, time, and tempo. He gives them an overarching design, moving from a tightly framed montage of a dangerous rock fight to an exhilarating wide shot of boys running alongside a passing train, and finally to an elliptical series of shots conveying dispersion and restless boredom. As he often does elsewhere, he starts with a close-up—in this case a boy using a piece of plywood or metal as a shield from rocks thrown at him—and gradually reveals the environment. Once the rock fight ceases, we see a kid's legs and feet standing on a patch of grimy, paper-strewn dirt. The kid knocks dust off his pants, and the off-screen sound of a train serves as lead-in to a wide, expansive traveling shot from the point of view of a railroad car as it traverses the dusty rail yard, making the entire space visible. On the far horizon are palm trees (this is, after all, sunny California), a few houses, and industrial power lines marking the outskirts of Watts. Suddenly, from over a mound of dirt, the boys run energetically into sight, racing the train and gradually passing it. Open-air exuberance ends with a stationary, reverse-angle telephoto of the slowing freight train as the boys line up along the tracks and throw rocks at it.

Once the train passes, we become aware of individuals: a boy stands beside a railroad sign, bored or sad, while another boy behind him listlessly throws rocks at a metal shed. An older boy with a cap and glasses suggests that they all go to a local bar and watch "hos" go in and out. One of the kids says no; if his mother were to see him there, "my ass is hers. You'd have to call the police to get her off me." In the next shot, the boy with cap and glasses is lying on a rail track, his neck against the wheel of a freight car, laughing and daring the other kids to push the train over him. (Burnett has said that in his neighborhood when he was growing up, "most kids did not believe they would live longer than twenty-one." In 1994, he added, "they do not believe that they will live longer than sixteen."[7]

A wide-angle, deep-focus shot positioned at ground level shows a boy walking down the tracks toward the camera away from the railcar. He reaches the foreground, ties one of his sneakers, and tells everyone that he's going home to get his BB gun. We don't know it yet, but this is Stan Jr., nearing his teen years and entering a rebellious, troubling phase. He's a sometimes-angry kid and virtually drops out of the later parts of the film. The camera follows him home as he walks down an alleyway behind houses, combing his Afro and observing the local sociology. Strolling along, he turns to look at two young men climbing over a fence, boosting a TV set.

An elderly gentleman in shirt and tie who is watering his back lawn also sees this, and the thieves chase him off: "What you looking at, punk?" they shout. "I'll kick your heart out!" Stan Jr. warns the thieves that the old gent is going to call the cops. (The call would do no good, because the LAPD was notoriously indifferent to Black-on-Black crimes.) One of the thieves tears a board from the fence, waves it like a weapon, and flies into nearly hysterical rage as his pal struggles to restrain him. Stan Jr. laughs. The thieves pick up the TV set, and the camera tracks backward as they race wildly down the alley carrying their loot, backlit by an afternoon sun. On the soundtrack, as counterpoint, we hear Cecil Gant's 1945 "race" record, "I Wonder." ("I wonder, my little darlin', where can you be, while the moon is shining bright?")

The sequence is characteristic of Burnett in its mixed emotional effects—a blend of humor, violence, beauty, and sadness, roughly like the great blues songs. The humor and beauty are underappreciated by commentators on Burnett's films; without them, *Killer of Sheep* would be unbearable. In the closing shot of the sequence, for example, there's a momentary beauty in the light of "the magic hour," a crazy violence and comedy in the thieves' run with the TV set, and a wistful sadness in the tune, which continues as Stan Jr. walks farther down the alley and passes a group of silent children looking over a wall at the film.

"I wonder, my little darlin'" bleeds into the next sequence, which introduces Stan and establishes his depression. We look down at his shirtless back as he kneels on the floor of his kitchen, laying linoleum and talking with a big fellow named Oscar, who stands mostly off-screen, restlessly slapping his fists together. "I'm working myself into my own hell," Stan says. "I close my eyes and don't sleep at night." (As one of Stan's friends later observes, trying to count sheep would do him no good.) The big man offhandedly asks, "Why don't you kill yourself?" Stan looks up—he's a handsome man with a slight bald spot and sad eyes—and wanly smiles. "No, I ain't going to kill myself," he says. "Got a feeling I might do somebody else tomorrow, though." He glances off-screen, and we cut to a surprising, almost surreal close-up of a child of about four or five, standing in a doorway, wearing a rubber Droopy-Dog mask, sucking a finger through the mask's mouth hole. She's Stan's daughter, impressively acted by Angela Burnett and the subject of some of the film's most memorable images. When Stan Jr. enters, he treats her roughly, squeezing the mask and asking where his BB gun is. "Mama threw it away," she says. Stan tells his son to stop acting like he has "no sense" and shoos him off.

If Burnett is underappreciated for his humor, he's equally underappreciated as a writer of dialogue, perhaps because people assume the conversations in his early films were improvised. Some of his lines have what Adrian Martin aptly describes as a "loopy" quality. A good example is when a woman named Dolores remarks that Stan would be good-looking if he didn't frown so much. Hearing this, a nearby fellow boasts, "Some sister just told me I look like Clark Gable!" Dolores looks wearily at him and mutters, "You about as tasteless as a carrot." Many of the speeches in *Killer of Sheep* have this wry, hard-boiled quality. In the scene at hand, Oscar notices two men approaching the back of Stan's house and makes a quick exit: "Here come Bracy and Ernie Cox. I don't want them asking *me* for money." The two men enter, and Bracy (Charles Bracy, a longtime friend of Burnett who was also responsible for the sound recording in *Killer of Sheep*) observes Stan scraping the floor with a kitchen knife: "I see your wife got you towing the cart. I see Oscar must have been here . . . He's the only one I know wears that Old Spice aftershave."

Bracy is a bumptious type, unmarried and unemployed, whose raucous personality makes Stan's depression more evident. (In his commentary on the Milestone DVD, Burnett emphasizes that the poor have little if any possibility to get medical treatment for depression.) Before the contrast between the two men is fully established, however, we briefly leave the kitchen for a sweet and humorous encounter. Stan's daughter, Angela, hears a whistle and runs outside, where she meets a shy little boy standing against a hurricane fence; she sucks her thumb through the hole in her mask, moves a little closer to him, and quietly bounces against the fence. Brief scenes involving her will become a motif. She's a key witness to adult behavior: innocent, not yet marked by the harshness and traumas of life in Watts, but coming to an awareness of her family's troubles.

When we return to Bracy and Stan, they're seated alone at a table in the poor but well-kept kitchen, sipping tea. Stan presses a warm teacup against his head and wearily remarks that it reminds him of "making love, how warm her forehead get some time." Bracy laughs; he thinks warm tea is nothing but "hot air" and doesn't care for "women with malaria." He and his pals have been walking the streets at night, he explains, hesitating to drop in; Stan says not to worry, he never sleeps. Another of Burnett's elliptical cuts shows the two men later in the evening, playing dominoes as somewhere in the night a dog barks (the sound design of the film is as effective as the photography, establishing an ever-present off-screen environment).

Stan's lovely wife, who has apparently been ignored during all this, appears in the kitchen doorway without speaking, her hair wrapped in a bath towel and an angry expression on her face. She turns and exits. Whatever nostalgia for intimacy Stan might feel, he doesn't act on it; he simply rubs his face in fatigue and says it's time to go to work. Bracy yawns and looks at his watch: "Maybe me and Ernest can luck up on a slave [i.e., a menial, part-time job] if we's lucky."

Each episode in the remainder of the film is relatively autonomous, illustrating typical events in the life of an ordinary but admirable man who is trying to cope. Like certain forms of jazz or modernist narrative, these episodes could be somewhat reordered without disturbing the fundamental unity or meaning of the film. The first two, however, are in dialectical contrast, representing male industrial labor versus female domesticity. To the music of William Grant Still's "Afro-American Symphony," we're given a montage of Stan at work in the slaughterhouse, hosing the floor and carrying sheep parts; then at home, we see his wife awaiting his return. The wife applies makeup while Stan's daughter, wearing a dress, sits on the back porch floor next to an old phonograph, playing with a white doll that has no clothing, happily singing along with Earth, Wind & Fire's recording of "Reasons."

The next sequence, also without dialogue, shows Stan at home and makes clear that his depression has affected not only his libido but also his will to express affection. The postures of the actors in Burnett's films are always communicative and are especially so here: Stan slumps in a kitchen chair, one arm dropped to his side, while his wife, wearing an attractive African print dress, sits across from him and leans forward, her legs crossed and her chin cupped in her hand. Angela enters, gets a glass of milk from the refrigerator, exchanges glances with her mother, puts her glass down hard, and exits. The wife stares at Stan, her head tilted, trying to get him to return the gaze. Stan lifts a teacup (a reminder of the earlier scene in the kitchen), and she reaches out to him. He rises, turns his back, and resumes work on the kitchen floor.

Burnett was fortunate in the casting of Stan and his wife. The man who was supposed to play Stan wound up in prison, and Burnett came across Henry Gale Sanders by accident in an elevator. "I thought Henry was [the] saddest-looking man I'd ever seen," Burnett has said. "I asked him if he'd ever done any acting."[8] Sanders had recently returned from two tours of duty in Vietnam, where he was injured, and was attending college under the GI Bill; his original ambition was to become a writer, but in Los Angeles he had begun to take acting courses. In *Killer of Sheep*, he radiates gentle strength and thoughtfulness, performing in a quietly naturalistic style. Kaycee Moore, on the other hand, had appeared only in theater (after *Killer of Sheep*, she acted in two films directed by Burnett's "students": Billy Woodbury's *Bless Their Little Hearts* and Julie Dash's *Daughters of the Dust*). She's a more vivid, ostentatious performer, and the slight difference in acting styles helps bring out the contrast between Stan's depression and his wife's vitality.

Moore's intensity is evident in one of the more improvised moments in the film, when a couple of gangster types—characters who seem to have entered from one of the blaxploitation pictures Burnett disliked—try to recruit Stan for one of their jobs. A shiny Cadillac with whitewalls comes to a lurching halt in front of Stan's small house, and in comic but sinister fashion, two slicked-up dudes named Scooter and Smoke exit the car and strut up the walk, calling out, "Hey, Stan, can you come out and play?" Laughing, bumping fists, acting cool, they knock on the door until Stan grudgingly emerges. They're wearing shades, leather, and bling; he's barefoot and wearing an undershirt and shabby pants. He sits on the front step, frowning while they gather around and tell him he's been recommended as a "third man."

In a ghostly close-up, Stan's wife is seen through the screen door as she watches Stan telling the two men he doesn't want to hear about their proposition. Scooter says he and his pal are looking for somebody "who wouldn't blush at murder" and asks to borrow Stan's "roscoe." When Stan says that he doesn't have a gun, the wife emerges. "Why do you always want to hurt somebody?" she asks loudly. Burnett frames the four actors as a group, and their postures and movements tell us everything: the wife stands in an assertive position, arms akimbo; Stan sits on the step, his head hanging down, lighting a cigarette and picking at his toe; the two hoods sway almost like dancers, gesturing with an air of flashy, easy confidence. Scooter speaks to the wife in a patronizing tone: "That's the way I was brought up! A man got scars on his face for being a man . . . me and Smoke are going to take our issue [i.e., what's ours]." Turning to Stan, he says, "You can be a man if you can, Stan."

At this, the wife marches down the steps and gets in Scooter's face, gesturing passionately and making a fiery speech, much of which Moore made up on the spot: "You wait just a minute! You talk about being a *man* if you can . . . scars on your mug!" Her finger points assertively. "Where do you think you are? In the bush or some damn where? You are *here!* You use your brain, that's what you use. You're not an animal. And both of you nothing-ass niggers got a lot of nerve coming here to ask him to do something like that!" When Smoke reaches out to grab the wife's arm and turn her toward him, she becomes nearly wild with anger and fear, jerking free and wordlessly rebuking Stan for doing nothing. Smoke and Scooter give up and wander off, complaining: "All we trying to do is help the nigger."

A threat of violence against the woman hovers throughout the scene, becoming evident in the veiled contempt Smoke and Scooter feel toward Stan's wife and their attempt to shame Stan into ignoring her. Ironically, the domestic male is the true "man," even though he looks shabby, passive, and worn down (we may recall that the theme of manhood was introduced in the film's opening sequence). Stan's job and his consequent depression have sapped his energy; he's in an inferior, seated position when his wife takes charge. There's also irony in the wife's speech. She passionately criticizes certain ideas about Black manhood but does so with the same language and imagery racists use: Smoke and Scooter, she says, are primitives who think they're in the jungle "bush." They're "nothing-ass niggers" with ugly mugs. They're "*here*," meaning the big-city United States, far away from Africa or the South, and they should be using their small brains. Smoke and Scooter deserve this abuse, but the wife has internalized racial images and language created by a long tradition of oppression.

Stan has better sense than to join up with thieves and killers, but it isn't clear that Stan Jr. will grow up to think the same way. Soon after Smoke and Scooter leave, the boy unsuccessfully asks his father for a dollar; in a later scene, he broods about the rejection of his request. We see Stan's little daughter putting on a dress in the bathroom and going into the kitchen, where her brother is eating cereal. "How clean I must be," she says, then sits at the table watching him. He scowls, pours what looks like half a box of sugar on the cereal, munches ferociously, and in close-up mutters, "I need some money." "What?" his sister asks. He pauses, stares at her with near hate, and speaks distinctly: "I need some money!"

Lack of money determines everything in the film. At one point, Stan confronts a man who owes him money, and the man walks away, saying, "I ain't got anything but my good looks." At another point, Stan gives a dollar and a can of peaches, wages he's received from "Miss Sally" for "cleaning up behind the garage," to his poor friends Gene and Dian. But the local economy is most evident when Stan goes to the only bank available to him—a liquor and convenience store—and tries to cash his paycheck from the slaughterhouse. Burnett introduces the episode with a striking image and a sad joke about the people hanging around on the street outside the store. A drunken man is reflected in a bewigged young woman's aviator sunglasses. "You a no-good woman," he says. "You get yourself in line," she sneers, and a close-up of her high heels shows her walking away to the sound of blues music. He follows, and the two squeeze into a beat-up car where four others are already sitting; there's a beer can on the hood of the car, and a fellow in the front seat reaches straight out to get it, revealing that the car has no windshield.

The only White person in the film is a big, tough-looking woman who manages the store. (Burnett found the woman working in a post office.) When a customer asks to cash a check, a middle-aged clerk behind the counter calls to her, and she emerges from a back room, seen in a floor-level shot that makes her look imposing. Shoving the clerk aside, she glances at the man's check and says "hell, no." Then the younger, better-looking Stan comes in with the same request, to which she responds with a sexual come-on. She *might* be able to cash the check, she says with a smile, and asks, "Why don't you come work for me?" Henry Gale Sanders does a nice job of conveying Stan's struggle to hide his discomfort and remain politely subservient; he shyly smiles and looks away, saying that he fears getting held up and shot. "Oh, I'll protect you," the woman promises. "You'll work in back with me." She nods toward the middle-aged clerk: "*He* takes care of the register." A close-up shows her hand stroking Stan's wrist. Stan doesn't pull away and manages to get out with his check cashed.

Possessed of a little money, Stan tries to help his friend Gene buy a used auto engine. This results in the longest episode in the film, a self-contained drama that serves as a virtual allegory of Stan's precarious situation in life. It's by turns bizarre, comic, sweet, suspenseful, and almost tragic. At the beginning, we see the two men, accompanied by Stan's daughter, drive an aged pickup to the edge of Watts and park on a steep hill outside a three-story stucco apartment house. Gene enters the building, heading up the steps to the top apartment. Before joining him, Stan worriedly counts cash from his paycheck and puts bits of it in different pockets to hide the amount. Stan's daughter, whom he leaves behind, sucks on a plastic toy. In the ambient street sounds, we hear the shouts of kids and faint music from an ice-cream truck playing "Yankee Doodle Dandy."

Inside the apartment is a strange collection of characters. Burnett introduces the scene with a close-up of a man with a bandaged head, lying on the floor. Gene knocks, enters, and asks what has happened. A wide shot reveals four other people: a slender, flashily dressed man playing with a deck of cards and consulting a hand mirror; a sullen young woman and her little daughter; and a teenaged boy picking his toes. According to Burnett's screenplay,[9] the man on the floor is named James, and the woman is named Dolores, although we never hear these names. We eventually learn that they're the nephew and niece of Silbo, the fellow playing cards. The boy's exact identity is unclear, but he seems to be part of the dysfunctional family. He explains to Gene that James was hurt when "Adolph and Boulevard jumped on him." Just then Stan arrives, winded from the long climb up the stairs. "What's happenin' ol' dude?" the boy shouts in welcome. Silbo unsuccessfully tries to get the morose Dolores to join him in a card game. Gene tells Silbo, "All I got is ten dollars." James, groggy from the head wound, complains of the noise and tries to go back to sleep. Burnett waits until this point to slowly zoom back and reveal that sitting on the floor next to James is an automobile engine atop a bunch of newspapers.

A large close-up shows Dolores, chin in her hand, quietly asking herself, "How did I ever get married to such a damn silly-ass family as this?" Before the zany situation can develop further, however, Burnett takes us outside with Dolores's daughter, who has gone to meet Angela in the truck. As in an earlier episode, we have a brief glimpse of childhood innocence apart from the adult world. The two girls sit together, chew gum, and play with the gum wrapper. "How come you don't come to school?" Stan's daughter asks. "I have been sick," the other little girl says. "You gotten far behind," says Stan's daughter.

Back in the apartment, Dolores, seated in a chair and wearing a short skirt, rubs lotion on her ample, attractive legs. The wounded James leers from his position on the floor and tries to make a pass, which results in bickering and then an angry quarrel between the two. During this, Gene confers with Stan and announces to Silbo, "All I got is fifteen dollars." He can barely be heard over the exchange of insults between James and Dolores, which escalates until James yells, "You just an all-day sucker, bitch," at which point Dolores gets up and kicks him (like most of the sequence, this is framed in a closeup—we see Dolores's face, but not where the kick lands). James cries out, Stan rushes to him, and Gene holds Dolores back. "Hey, Silbo," Stan says. "Take care of your nephew here, man! . . . He's bleeding!" In response, Silbo picks up his hand mirror and studies himself. "I've got more important things to do," he says. "My hair's falling out." Then he half rises, disgusted with his niece and nephew, and accepts Gene's offer of fifteen dollars for the motor.

The remainder of the episode concerns Stan and Gene's grueling, reverse-Sisyphean attempt to get the engine down to the street and load it onto the pickup. Burnett devotes nine shots to the journey, negotiating the tricky space of a long stairway, creating a downward spiraling movement, and generating a fair amount of suspense. (The sequence was shot on two different stairways, making the trip down look especially complicated.) Given the world of this film, we fear disaster—and not the comic disaster of Stan and Ollie moving a piano. Burnett begins with a close, handheld view as the two men struggle to get the engine out of the building. They move through the apartment door, out a hall entrance to a stairway, and then start down. Good Samaritan Stan is predictably at the heavy end, moving backward along the rickety steps. They reach a landing, turn slightly, and encounter another flight of steps. Slowly they continue down, pause, turn, and face a third set of steps. Stan, wearing work gloves, is beginning to wince from the effort. "One more," Gene says as they reach the bottom. They put the engine down for a moment's rest, then pick it up and struggle toward the truck. Arriving, they heave the load up onto the flatbed, which lacks a gate, and Gene, who has no gloves, cries out because his finger is caught. He extracts the finger from the engine and winces, saying, "Just leave it there. It'll stay there." Stan disagrees, and they shove the engine forward a bit. Still nursing his finger, Gene insists that they've done enough—no more pushing.

On the soundtrack there are ambient sounds of a passing airplane and kids at play. A low, street-level shot shows the two men walking up the hillside toward the doors of the truck. Dolores's daughter gets out, and the two men get in, Gene taking the driver's seat. He starts the truck, but when he puts it in gear, it lurches, causing the engine to tumble off the flatbed and crash into the street. (The engine nearly hit Burnett and his camera when it rolled toward him as he lay on the ground for the street-level shot.) The truck stops, and the two men get out, silently surveying the wreckage. Without speaking, they climb back in and drive off, to the poignant piano music of Scott Joplin's "Solace." Burnett ends the episode with Angela looking sadly out the back window as the truck moves away. From her point of view, we see the engine lying dead in the street, receding into the distance.

The sexual problems between Stan and his wife reach a crisis sometime later, when they're alone at home, embracing and slowly dancing. For this sequence shot, Burnett originally used Dinah Washington's sensual, hauntingly romantic rendition of "Unforgettable," but he was unable to secure the rights for distribution; instead we hear Washington's hit 1960 recording of Clyde Otis's "This Bitter Earth," which creates a sensual mood tinged with lament, pain, and sorrow. ("What good is love that no one shares? . . . My life is like the dust that hides the glow of a rose.") The music is mixed in a style that makes it seem non-diegetic, yet it collaborates with the expressivity of the actors and the choreography. Stan and his wife are framed in profile, half silhouetted against a lighted window; at left, atop a table, are a lamp and a pair of preserved baby shoes. The actors only slightly change their position, and the camera doesn't move. Stan, shirtless and wearing loose pants that almost expose his buttocks, stands slightly apart from his wife; she looks lovingly at him, but he doesn't return the look. They slowly turn to the music so that his bare back is to the camera; she runs her hand along his back, puts her head on his shoulder, and moves close. As they continue to turn, we see that his hands are held loosely around her and his expression is zombielike. She strokes his chest and moves a hand behind his neck. They turn again, and she seems to reach down into the front of his pants. Then she embraces him with both arms, kissing his neck and cheek. When the song ends, she kisses his chest, grasping him tightly, subtly grinding against him, on the verge of tears. He pushes her gently away and exits, leaving her alone.

Stan's wife moves to the window and strikes a somewhat melodramatic pose of grief that suits the inherent musicality of the scene. Turning, she sits on the windowsill, and we're given one of the film's most unusual narrative devices, a brief internal monologue that also has musical or lyrical qualities. The monologue deals openly with themes that until this point have been treated only indirectly, revealing the wife's deep memories of the rural South, an impoverished world she and her husband had left behind for the sake of opportunity, only to find alienation and struggle: "Memories that don't seem mine, like half-eaten cake: rabbit skins stretched on the backyard fences; my grandmother; mother dear, mot dear, mot dear, dragging her shadow across the porch." (An insert shows the wife picking up the baby shoes on the table.) "Standing bare-headed under the sun . . . Cleaning red catfish with white rum." As she embraces the shoes and walks off, the plaintive sounds of Rachmaninoff's "Piano Concerto Number 4" form a sound bridge into a montage of sheep being herded to slaughter.

When Stan returns from work on a subsequent day, tension is conveyed by a silent tableau around the dinner table. He once again slumps in his chair, and his wife looks dejected. Stan Jr. stretches his arms, rises, slams his chair against the table, and walks out, barely noticed by his father. As Angela tries to clear away the dishes, Stan breaks the silence by glancing at his wife and asking, "So, what'd you do today?" She smiles sadly, shakes her head, and worries the napkin in her hands. "Got to find me a job," he mutters. She grasps his wrist, gently reminds him that tomorrow is Saturday, and suggests they go to bed. He doesn't respond. The remainder of the scene is played silently through an exchange of gazes between husband, wife, and child. Stan shifts his chair around toward his wife as she clears the dishes, and Angela comes to him, standing between his legs. He gives her a gentle touch and one of his rare, half-hearted smiles. His wife exits, looking back as he embraces his daughter, who looks off-screen toward her mother. The wife goes to the next room, sits on a couch, anguished, and looks toward the kitchen. Angela looks at her mother and softly strokes her father's face, taking on a maternal role, trying to comfort both parents.

The catalog of frustrations and disappointments carries over into the next phase of the film, which begins with a richly detailed deep-focus shot: Stan's skinny friend Gene leans far over the open hood of his car while his enormous wife Dian watches him and complains that he's spending too much time and money on the project; in the foreground, a boy straddles a bike decorated with an American flag and tries to push it forward as another boy pushes back against the handlebars; and in the far distance, Stan comes around a corner and jogs uphill toward Gene and Dian, bringing them a dollar and a can of peaches. A close-up shows the freckle-faced Dian smiling in tender gratitude. "It's getting late," Gene says. "Let's go have some coffee and see what my guests are doing." He and Stan load a battery and a spare tire into the car's trunk, and the camera pans as they head toward the house, passing a stray dog. Then the camera pans back to the closed trunk, portending trouble.

In Gene's kitchen, the guests are having a parry: blues music is playing, a crap game is in progress, and the camera is set almost level with the floor, looking up at the large posterior of a woman who embraces a fat man. The man proposes marriage and then joins the crap game. Dian approaches the woman, smiles, and asks if she's happy. A big fellow on the floor grins and winks at another woman as he rolls the dice. Stan and Gene stand apart and look miserable.

The theme of gambling continues into the next episode. It's a bright Saturday morning, and seven characters—Gene, Dian, and their baby; Stan, his wife, and his daughter; and Stan's pal Bracy—prepare for an outing at the racetrack. Dressed in their good clothes, they begin packing themselves into Gene's car, which is now in working order, while a bunch of kids play and fight in the far distance and the apparently drunken Bracy, sporting 1970s-style stacked heels, shouts incoherently about his last night's adventures. In the back seat, Stan's wife fixes Angela's hair and wipes her face. Once everybody squeezes aboard, the car drives off to the sound of Louis Armstrong's rendition of King Oliver's "West End Blues," upbeat in tempo yet also mournful. On the road, Dian tells Gene to slow down, Bracy studies a racing form, and Stan's wife enjoys the air from an open window as her weary husband sleeps on her shoulder.

Soon trouble strikes. Out in the countryside, the car gets a flat tire, and Gene discovers that his spare has been stolen from the trunk. Angela gazes sadly out a window, just as she did in the sequence involving the wrecked engine. We look down the side of the car as Bracy paces back and forth on the road, gesturing wildly and berating Gene: "Look, man, I told you to have a spare tire and don't be comin' out here in the middle of nowhere . . . In the ninth race, man, I got me a nag that I *know* is going to come in! I got me some money, man! And you ain't got no spare! Look, aw shit!"

Here Burnett makes excellent use of off-screen space. Stan's wife, nicely coiffed and made up, slowly emerges from below the frame into a big close-up, looking grimly down at the wheel of the car, while behind her Bracy (whose voice sounds postsynchronized) breaks into rap: "Man, I'm out here singin' the blues, got me a horse that can't lose! Always told you to keep a spare, but you's a square!" Gene studies the situation and softly replies, "I guess we have to ride back on the rim, that's all. Ain't got no spare." Everybody gets back in the car, which makes a U-turn and drives off on the rim; once again, Gene's fixation with his auto has resulted in a kind of tragicomedy. Despite all the discord and trouble, however, there's a sweet quality in the scene: the sharply delineated, flawed characters remain friends, moving through life in the same boat (more accurately, car), facing disappointment together.

We are now at the closing moments of the film, in which Burnett emphasizes the theme of survival and creates a modest sense of ongoing strength. After arriving home from the abortive trip to the racetrack, Stan slumps wearily on a couch as his wife remarks that rain is coming and the roof needs repair. Angela stands with her arms akimbo and then turns and opens the screen door. "Daddy," she asks, "what makes the rain?" Stan softly replies, "Why, it's the Devil beating his wife." Angela smiles, and a large close-up shows Stan's wife also smiling, happier than she's been at any point. She crosses to Stan and sits close to him. They share a soft smile (his third in the film, and the most genuine), and he touches her knee.

I grew up in the South not far from where Burnett was born, and whenever it rained while the sun was shining, my White father would remark that the devil was beating his wife. It's an expression peculiar to the Deep South, and Burnett's use of it here is significant. Stan is making a slightly dark joke but also acknowledging his roots in the folklore of a world he's been trying to escape. For the moment, father, mother, and child feel a happy bond.

The only member of the family who isn't present is Stan Jr., and in the next scene, we see the wife standing behind their house, calling him. "I know you hear me calling you, boy," she says loudly, and then talks to herself: "I know that boy heard me calling him." As she goes inside, the camera pans up to the roof and reveals Stan Jr. and another boy. Cut to the front of the house. On the tiny porch, a girl sitting in a chair is having her hair arranged by Angela, and two other girls are perched on the steps. A pretty young woman enters the shot, supporting herself with a cane, and as she moves up the front steps we see that her right leg is in a brace. She knocks at the screen door, and Stan's wife welcomes her, giving her a delighted hug when she whispers something. Inside, two women are visiting. One of them brandishes a cigarette and asks the new arrival why she's wearing a pretty smile. The lame young woman looks down at herself shyly. Stan's wife beams and announces, "She's going to have a baby!" One of the women remarks, "Well, I thought her old man was shooting blanks, but I see he's dropping bombs on occasion, I guess." Stan's wife laughs, and the young woman looks proudly at her stomach, moving her hand in an arc over it, indicating how it's going to grow.

This is the first scene involving female friends of Stan's wife and the only scene, apart from a brief early one between Stan's wife and daughter, made up entirely of women. It's also a rare example of a scene that ends on a happy note. Unlike a typical Hollywood movie or "well-made" drama, it doesn't identify the new characters and doesn't explain the pregnant young woman's disability. In fact, the disability motivates nothing and isn't necessary to the scene; it's simply there: an undiscussed, unusual, harsh fact that will probably complicate motherhood. The scene is pregnant, one might say, with unstated meanings that have little to do with plot. It celebrates new life and the endurance of the community, but at the same time, partly by means of the young woman's leg, dramatizes an ongoing struggle.

Burnett ends with a montage of Stan and his fellow workers on the killing floor of the slaughterhouse. Once again we hear Dinah Washington singing "This Bitter Earth," this time as a background to images of dead and bleeding sheep. There's a small flaw that Burnett was unable to correct. As Stan herds animals to their death, he's broadly smiling, almost laughing; during the shooting, Burnett has explained, Henry Gale Sanders split his trousers wide open and couldn't control his amusement. Even so, the somber music and the montage are anything but uplifting, and the film leaves Stan in virtually the same circumstances as at the beginning. The screen goes dark, and over the closing credits we hear Paul Robeson's rendition of Antonin Dvorak's "Going Home," a hymn inspired by what Dvorak called the "great and noble music" of nineteenth-century African Americans. Like the film, it's pathetic, tender, passionate, and melancholy; it bestows grace and importance on Stan, his family, and his community.

Notes

1. Catherine Arnaud and Yann Kardau, "An Artisan of Daily Life: Charles Burnett," in *Charles Burnett: Interviews*, Robert Kapsis, ed. (Jackson: University Press of Mississippi, 2011), 5–9.

2. David Lowery, "A Conversation with Charles Burnett," in *Charles Burnett: Interviews*, Robert Kapsis, ed. (Jackson: University Press of Mississippi, 2011), 161–167.

3. Michael Sragow, "An Explorer of the Mind Looks Back, but Not in Anger," in *Charles Burnett: Interviews*, Robert Kapsis, ed. (Jackson: University Press of Mississippi, 2011), 95–100.

4. Manthia Diawara, "Black American Cinema: The New Realism," in *Black American Cinema*, Manthia Diawara, ed. (New York: Routledge, 2003), 3–25.

5. Ibid., 10–11.

6. Max Evry. "Killer of Sheep: Interview with Charles Burnett." April 9, 2007. http://www.blackfilm.com/20070406/features/charlesburnett.shtml.

7. Aida A. Hozic, "The House I Live in: An Interview with Charles Burnett," in *Charles Burnett: Interviews*, Robert Kapsis, ed. (Jackson: University Press of Mississippi, 2011), 75–95.

8. Dave Kehr, "Shadows of Watts, in the Light," in *Charles Burnett: Interviews*, Robert Kapsis, ed. (Jackson: University Press of Mississippi, 2011), 141–144.

9. Phyllis Rauch Klotman, *Screenplays of the African American Experience* (Bloomington: Indiana University Press, 1991).

9

KILLER OF SHEEP

Jeffrey Skoller

THE NEED TO CONFRONT THOSE SPECTERS OF A past that, though unseen, still powerfully impacts the present becomes even more necessary as the events themselves recede into a distant past. Whereas the events of the Shoah lasted less than ten years and occurred more than seventy years ago, the catastrophe of African American slavery, on the other hand, lasted for hundreds of years and visibly ended generations ago. Understanding the ways in which events of the past continue to inhere in the present becomes even more difficult to pinpoint and harder to represent visually. It has been the challenge for some artists to find different ways to speak about the spectral nature of such events in an attempt to produce more complex and deeply felt representations of people as beings who are affected and transformed by the movement of time.

The film *Killer of Sheep* by Charles Burnett (1977) reveals the ways in which legacies of events from the past actually inhere in the present, invisibly inflecting daily life with a force that is powerfully tangible. This film can be seen as an attempt to understand how elements of a past come to bear on the present in ways that are not always identifiable. These are the "hauntings" of the present, which, although invisible in positivist social science notions of historicism, when given close attention, begin to reveal just how dynamic the relationships are between past and present. As Avery F. Gordon suggests, "Invisible things are not necessarily not-there [and] encourage the complementary gesture of investigating how that which appears absent can indeed be a seething presence."[1] This suggests a need to refocus attention away from what is simply visible toward the temporal as the meanings of an event, its legacies and effects, transform in time. For a medium like film, in which its indexical literalness is the basis for its historiographic authority, conventions of historical narrative are harnessed to that of the seeable. The larger problem of narrating the history of African American slavery is compounded not only by the formal problems of how to show it but also by American society's reluctance to integrate its history of slavery into narratives of the present. This is why these histories tend to produce such powerful boundaries that close off the past. The insistence on closure limits the complex ways that different moments of time commingle, inscribe, and inflect each other. This often forecloses possibilities of understanding the continuing effects of such a past as they impact the present. To take up daily life in the present in relation to the specters of the past is to counter the notion that African slavery is a closed chapter in American history and to show that its haunting legacy continues to be a powerful part of the present—a force that continues to brutalize Black America and unsettle the entire nation.

The vision of a life and a community haunted by the cultural inheritance of the catastrophe of slavery and hundreds of years of racist brutalization permeates the images in *Killer of Sheep*. While it does not appear to fit into many of my criteria for materialist avant-garde film practices, I find that the film's formal and aesthetic style not only is cinematically innovative and perhaps unique but also reflects an aesthetic designed to evoke the haunting legacy of American slavery. As Ernie Gehr does in *Signal—Germany on the Air*, Burnett uses cinematic duration, especially the continuous take and long shot, as the central formal element of the film's visual style, allowing viewers to engage their own thoughts in relation to what is seen and heard. But while *Signal* remains staunchly materialist, *Killer of Sheep* produces both a representation of a state of being in the film's fictional characters and a concrete real-time experience for the viewer. The film evokes, rather than represents, the daily rhythms and psychological conditions of the film's central character and community. A good deal has been written about the emerging PanAfrican cinema of the last thirty years. Much of this writing has focused on the social and political contexts of these films, either as artifacts of marginalized cinematic practices or as communities within a larger context, as does Thomas Cripps, for example, when he writes about African American cinema as a genre within the larger context of American film: "We shall seek to define black genre film through social and anthropological rather than aesthetic factors. In this light, films are different from those fine arts in which the artist and his audience share a fund of common knowledge and experience. Rather, films bridge the gap between producer and mass audience, not through shared arcane tastes, but because a team of filmmakers shares a knowledge of genre formulas, more than an artistic tradition with its audience."[2]

Here Cripps implies that because African American cinema is specifically a minority cinema, the films should largely be understood in sociological terms or as artifacts because marginalized Black sensibilities and "tastes" are inaccessible to wider audiences outside Black culture, or worse, that the only ground Black filmmakers and their audiences share is the knowledge of cinematic genre formulas. The danger with Cripps's contention is that it implies that Black cinema is simply a subgenre working off the dominant ones, rather than a dynamic and innovative cinema capable of creating complex and nuanced expressions of an individual filmmaker and his or her community in the context of other advanced work in contemporary world cinema.

In *Killer of Sheep*, Burnett innovatively uses the cinematic element of duration instead of literary elements of emplotment to show the intimate details of the daily lives encountered in the film's characters. He has also pared down plot elements to the barest minimum in order to reveal other elements within the film as complex components in the production of the film's meanings. In *Killer of Sheep*, the depiction of place as opposed to events is foregrounded. The characters' interaction with the environment in which they live reveals their psychological or emotional condition rather than the forward movement of melodramatic conflict-resolution forms so common to conventional dramatic films. The film places the main characters' psychological states in the context of larger social conditions, suggesting that social contexts are what have produced the characters' personal condition. *Killer of Sheep*, however, is not a sociological study. Rather, the attempt is to produce the experience of the characters' conditions as a cinematic experience for the viewer. To do this, the film departs radically from the cinematic conventions of film melodrama, such as the continuity constructions of the classical Hollywood form, with its seamless flow of time moving from one scene to the next according to the dictates of plot requirements. The film has reduced to a minimum spoken dialogue between the characters as a way of propelling the narrative forward. Rather, the film shows the characters in detailed visualizations of their daily activities and their physical relationships to the people around them.

The narrative form of the film's story is more typically modernist than classical. The story in *Killer of Sheep* is episodic and fragmentary, constructed through a series of loosely knit sequences depicting the daily life of this working-class African American family, each separate scene a self-contained narrative with its own formal logic. While the accumulation of these sequences produces specific meaning as a whole, each shot has its own integrity temporally and compositionally. Narrative time is constantly being constructed within each shot and then broken by colliding with another. As in the films of James Benning and Jean-Luc Godard, the narrational intensity comes from the accumulation of discrete shots, each successive one de-framing the next. This is a quintessentially anti-illusionist gesture that fractures narrative continuity and repeatedly throws the viewer back into the context of his or her own present by constantly having to work to reconnect one sequence to another.

In *Killer of Sheep*, the formal style is constructed around two major kinds of shots: the long shot, in which the entire object shown is contained in the frame, and the long take, in which the duration of the shot is continuous. These shots emphasize complete actions and images of whole objects. These types of shots emphasize the real-time continuity of an action rather than the expansion or elision that results from putting together individual shots to make up a whole action. These two shots are deviated from in the occasional use of the close-up or moving camera. The long shot and the continuous take, however, create the rhythms of the film, which are languid and produce a contemplative relation to the events in the story.

Killer of Sheep produces interesting tensions between traditional modes of storytelling and more purely visual and experiential modes of filmmaking. It shows, through a loosely connected string of sequences, elements of daily life in a working-class Black community. The story is structured in alternating sequences between the activities and interactions of the adults in the family and neighborhood and the play of the children in its streets and buildings.

The film centers on Stan, who has a wife and two kids and works in a slaughterhouse. We see him interact with family members and friends. We see him involved in different activities that show the uneventful, prosaic quality of his life. He is repairing the kitchen sink, cashing a check, disciplining his son, going through the routinized activities at work. The adults talk to each other about their lives either in stammering, soul-searching discussions or by arguing. In both cases, they seem to be trying to articulate their emotional condition, but with little success. Through objective positioning of the film's mostly static camera and long takes, the viewer is given the time to see the characters' eyes, expressions, and bodies. We see what cannot be expressed verbally. In contrast to the adults, we see the children of the neighborhood playing in the streets, in vacant lots, and in buildings. The children are pure motion, like kinetic apparitions who are defined by movement. There is little for them to do or play with, so they play with each other, inventing games, running and biking around the neighborhood. Their youthful energy and constant invention of activities keep them in motion and occupied. No one, adult or child, is doing anything out of the ordinary, and nothing particularly dramatic happens, again emphasizing the prosaic nature of life in this neighborhood. Intermittently we see Stan at work, herding the sheep to slaughter. These moments at the slaughterhouse that show the sheep unknowingly being led to slaughter are placed in relief against the activities of the adults and children. The metaphor of the archetypal image of the innocent lamb being led to slaughter is the only specific comment the director makes about the condition of his characters. Otherwise the activities of the people are recorded objectively with a static camera shot largely in a series of long shots with the occasional cut to a close-up of a face. Burnett rarely leads the viewer to specific conclusions through conventional master-shot/closeup combinations but rather lets his or her eye wander through the details of a shot's richly composed framing.

Killer of Sheep creates rhythms rather than stories. It is in the contrast between the alternating rhythms created by the kinetic energy of the children at play and the slow movements of the quietly serious adults placed in the unremarkable, crumbling environment of South Central Los Angeles that the condition of many African Americans in the late-twentieth-century United States is most profoundly articulated. These rhythms emerge as the central element of the film, giving *Killer of Sheep* a strange, otherworldly quality. While the film is located specifically in South Central Los Angeles, in the present day, the highly formalized rhythms render the place and time slightly unfamiliar and ephemeral. Rather than being realistic, the film produces a spectral-like aura around the characters that makes them appear to be slightly out of time.

In his essay "New Black Cinema," Clyde Taylor, who has emphasized the realism and documentary quality that characterizes the visual style of *Killer of Sheep*, writes: "The basic palette of the indigenous Afro-screen is closer to that of Italian Neo-realism and third world cinema than to

Southern California. Charles Burnett, in *Killer of Sheep* for instance, makes effective use of the open frame, in which characters walk in and out of the frame from the top, bottom and sides—a forbidden practice in the classical mode of Hollywood."[3] The realism of the film's mise-en-scène, with its unadorned locations and real interiors instead of sets, is unmistakable. The film, however, is also a tightly controlled and formally rigorous construction, which defies the documentary-like quality associated with early neorealist cinema, such as *The Bicycle Thief* by Vittorio De Sica (Italy, 1948) or *Rome, Open City* by Roberto Rossellini (Italy, 1945). Rather, *Killer of Sheep* can be seen more productively in relation to later highly formal and stylized modernist films that grew out of neorealism, such as *L'Eclisse (The Eclipse)* by Michelangelo Antonioni (Italy, 1962). *L'Eclisse*, while using real locations, also expresses the traumatized, outof-time quality of its characters, who in the wake of World War II are no longer able to express a sense of personal agency. As with Stan in *Killer of Sheep*, they seem to be disconnected from the lives they lead and are seen in rigorously composed shots existing in depersonalized urban landscapes.

Unlike the more spontaneous style of neorealism, in *Killer of Sheep*, every shot is formally composed using the graphic elements of the frame to compositionally foreground the interplay between characters and their environment. This relationship can be seen in one paradigmatic sequence of four shots (figs. 9.1, 9.2, 9.3, and 9.4), which opens as a deep-focus long shot of children playing in the stairwell of an apartment building. Far in the background, we see three boys on a bicycle. In the foreground, there are more kids wrestling each other. The bicycle approaches the stairs. The boys dismount and walk the bike down the stairs. The camera is static and holds its fixed position. The boys remount the bike and proceed to ride forward toward the camera. Shot 2 is a medium shot reframing from the same camera angle. All the boys are still in full frame. The bike and riders continue to move toward the camera. The scale changes, with the wrestling kids now in the background, and the new angle emphasizes the narrowness of the walkway, while the bikers are getting larger as they approach the camera and finally ride out of frame left. Shot 3 is a reverse shot of the bike now in a different location—a large boulevard on which the boys are riding away from the camera. This is a long shot in which we see a car approaching. Then two dogs enter frame left and start chasing the bike. The boys swerve into the car's path to avoid the dogs. As they are about to run into the car, they all jump off the bike and leave it lying in the street and run out of frame left. Shot 4 follows the boys running down the street.

Fig. 9.1

Fig. 9.2

Fig. 9.3

Fig. 9.4

In the case of the first three shots, the static full frame reveals the intricacies of being a child in an urban environment. Shot 1 uses a wide-angle lens that accentuates the narrowness of the walkway through which they must ride. Shots 2 and 3 use a telephoto lens, which flattens the space, collapsing the elements of the mise-en-scène together and emphasizing the lack of open space in the city. Even children at play are constantly being forced to negotiate the constricting reality of inner-city life with its buildings, narrow stairways, sidewalks blocked with other children, dogs running uncontrolled, and boulevards filled with cars. In these tightly composed framings—rather than documentary spontaneity—we see the thwarted desire for the freedom of open spaces that characterizes inner-city life. This becomes a graphic cinematic metaphor for the African American lives that are filled with compromise, the negotiation with a hostile environment, and the ultimate inability to live the way one wants.

The high-contrast black and white used in the film emphasizes the graphic compositional elements of the shots as opposed to the use of black and white to heighten a sense of realism, another element often ascribed to early neorealism. From the beginning of the film, the black and white are used to create contrasts, producing otherworldly spaces and separations between people and cultures. From the opening, the images of a father chastising his son are shot in low-key expressionist lighting in which space is deterritorialized, as in a dream. The next sequence begins with the screen literally divided between black and white. It is a rock fight in a sandlot, and a boy is using a sheet of plywood as a shield. By framing the plywood to completely cover half the frame, Burnett uses the flatness of the screen to create divisions between dark and light. Throughout the film, the high contrasts of the black and white make palpable the sense of claustrophobia and frustration of daily life in this ghetto. In this sense, the black and white of the film creates a much more abstract and metaphorical world than a realistic one. There is no clearer instance of this than the graphic quality of the white sheep disappearing into the black space of the chute in the slaughterhouse. The contrast between black and white is made even more potent when the image of the white sheep going to slaughter is reversed in the viewer's mind—through the film's central metaphor—into the black skins of the film's subjects.

The metaphor of innocence then continues as the sheep silently go off to slaughter, intercut with images of the also-innocent Stan helplessly watching the neighborhood children. Stan, as the killer of sheep, is at once murderer and victim as he bears witness to the trauma of the African American experience. Stan's silence comes from the slow and steady diminution of a sense of self through the lack of control over his life. As the killer of sheep, he kills, as he himself is being killed by the lack of possibilities and his lost dreams. In *Killer of Sheep*, this can be seen as his trauma—and also the collective one—embodied by his silence and listless gaze.

In his essay "Notes on Trauma and Community," Kai Erikson describes traumatized subjects as those who "look out at the world through a different lens. And in this sense they can be said to have experienced not only changed sense of self and changed way of relating to others but a changed worldview."[4] Looking out at the world through a different lens is an apt way to describe a film like *Killer of Sheep*. It is one that presents a completely different image of the Black experience in America by looking closely, carefully, and intimately at the rhythms of daily life in an American community. In the film, Stan's silent gaze can be seen as that of the traumatized subject, through whom the viewer bears witness both to the spirit of endurance and to the abjection in African American life. Through Stan's silence, the film privileges the visual over the written, opening the film and its viewers to insights and modes of expression perhaps not possible by literary means. Because of the film's prosaic and quiet qualities, we are able to see the world around Stan. Nothing much happens to him, and he does little besides his job. This invites us to move beyond the actions of the protagonist and to look at the world around him.

In one of the most moving scenes in the film, Stan tries to speak in a way that reveals his deep sensitivity, however clotted and sedimented under his silence it may be. Late one night, he is sitting at the kitchen table playing dominoes with a friend; they are drinking tea out of china cups. Stan has the friend put the hot teacup against his cheek and asks what it reminds him of. The friend says he has no idea. Stan ventures that it feels like a woman's forehead while making love. The friend bursts out laughing incredulously. We see in the background his longing wife in the darkness of the hallway, silently observing this exchange. The camera holds on Stan as he rubs the cup against his cheek; we see him struggle with his emotions as if he is using the hot cup to evoke the memory of another world now inaccessible to him. Throughout the film, despite the advances of his wife and other women, he shows little interest in sex or sensual experience of any kind. So the realization of the warm cup as something connected to pleasure takes on much larger symbolic proportions than a sexual fantasy. In the disparities between his quietly reflective attempt to describe an ephemeral sensation, the boisterous ridicule of the uncomprehending friend's laughter, and his wife's silent presence, the viewer can see evidence of Erikson's notion of a worldview changed by trauma. All bear witness to Stan but are unable to perceive as he does the memory evoked by the heat of the teacup, thus separating Stan from his wife, his friend, and the viewer, isolated as he is in his own world.

The relationship between a traumatized subject of catastrophe and the act of witnessing is central to understanding this reading of the film's form. The fixed camera quietly records these poignant moments in Stan's domestic life in which his wife and children try to find ways of crossing into the isolated world that surrounds Stan. In a single fixed-camera shot, Stan and his wife are seen alone in their darkened living room. She is trying to get him to dance with her. They are in silhouette, framed by a window through which nothing can be seen but the bright white light of the overexposed outside world. In this heartbreaking scene, he spurns her attempts at lovemaking and walks away. Like a moth to the light, she rushes to the window, throwing her body against it as if she might crash through. Such otherworldly images graphically open the film beyond the present. In Burnett's formal style of real time observed through the continuous take, we are able to sense the specters of past trauma in the present.

The African American community is haunted by the specter of the trauma slavery. As Avery Gordon writes, "Slavery has ended, but something of it continues to live on, in the social geography of where peoples reside, in the authority of collective wisdom and shared benightedness, in the veins of the contradictory formation we call New World modernity, propelling, as it always has, a something to be done. Such endings that are not over is what haunting is about."[5] The profound accomplishment of *Killer of Sheep* is its quiet construction of the rhythms of the quotidian. It creates the sense of the wavering present by asking the viewer to think beyond what is represented and perhaps opens up a space where one can experience the ways in which ephemeral and ungraspable elements of the past are always present and inflect daily life. Through the long and lingering shots of his camera pointed at his own community, Burnett creates a conjuring tool with which to witness a present that evokes a past far from over.

Burnett is committed to an image of time as a way of exploring a prosaics of the quotidian that might sensitize the viewer to the complexity and richness of African American cultures past, present, and future. Certainly

Killer of Sheep is a politically situated expression of the African American reality in the late twentieth century—coming at the end of the civil rights and Black Power movements of the sixties. The film can even be seen as social realist in the ways some critics have cited. As I have argued, however, the film's power lies in what remains unseeable but is felt through Burnett's use of the formal elements of duration, composition, and the contrasts of black, whites, and grays that evoke in the present the specters of the catastrophic past of slavery that continues to haunt America.

Notes

1. Avery F. Gordon, *Ghostly Matters: Haunting and the Sociological Imagination* (Minneapolis: University of Minnesota Press, 2008), 17.
2. Thomas Cripps, *Black Film as Genre* (Bloomington: Indiana University Press, 1978), 9.
3. Clyde Taylor, *Jump Cut*, no. 28 (April 1983): 46–48.
4. Kai Erikson, "Notes on Trauma and Community," in *Trauma: Explorations in Memory*, Cathy Caruth, ed. (Baltimore, MD: Johns Hopkins University Press, 1995), 183–199.
5. Gordon 2008, 139.

10

REVENONS À NOS MOUTONS
Regarding Animals in Charles Burnett's Killer of Sheep

Sarah O'Brien

*K*ILLER OF *SHEEP* (CHARLES BURNETT, 1977) IS A neorealist drama loosely centered on a slaughterhouse worker and his immediate circle of family and friends in post-riots Watts, Los Angeles. The film's penultimate slaughterhouse sequence contains a shot of some dozen sheep being herded into the paddock where they will await their death: the camera lingers on several of the animals, and they turn slightly and look directly at it (fig. 10.1). Like the direct address employed by the showman-like exhibitors and performers of the early cinema of attractions, their look back is unsettling insofar as it reminds us of the presence of the camera and thus precludes our complete absorption in the film. More than that, their gaze is unnerving because it expresses a solemn curiosity that goes beyond a basic awareness of the surroundings and because, in its odd placement in the sequence and the sequence's relation to the preceding sequences of slaughter, it seems to direct a look of supplication not only to the slaughterhouse workers but also to us, the audience. Rather than appearing at the beginning of the sequence, as the linear narrative logic of slaughter would insist, the image of the sheep being led to slaughter follows a series of shots detailing the various processes of disassembly (hide removal, dismemberment, cleanup); this image comes at the film's third of four sequences in the abattoir. Within this reshuffled syntax of slaughter, the sheep appear to look back at—to witness—their future death and dismemberment. Through this

Fig. 10.1

disruption, the film and its maker register the possibility that, in Jacques Derrida's words, the "animal could, facing them, look at them, clothed or naked, and in a word, without a word, address them."[1]

Derrida's reference to nakedness belongs to the specific context of his daily encounters with his cat in his bathroom and speaks directly to the shame of feeling shame before a being that, within the framework of traditional humanist thought, is held to be incapable of shame. Yet his remarks on the denuding potential of the animal's address are also bound up with his use of the French *dressage*, "training," to describe "a habit or a convention that would in the long term program the very act of thinking."[2] The way we come to see the world can certainly be thought of as a *type* of *dressage*—a training that in the long run programs the very act of looking and specifically the act of looking at animals and at violent animal death. (I am thinking here of Walter Benjamin's observation that modem technology—and particularly cinema—"has subjected the human sensorium to a complex kind of training.")[3] Certainly the English usage of *dressage*—a type of equestrianism that emphasizes obedience, flexibility, balance—calls to mind a focused rationalization of our relationships, visual and otherwise, to animals and particularly to animal bodies. And, as David Wills allows by parenthetically retaining the French *dressage* in his translation of "The Animal That Therefore I Am," the French term also has the curious advantage of evoking the English *to dress*: we dress ourselves up in clothes and also in logic, language, and reason—in short, all the accoutrements of "the human."[4] Read in the context of current, ethically charged discussions of animals and visuality, the term *dressage* intimates that the way we train our gaze on animals has much to do with our desire to distance ourselves from them. In this essay, I focus on the idiosyncratic formal strategies Burnett employs in *Killer of Sheep* both to render animal slaughter unfamiliar and to effectively bind this site (sight) and its animal constituents to the lived reality—and particularly to the domestic space—of the film's human players. The film, I argue in dialogue with Derrida, thus reconfigures our relationships to animals in the terms of a faltering, undecidable proximity.

The sheep's arresting gaze is but the starting point of my analysis of *Killer of Sheep*. This literal, even stark, instantiation of the reciprocal gaze Derrida seeks prompts my consideration of the film's form as a whole, particularly the way it joins defamiliarizing gestures with techniques of alignment, juxtaposition, and abutment; in this way, the film not only undresses our habits of looking at animals but also suggests how we might redress this training. Steve Baker asserts that for Derrida, "it is clear that the killing of animals can indeed be productively addressed through the turning of the looking and through philosophy's adoption of the vantage of the animal."[5] It is less clear exactly how one makes this turn. How, in effect, does one cultivate *animalséance*—Derrida's word for the unease one feels when looked at by an animal (from *malséance*, "unseemliness")?[6] *Killer of Sheep* generates a powerful methodology for this project through its surrealist-tinged approach to coupling radical difference and contradiction. Although the film neither begs the label "surrealist" nor fits squarely into that movement's genealogy, it shares what Adam Lowenstein describes as surrealism's commitment to "a radically altered vision [that] restores unseemliness."[7] Lowenstein makes this remark in reference to *Le sang des bêtes* (*Blood of the Beasts*, Georges Franju, 1949), a categorically surrealist documentary that weaves together scenes of World War II–era Paris and its slaughter complex La Villette; this film opens, as Lowenstein puts it, with "a kaleidoscope of wildly contrasting Surrealist images that underline the impossibility of a soothingly familiar world to comfort us before we descend into the nightmare of the slaughterhouse."[8] *Killer of Sheep*, I contend, achieves a similar end through different means.

The crux of my argument is that the film's distinctive engagement with a constellation of boundaries—between sound and image, waking and dreaming life, human and animal—works to loosen the visual field and to make room for an ethical recognition of the complex relationships involved in the practice of slaughter. This loosening realizes visual artist Eduardo Kac's recommendation that "more than making visible the invisible, art needs to raise our awareness of what firmly remains beyond our visual reach but, nonetheless, affects us directly."[9] Kac offers this prescription in a manifesto about contemporary transgenic art, yet it serves equally well to describe the operations at work in the comparatively lo-fi registers of *Killer of Sheep*. While Burnett makes use of a number of film styles (an admixture I explore presently), his method of filmmaking is best characterized as an expression of Bazinian realism. According to George Kouvaros's eloquent summation, for André Bazin, realist cinema is "not an attempt to 'show things as they are,' but rather [is] grounded in moments of sensory experience in which the contingency and finitude of everyday life is brought to the fore."[10] As he puts it, Bazin prizes the "capacity of the cinematic image not simply to represent a sense of material contingency, but to make it present on screen."[11] Read together, Kac's prescription and Kouvaros's description confirm that defamiliarization alone is insufficient for rethinking the predominantly violent relationships between humans and animals in our postindustrial, postmodern, and arguably post-humanist society. Cinema can participate substantively and ethically in the reconfiguration of those relationships by making present or perceptible—which is distinct from making visible, knowable—the contingencies and limits that bind humans and animals.

The borrowed imperative of this article's title, *revenons à nos moutons*, phrases this potential in slightly different terms. Sergei Eisenstein, director of what may be cinema's most iconic scene of animal slaughter (*Strike*, 1925), uses this idiomatic expression to guide readers back to his constant concern—the physiological and emotional effects of montage.[12] As translators Richard Taylor and William Powell explain, the phrase means "literally, 'let us return to our sheep,' and metaphorically, 'let us get back to the point.'"[13] Eisenstein's willful affectation of the French reminds me, perhaps not altogether arbitrarily, that one of Ferdinand de Saussure's primary proofs for the interdependence of linguistic values is *mouton*. He observes that in modern French, "sheep" and "sheep rendered into 'a

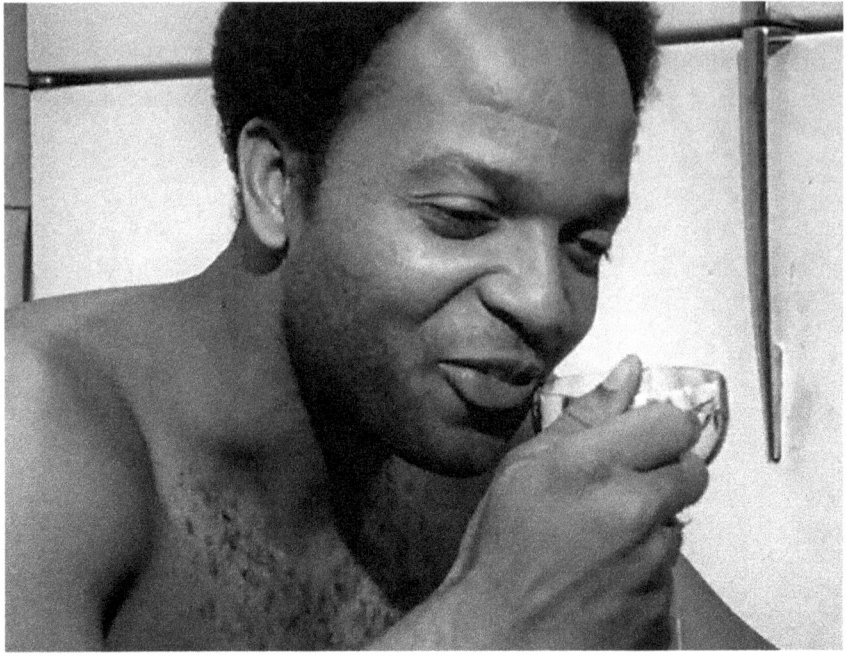

Fig. 10.2

piece of meat ready to be served on the table'" share the signifier *mouton*, whereas in English, the former is signified by *sheep* and the latter by *mutton*. This observation leads Saussure to write, "Within the same language, all words used to express related ideas limit each other reciprocally . . . Conversely, some words are enriched through contact with others."[14] That is, the meanings of words (or of any other linguistic unit) exist only in relation to other words and/or units. Saussure's insight into the constitutive difference of language informs much of the Derridean work on which this article draws. Moreover, it directs our attention to the animals whose bodies—whose fleshly meat, or *mouton*, are made to produce meaning and metaphor through their disassembly and reassembly on-screen—urge us, then, to get back to the meat of cinema.

Set in Watts, Los Angeles, roughly five years after race riots convulsed the neighborhood, *Killer of Sheep* principally follows Stan (Henry Gale Sanders), a man who supports his family by working at a slaughterhouse. Stan suffers from insomnia, a condition presumably induced by the anxieties of his domestic life and the deadening conditions of his job (fig. 10.2).

The film's title thus introduces its organizing pun: by day Stan kills sheep, and by night he counts them. This conceit is at once playful and damning. It functions, on one level, as an ironic critique of the new strain of metaphorical and material violence that late capitalism has introduced into human-animal relationships; after all, if Stan were a shepherd, a gentle husbandman in a premodern pastoral economy, he would count sheep literally rather than figuratively. This wordplay also serves more generally to anchor Stan and the sheep in an ineluctable and decidedly imbalanced relationship: Stan plays a decisive role in the lives of the sheep (he slaughters them), just as the sheep play a decisive role in his (their existence as a class of heifers that elicits a "noncriminal putting to death," as Derrida would put it, debases his life).[15] In its title alone, then, the film initiates a critical engagement with, on the one hand, long-standing anxieties that the human labor of animal slaughter threatens to contaminate human life, and, on the other hand, abiding associations between marginalized, disenfranchised humans and powerless animals. The film's power lies in its refusal to tidily confirm or discredit these overlapping spheres of influence and association between humans and animals.

Killer of Sheep's placement in and negotiation of these spheres is best approached through a thick description of the film's production context, its narrative and style, and the criticism it has so far received. It bears stressing at the outset that this negotiation is embedded in a particularized context of race and class relations. The film is, first and foremost, a political expression of the lived reality shared by a community of working-class African Americans in South Central Los Angeles in the wake of the turbulent 1960s, and it demands to be read not only in relation to the fallout of the civil rights movement, the Black Power movement, the Watts riots, and the general social upheaval of the era, but also as a response to the racially exclusionary practices of Hollywood film, to that cinema's perpetuation of the stereotype of disempowered Black masculinity, and to more broad-based initiatives (namely, the Moynihan Report of 1965) that condemned African American families and communities as pathologically self-destructive.[16] Because it is more of an expression of a time than a carefully plotted story, *Killer of Sheep*'s narrative resists retelling. It is episodic and consists of three outwardly disparate strands: mostly interior scenes of Stan, his family, and his friends engaged in the mundane details of domestic life and the prosaic activities of the neighborhood; interior scenes of Stan working at the slaughterhouse and exterior scenes of children, including Stan's son and daughter, playing in back alleys, train yards, and razed lots. These threads are stylistically dissimilar: conforming most closely to the conventions of cinema verité, the domestic scenes play out in long, static takes with seemingly little directorial intervention; the scenes of Stan's work life, meanwhile, are characterized by frenetic camera movement and relatively rapid editing; finally, the scenes of children at play are distinguished by a deeper focus and looser framing, and thus by a greater sense of movement and space. Burnett does not fit these strands into a conventional narrative arc; things happen in the film but not in the typical storytelling terms of cause and effect, conflict and resolution. The film is thus more effectively described through a consideration of its form and of the ways in which Burnett's formal choices relate to both the human and nonhuman subjects of his film. As indicated, key to this descriptive reading is the way the film represents this family and this community through an assemblage of idiosyncratic styles.

Burnett made *Killer of Sheep* as his thesis film for his master of fine arts degree at UCLA's School of Theater, Film, and Television, and it has since become, according to the words of one critic and to the mythologizing flourishes that tend to adorn its reviews, "the world's most legendary student film."[17] Yet the film did not come out of nowhere. At UCLA, Burnett belonged to the first wave of the LA Rebellion (also known as the Los Angeles School of Black Filmmakers), a cohort of up-and-coming African American and African graduate film students and filmmakers that included Haile Gerima, Billy Woodberry, Larry Clark, and Julie Dash, to name just a few. In its move to forge a Black independent American cinema, the LA Rebellion rejected the representational norms of Hollywood cinema, particularly the then-emergent genre of blaxploitation films, and embraced as its primary influence the anti-colonialist ideology and esthetics of Third Cinema. Ntongela Masilela, a member of the group, characterizes its films as being imbued with the sense that "imagination [is] explicitly wedded to political and cultural commitment."[18] He observes that its early output, of which *Killer of Sheep* is a cornerstone, is moreover preoccupied with "redefining the relationship of history to the structure of the family."[19] Burnett came to UCLA in 1967 and began work on *Killer of Sheep* soon thereafter, with a budget of less than $10,000 and a cast of nonprofessional actors. The film's completion was considerably delayed because of the incarceration of one of those actors. When Burnett managed to complete the film in 1975, he could not afford to secure the rights to the music, and consequently the film's official 1977 release was limited to the festival circuit. It garnered high praise, including the

International Critics Prize at the 1981 Berlin International Film Festival and the honor of being among the first fifty films chosen for the National Film Registry of the Library of Congress in 1990. Despite this acclaim, the film more or less languished in storage facilities until 2007, when UCLA restored it to 35mm and released it in theaters. It was subsequently released on DVD and is only now beginning to reach larger circles.[20] Largely as a result of its troubled reception history, *Killer of Sheep* has received relatively little scholarly attention. Its recent rerelease garnered unanimously glowing reviews, but it has, at this writing, so far been rigorously discussed in only two journal articles and one book chapter (passing mention of it is regularly made in scholarship on Black independent American filmmaking). Fortunately, the three detailed analyses offer a great deal of insight into the film, and I position my own examination of the film in dialogue with them.

The existent analyses of *Killer of Sheep* are remarkably coherent in their reading of Burnett's distinctive visual and aural style as a direct engagement with the race dynamics that subtend the past, present, and future of this community and the United States at large. Paula Massood focuses on the film's local contexts—its setting in Watts and its place in the LA Rebellion—and demonstrates that Burnett's assemblage of a range of filmmaking styles creates a potent and profoundly nuanced filmic antidote to the sensational and racially charged televisual images of the riots, which since 1965 have laid claim to the public imaginary of Watts.[21] She mines the film's recognized resemblances to Italian neorealism and to Third Cinema and cogently establishes its significant debt to and departure from both Griersonian observational documentary and cinema verité.[22] Within this frame of references, she situates Burnett's alternation between such disparate techniques as static long takes and handheld camera work, vernacular speech and stilted, patently scripted conversation, and direct sound and sync-sound as a measured "formulation of an aesthetic that dialogue[s] with and refract[s] a unique set of cultural conditions."[23] Massood also makes the persuasive argument that the film's narrative, the episodic nature of which draws as much from African oral traditions as it does from the films of Vittorio De Sica and Roberto Rossellini, "expand what first appears as a sole focus on a singular hero and suggests that Stan's existential dilemma is undeniably linked to a larger community crisis."[24] Meanwhile, Inez Hedges positions *Killer of Sheep* as an example of "signifyin'," a set of rhetorical strategies in African American vernacular speech that, in Henry Louis Gates Jr.'s formulation, are "not engaged in the game of information giving. Signifyin' turns on the play and chain of signifiers, and not on some supposedly transcendent signified."[25] (To put it another way, signifyin' exploits the gaps between denotative and connotative language.)

Hedges contends that Burnett and other independent Black filmmakers of the period deploy signifyin' as a counter-hegemonic strategy; *Killer of Sheep* not only represents characters in the act of signifyin' (in, for example, the many scenes that revolve around jokes and put-downs) but also absorbs signifyin' into its visual and aural style. Hedges identifies the following as formal examples of signifyin': Burnett's ambiguous treatment of the trope of innocent sheep, his use of music as an ironic counterpoint to the image track, his way of framing shots so as to heighten their affective intensity and his eschewal of point-of-view shots. She contends that these stylistic choices "decenter the spectator, creating uncertainty about the image" and open up a critique of hegemonic culture.[26] Finally, in a chapter of a book dedicated to demonstrating avant-garde film's oft-overlooked commitments to political history, Jeffrey Skoller locates *Killer of Sheep* within the discourse of trauma and argues that its visual style works to evoke or make present the inheritances of slavery, a centuries-long regime of violence that "visibly ended generations ago" but continues to shape the present in profound, often invisible, ways.[27] He identifies Burnett's use of duration (both the continuous take and the long shot) and high-contrast, black-and-white film stock as the primary means by which the film "reveals the ways in which legacies of events from the past actually inhere in the present, invisibly inflecting daily life with a force that is powerfully tangible."[28]

Together these readings demonstrate that *Killer of Sheep*'s idiosyncratic form develops—in the photographic sense of making visible or perceptible but also in the musical and mathematical senses of elaborating, modifying, or expanding a theme—connections between the local and the diffuse, the individual and the collective, the past and present, and the dominant culture and its margins. For all their focus on the film's work of decentering, though, they remain firmly centered on its human elements. My reading offers a vital supplement. It is only by attending as well to the presence of animals in *Killer of Sheep*—to, specifically, the means by which it renders animals' presence alongside humans—that we may fully comprehend the film's concurrent proliferation and destabilization of a diffuse network of boundaries. My aim is not to efface the established analytical frame of race but rather to thicken it. As Cary Wolfe puts it, "You can't talk about race without talking about species."[29] By this he means that one cannot disentangle discourses of race and species, because "both categories—as history well shows—are so notoriously pliable and unstable, constantly bleeding into and out of each other."[30] The flip side to this recognition is that talking about race strengthens discussions about animals, just as talking about animals enriches discussions of race. In the context of *Killer of Sheep*, for example, Massood's contention that "Burnett shifts conventional narrative identification from the individual to the community" and thereby "disput[es] blaxploitation's assertion that an empowered lone male figure leads to salvation" is only bolstered by the acknowledgment that the community to which Burnett shifts focus decidedly includes animals.[31] If we allow this enlarged view, it becomes apparent that the film unseats the individual human hero precisely by, among other things, extending its regard to animals.

With the supplementarity of race and species in mind, my reading, alongside the nascent scholarship on *Killer of Sheep*, can be understood as complementary efforts to read and understand the film's limitrophy. Derrida appropriates this term to characterize his aspirations for his "Animal I Am" address and defines it as "what abuts onto limits but also what feeds, is fed, is cared for, raised, and trained, what is cultivated on the edges of a limit."[32] He maintains, moreover, that his address "is designed, certainly not to efface the limit, but to multiply its figures, to complicate, thicken, delinearize, fold, and divide the line precisely by making it increase and multiply."[33] As Massood, Skoller, and Hedges persuasively demonstrate, the limitrophic nature of *Killer of Sheep* emerges in Burnett's pronounced movements in, around, and across the edges of film form. My analysis concentrates on the film's peculiar juxtapositions of sound to image and its distinctive cinematography and editing. These gestures populate the limits between on- and off-screen space, past and present, and waking and dreaming life, as well as between the outwardly disparate narrative threads. It is my contention that in doing so, these movements "complicate, thicken, delinearize, fold, and divide the line" between humans and animals.

As indicated earlier, Stan's job at the slaughterhouse introduces two significant sites of potential human-animal association: on the one hand, Stan's life is presumably debased by his work of killing animals, and on the other hand, the conditions of his life and the lives of the humans around him—in particular, his own children and the kids in the neighborhood—are, arguably, made comparative to those of animals. (To put it another way, the presence of the sheep renders the human characters susceptible to zoomorphic metaphor.) My analysis is ultimately more concerned with the latter—that is, with Burnett's gamble with the trope of animalization. Yet insofar as these sites or spheres feed into one another, it is worth addressing the former in some detail. Anxiety over the interpersonal effects of killing animals dates at least as far back as Thomas More's *Utopia* (1516), in which the leaders of the eponymous society "suffer none of their citizens to kill their cattle, because they think that pity and good-nature, which are among the best of those affectations that are born with us, are much impaired by the butchering of animals."[34] In Upton Sinclair's *The Jungle*, the belief that violence against animals begets violence against humans is expressed as a commonsensical rule of nature: "There is but scant account kept of cracked heads in back of the [stock] yards, for men who have to crack the heads of animals all day seem to get into the habit, and to practice it on their friends, and even on their families, between times."[35] Finally, the formative nature of slaughter serves as the premise —and arguably a parodic one— of *The Texas Chainsaw Massacre* (Tobe Hooper, 1974), a pioneering slasher flick released to cult acclaim while Burnett was completing *Killer of Sheep*. In Hooper's film, a group of day-tripping friends pick up a hitchhiker, and as they pass by a slaughterhouse, he spells out their fate with the proud declaration, "my family's always been in meat." Sure enough, the friends soon fall into the chainsaw-wielding, cannibalistic clutches of the hitchhiker, his brother Leatherface, and the men's grandfather.[36]

In contrast to these earlier texts, *Killer of Sheep* is distinguished by its refusal to neatly assert that the practice of slaughtering animals engenders violence toward—or cruel detachment from—one's fellow humans. To be sure, the film repeatedly attests to the connectedness of Stan's work and home life: at the start of the film, Stan's friend Bracy half-jokingly riffs on Stan's entwined activities of killing and counting sheep and Stan suggests several times that finding a new job will solve his problems at home. Yet the associations the film draws between Stan's work and domestic malaise are multiple and profoundly ambivalent. According to the texts cited here already and to the popular myths in which they are embedded, violence against animals automatically gives rise to violence against humans. Yet Burnett goes to great lengths to portray Stan as both a competent slaughterhouse worker and a man—a son, a father, and a husband—who is opposed to violence.

The film opens with a dream sequence that is only loosely tethered to the narrative: A man chastises his adolescent son, whom the audience will likely later presume to be a younger version of Stan, for not jumping into a fight between his brother and a bully. The son's unfaltering stare simmers under the father's tirade—"you let anyone jump on your brother again and you just stand there and watch, boy, I'll beat you to death . . . Boy, you get a stick or a goddamn brick—get anything—and you knock the shit out of whoever is fighting your brother." If this obscure introduction to the world of *Killer of Sheep* establishes anything, it is that Stan quietly resists the violence around him. The film never returns to this primal scene but rather alludes to it in later episodes: in one, Stan tries to reprimand his own son for bullying his sister, and in another, he refuses the attempt of some neighborhood toughs to enlist him in a murder and robbery. In both cases, Stan's reticence causes him to fall short: Stan Jr. runs off before he can voice his disapproval, and Stan's wife intervenes to disabuse the thugs of their recruitment plans.

Stan's attempts to quietly refuse violence brush up against the images of him at work. As Massood astutely observes, Stan appears most active and alive when at work in the slaughterhouse: in these sequences, the otherwise mostly immobile camera swings into action, following his purposeful movements and once even catching him with a "rare smile." Massood asserts that the formal incongruity between the oppressively static domestic scenes and the almost exuberantly mobile slaughterhouse sequences disproves readings of *Killer of Sheep* that focus on Stan's job as the primary cause of his crisis.[37] More radically, this dissonance could be read to suggest that his work of killing and disassembling sheep constitutes a reprieve from a life of overwhelming monotony and hopelessness. It is impossible, however, to press this observation further and to argue that Stan finds any sort of escapist, sadistic pleasure in slaughtering sheep. In summary, *Killer of Sheep* elaborates a frame of connections—Stan practices nonviolence with people but capably slaughters animals; his malaise is partly by caused by a job at which he sometimes seems comfortable and even content—that does more than confirm the formative nature of killing animals and/or highlight the hypocrisy of a politics of nonviolence that does not extend to animals. The film works precisely to make present or palpable the connections between Stan's work and his generalized unease, and it works because it refrains from concretizing or synthesizing them in a definitive critique.

It is worth pausing here to question the decision to cast Stan as a killer of sheep. To create the film, Burnett drew largely on his own experiences as a longtime resident of Watts, and it would have been just as easy—if not easier—for him to develop a protagonist who, say, worked as an electrician, just as he had before attending film school (of course, this would have left him with a much less provocative title and thematic underpinning). What I am getting at here is that Burnett made Stan a slaughterer, and he made a number of formal choices that link the animals he slaughters (in addition to the other animal figures in the film) to the lives of the people that circulate around him; that is, he made a film that invites the simile "like animals." To my mind, the most significant question asked by the film is, then, what do we do with this potential metaphor? How do we read its very suggestion? A number of critics take it at face value. Skoller affirms, for example, "these moments at the slaughterhouse that show the sheep unknowingly being led to slaughter are placed in relief against the activities of the adults and children. The metaphor of the archetypal image of the innocent lamb being led to slaughter is the only specific comment the director makes about the condition of his characters."[38] Burnett's comment is supposedly so specific—so explicit, so unequivocal—that Skoller deems it unnecessary to recapitulate it; we can surmise, however, that he thinks Burnett uses images of the soon-to-be-slaughtered sheep as a potent visual metaphor for the collective sociohistorical trajectory of his disempowered human characters.[39] Reading *Killer of Sheep* as a film that uncritically likens its human characters to animals holds dangerous implications. To begin, such a reading suggests that, in the impoverished conditions of a racially stratified society, life is pared down to some sort of brute essence—to mindless toil and emotionless interpersonal exchanges or, as Armond White puts it in his written commentary for the DVD release of the film, "to random scenes of stasis and anomie."[40] Such a reading implies, in the extreme, that the humans are reduced or degraded—that they "animalized." The trope of animalization is of course enormously vexed, perhaps nowhere more so (with the exception of the Holocaust) than in discourse surrounding racial oppression and, specifically, African American slavery. The very suggestion of any resemblance between animals and African American slaves constitutes "the dreaded comparison," to borrow the title of Marjorie Spiegel's book-length consideration of this abiding trope.[41] To affirm that *Killer of Sheep* simply trades in this comparison is to overlook the myriad ways in which the film critically engages with the sociohistorical legacy and present-day reality of human-animal comparison.

Hedges moves toward an acknowledgment of *Killer of Sheep*'s self-reflexive treatment of the trope of animalization with her observation that "it's never clear that the fate of the children is equated with that of the sheep—it's just a nagging anxiety."[42] It is my contention that the film not only instills this anxiety, but also—and more importantly—presses the spectator to question it. In the context of current discussions about how one might ethically regard animals, the trope of animalization poses a specific danger: condemning the reduction of humans to beings that are "like animals" threatens to subsume any ethical recognition of the deplorable conditions in which many animals live and die. In his explication of the term *speciesism*, Wolfe develops a small lexicon that helps explain this point. He explains that the term, famously codified by Peter Singer in *Animal Liberation* (1975), "suggests (like its models racism, sexism, and so on) not only a logical or linguistic structure that marginalizes and objectifies the other solely based on species, but also a whole network of material practices that reproduce that logic as a materialized *institution* and rely on it for legitimization."[43] Wolfe envisions this network or institution as a grid and maps onto it four increasingly polarized categories: animalized animals, humanized animals, animalized humans, and humanized humans.[44] These designations elucidate a rhetorical move that is too frequently overlooked in discourse around animals: to animalize humans, we must first animalize animals; likewise, to humanize animals, we must first humanize humans. The failure to recognize this hierarchical exchange makes possible a profoundly speciesist ethical contradiction: it allows one to condemn systems or instruments of power that reduce humans to the state of animals (e.g., slavery), all the while taking it as given or natural that animals exist in conditions of extreme violence, deprivation, and suffering. This speciesist logic holds in readings of *Killer of Sheep* that maintain that the film depicts a society that reduces humans to the status of animals. More to the point, it effaces what I take to be one of the film's definitive ethical gestures: its refusal to subsume the animalization of animals within the animalization of humans.

This refusal emerges in Burnett's careful positioning of animals in the visual and aural registers of the film. The presence of animals in *Killer of Sheep* is initially perceptible on the soundtrack: the viewer is introduced to Stan, drinking tea in his kitchen with his friend Bracy (Charles Bracy), their ebbing conversation competing with the noises of dogs barking and, as the night wears on, crickets chirping and a car engine wheezing. Animals are regularly invoked in the characters' dialogue, appearing as the stuff of metaphor in insults, nursery rhymes, and poetic reverie: a woman calls her bawdy nephew "a dirty dog," children recite "knick-knack, paddywhack, give a dog a bone," and Stan's wife (played by Kaycee More, she appears frequently but remains unnamed) likens her memories to "rabbit skins stretched on the backyard fence." More often than not, these references are expressed in voice-over dialogue, and thus the invocations are twice removed. Animals likewise play a figurative role on the image track: Stan's young daughter, Angie, for example, first appears wearing a rubber dog mask, her own hangdog expression veiled by a surrogate animal one (in the background, birds chirp in unison with the squeak of a chain-link fence). Finally, animals sporadically appear on-screen in the flesh—the sheep in the abattoir, a pack of feral dogs in the street. In summary, animals populate various registers of the film, yet they remain always at the periphery. The placement of the animals at the limits of the narrative and the edges of the screen manifests a sort of Derridean supplementarity. Through choices of sound, framing, and editing, the film explicitly codes its nonhuman subjects as marginal. Yet it does so precisely to fold the underlying logic of this move back on itself, making visible the indivisibility of the supplement and that which it ostensibly augments—or, to use Derridean shorthand, rendering undecidable the reciprocity that binds human and nonhuman animals.

Burnett's peculiar combinations of sounds and images in and around the slaughterhouse sequences lay bare this supplemental relationship. More precisely, they make present the highly ambivalent relationships between the domestic sphere and the killing floor. An extended description of these sequences and the ways in which they are embedded in the film is here in order. To begin, a number of sound bridges and graphic visual rhymes bind these sequences to the other parts of the film, with the end result being that they unfold as diffuse yet connected episodes. The aforementioned scene of Stan and Bracy's dilatory conversation ends when Stan's wife enters the kitchen, whistling, and the film cuts abruptly to images of Stan cleaning up at the slaughterhouse. Our first glimpse of this grungy, industrial space is presumably taken from the end of Stan's workday, and—save for a skinned carcass and a tray of cutlets—the sheep are markedly absent. As Massood observes, Burnett makes two significant deviations in this and the following slaughterhouse sequences: he trades the static camera and direct sounds (conversations, background noises) of the domestic scenes for rapid, handheld camera work and an asynchronous, non-diegetic musical soundtrack.[45] In this first sequence, the swing-like second movement of William Grant Still's "Symphony No. 1:

Afro American" (1930) accompanies the images of Stan working, and as if to keep up with the score, the camera becomes almost exuberantly mobile, with several jarring swish pans announcing that the slaughterhouse is not exclusively a space of regimented movement. On the one hand, the playful melody and camera movement seem an incongruous accompaniment to the site of slaughter, with its cold, metal surfaces and rationalized activity of killing; on the other hand, the music and enlivened camera movement are a welcome reprieve from the preceding scene in Stan's kitchen, in which the lengthy silences and claustrophobic, static framing border on oppressive. Burnett reverts back to the more sedate stylistic conventions of the home and the neighborhood immediately upon leaving the slaughterhouse: the voices of children singing "This Old Man" play over a series of oddly placed establishing shots of the weathered facade and ruinous postindustrial surrounds of the Solano Meat Co., and the desultory lullaby leads back to the kitchen, where Stan's wife arranges her hair in a dulled reflection cast by the lid of a pot. Massood observes that the lullaby functions as a sound bridge that "links the abattoir with the kitchen not only because both spaces are connected to Stan, but because the spaces affect his psychological state. [It] relates Stan's job to the themes that most define the family scenes, fatigue and malaise, thus suggesting that his condition has become a vicious cycle in which work effects [sic] home and vice versa."[46] I agree, yet I think we can press these sites of connection further. For one, home and abattoir are bound not only by the lullaby but also by the faint echo of Stan's wife's whistle in the melody of Still's "Symphony." Indeed, the prosaic sounds of Stan's wife whistling and the children singing aurally bookend the melody that accompanies the images of Stan working. Burnett stitches the site (sight) of slaughter ever more closely into the domestic and social realms in subsequent sequences featuring Stan at work. Footage from the slaughterhouse next appears in between a scene of children playing in a vacant lot and the aforementioned scene in which the neighborhood toughs try to recruit Stan. The improbably deep bass of Paul Robeson serves as the sound in this sequence. His rendition of "The House I Live In" plays over the images of the desolate lot, his words "the children in the playground, the faces that I see, all races and religions, that's America to me" layered—perhaps ironically—over a close-up of a top spinning and a long shot of boys seated on a rumbling wall, aimlessly throwing rocks. Burnett cuts to the slaughterhouse, where a White worker hangs and wipes down the hooks onto which the bodies of dead sheep will be hoisted, and Stan in turn spaces out the hooks. Robeson's voice is cut off by the sound of forced air and the cold, metallic whir of the hooks skating against the track. A close-up shows the torso and hands of the White worker as he whets his knives, and a longer shot follows him from behind as he turns and exits. Burnett cuts to silence and to a corridor in which two rams stand, seemingly undecided; the space is clearly a part of the meat production facility, but its precise geographic relationship to the killing floor is unclear. Robeson's voice returns, this time singing the lines "lots of folks gathered there, all the friends I knew" from the spiritual "Going Home." Burnett holds the shot, and some dozen sheep traipse down the corridor, toward the rams; the animals turn first right, then left, and the line "all the friends I need" repeats. Finally, Burnett cuts to silence and an exterior shot of Stan's house. As in the previous sequence, the sound serves as a bridge on either end of the slaughterhouse footage, yet here Robeson's voice links the abattoir not only to Stan's home but also to the nation ("The House I Live In") and to home, i.e., heaven ("Going Home").

The third iteration of the slaughterhouse footage integrates visual rhymes in addition to aural linkages. It begins with the image described at the beginning of this section of the sheep turning and looking. Burnett then cuts to a streetscape shot with a telephoto lens so that its contents—three mangy dogs, an abandoned bicycle, a beatup car—appear flattened into one plane. Three boys run out of the frame, and a closer tracking shot follows them as they round a corner, laughing (fig. 10.3). Burnett matches to a shot of a homologous mass of sheep being hoisted onto the hooks (fig. 10.4). Little Walter's single "Mean Old World" begins to play over images of human hands grasping at the hides. A longer shot reveals a row of men skinning the animals, and a choppy series of shorter shots shows that a few deft cuts and yanks are all that is needed to strip the sheep (fig. 10.5). A shallow-focus shot frames the skinned heads and necks of two sheep, backed by a blurred-out row of similarly sickening shapes; here, Little Walter's bluesy harmonica momentarily aligns with the image track to suggest that the bobbing carcasses are dancing. Burnett then cuts the film's most graphic image: a shot of a sheep's skinned head, staked upside down on a metal post. A worker neatly slices out its gullet and tosses it into a bin. The music tapers out, and Burnett cuts back to the footage of the live sheep, which, as before, occupy a disparate and geographically indeterminate part of the facility. The direct sound recommences; the sheep bleat and again look at the camera. The sheep turn right and, as if startled by an offscreen

Fig. 10.3

Fig. 10.4

Fig. 10.5

sound or movement, quickly turn left and start to run. A static medium shot frames the long line of animals as they cross and exit the horizontal frame en masse.

This composition replicates the soporific, bedtime-story image of sheep bounding over the horizon, and the introduction of a boy's voice counting ("one Mississippi, two Mississippi") confirms the resemblance and ties it to the film's title and central conceit. Burnett cuts to a porch: two of the boys who were previously running have flung themselves upside down in a handstand contest (fig. 10.6). The third boy crouches to the side, counting; when he falters, one of the upturned boys chides him: "Boy, can't you count?" This sequence bleeds into the fourth and final iteration of slaughterhouse footage, and the two can thus be read as one long, diffuse sequence. A medium shot frames a girl hanging white sheets on a line, and she looks back at a group of boys who have just thrown dirt at her clean laundry. Burnett cuts to the slaughterhouse, to yet another shot of a sheep looking back; this time, a ram nuzzles an older female. The lilting voice of Dinah Washington singing "This Bitter Earth" plays over images of sheep

Fig. 10.6

being hoisted onto the line. It is a deliberate repetition: the same song accompanies a previous scene in which Stan and his wife slow dance and Stan quietly refuses her romantic advances. This last glimpse into the abattoir ends with a shot of Stan brandishing a white cloth as he herds the sheep down a narrow hall.

This description of the slaughterhouse sequences begins to explain the logic according to which the disparate actors and scenes of *Killer of Sheep* are made to abut one another. I will return to Burnett's peculiar use of sound, but I first want to highlight the way his editing and cinematography generate a series of morphological consonances between the film's humans and animal actors or agents. The last sequence described just above typifies the film's use of modified matches on action and graphic matching. The subject in a typical match on action remains the same from one shot to the next; indeed, the point of this continuity-editing device is to produce the illusion of an individual subject's continuous movement. In *Killer of Sheep*, in contrast, Burnett uses matches on action to join the movements of disparate subjects—namely, to make continuous the movements of human

Fig. 10.7

and animal actors. In the sequence scored to Little Walter, he uses matches on action to connect first the running boys to the swinging sheep and then the upended sheep back to the upside-down boys. These matches do not seamlessly blend the boys and the sheep together, but rather, with a sort of clumsy elegance, make them adjacent, contiguous. Moreover, they join the film's disparate narrative threads—the abattoir, the neighborhood, and more tangentially, the home. Burnett makes use of the technique of graphic matching or rhyming to similar ends. The sharpest example in *Killer of Sheep* occurs near the end, in an exterior sequence that shows children leaping from one tenement roof to another. Burnett films the children from below, positioning the camera at ground level and between the walls of the buildings. The effect is eerie: one by one, the children leap over the open threshold, their graceful bodies recalling, again, the sleep-inducing image of sheep bouncing over the horizon (fig. 10.7). Shots of children bounding over the firmament are among several instances in which the human characters are made to graphically rhyme with their animal counterparts: in the sequence described earlier, a young girl hangs laundry in a dusty yard, and the billowing sheets recall the images of the sheep suspended from hooks (this rhyme also refracts the image of the boys holding headstands).

We could allow that Burnett constructs these moments to represent a society that imposes equivalent limitations on certain of its human and animal subjects. Yet this would gloss over the film's much more nuanced critique of the very field of human-animal comparison. The desire to engage that critique prompts my earlier characterization of *Killer of Sheep* as a film that adheres to Bazin's ideals of realist filmmaking. What I have in mind here is not simply that Burnett abides by the tenets of duration that have come to be associated, somewhat reductively, with Bazin, but that he practices an idiosyncratic form of cinema that realizes Bazin's advocacy for "a film narrative capable of expressing everything without chopping the world up into bits—to reveal the hidden meanings of beings and things without breaking up their natural unity."[47] Readers may object that my coupling of Bazin and Burnett is somewhat perverse: Burnett may achieve Bazin's ideal, but it is only by using the very techniques—namely, editing—that Bazin eschewed. I would respond that *Killer of Sheep* documents a set of specific sociohistorical conditions in which the shared reality of humans and animals (among other ontological categories or fields) is always already chopped up into bits, and the film therefore works not to uncover a natural or objective unity but to remind us that connections persist and even proliferate within this highly fragmented field; to this end, Burnett has no choice but to rely on inventive (in Bazin's terms, additive) techniques of editing, as well as imaginative cinematography and asynchronous sound. I would add that while Bazin is most frequently remembered for his aphoristic disavowals of editing, he in fact viewed it as a perfectly acceptable element of film language but one that should be used sparingly and only when other means (deep focus, extended takes) were unavailable. The strict letter of his preference reads, "Whenever the essential aspect of an event depends upon the simultaneous presence of two or more agents, editing is prohibited."[48] Burnett violates the letter but not the spirit of Bazin's proscription. In fact, as my description of the slaughterhouse sequences suggests, Burnett uses editing (as well as cinematography and sound) precisely to make present the two agents—human and animal—on which his filmic reality depends. Moreover, he bends editing—which, according to Bazin, "by its very nature, is opposed to ambiguity"—into the service of fostering ambiguity.[49]

To pursue a slightly different tack, *Killer of Sheep* resonates with Jennifer Fay's assertion that Bazin's particular "ethos" as a film theorist and critic hinges on "his surrealist attraction to films that momentarily showcase the objective co-presence of radically different entities."[50] Fay is not alone in noting the surrealist undercurrent of Bazin's realism; Lowenstein asserts, "Bazin must be understood not as the naive realist he is so often mistaken for, but as a complex film theorist whose work reminds us of the realism within surrealism, and reveals to us the surrealism within realism."[51] These characterizations of Bazin find an uncanny echo in *Killer of Sheep*'s central stylistic tension, as the film shifts between gritty neorealist melodrama and the somewhat unlikely bedfellow of surrealist art and filmmaking. As Massood observes, *Killer of Sheep* makes use of almost every signature formalized by the Italian school of neorealism: it was shot on location amid urban ruin, it employs nonprofessional actors in scenes that are both more and less scripted, it favors natural lighting, and it unfolds as an episodic narrative.[52] Yet if the film adopts the principal conventions of neorealist filmmaking, it also draws on visual and aural techniques more readily associated with the avantgarde and particularly with surrealist filmmaking. These latter techniques provide the motivating force of the film's limitrophy.

Killer of Sheep works, by and large, in the low registers of understatement. Against this backdrop of restraint, Burnett's use of an asynchronous and wildly incongruous musical soundtrack in the slaughterhouse sequences emerges as the film's most arresting formal feature. In its deliberate incongruity, Burnett's use of sound and image to link Stan's home and work life resembles an analogous, albeit even less subtle, gesture from *Un Chien Andalou* (Luis Bunuel and Salvador Dali, 1929), a surrealist masterpiece that likewise couples overwhelmingly sinister images and jaunty music. Toward the middle of Bunuel and Dali's frenetic associative free-for-all, a reveal discloses that the male protagonist is dragging not just two pianos, but two pianos stuffed with the bodies of two slaughtered donkeys. Like Burnett's incongruous pairings of sound and image, this surrealist image ushers into the domestic realm all the terror that humans daily inflict on animals. In both cases, the introduction of slaughter into the home remains unsettling—indeed, terrifying—precisely because the films do not explain it away. In *Un Chien Andalou*, the material of slaughter seems to lodge itself in the living room, the inert bulk of the dead donkeys unreadable, unmovable. The connections Burnett forges are comparatively more dynamic, as they suggest an incalculable give-and-take between the spaces in which humans live and animals are killed. To be sure, the use of incongruous sounds and images to connect sites of radical difference is not an exclusively surrealist practice. Massood asserts, for example, that Burnett's juxtaposition of sound and image is an adaptation of a Soviet approach to filmmaking for an African American cultural context.[53] She does not qualify her reference, and I assume she alludes to Eisenstein, V. I. Pudovkin, and G. V. Alexandrov's "Statement on Sound," wherein they decry the use of additive or explanatory sound that serves "the satisfaction of simple curiosity" and in its place advocate a "contrapuntal" use of sound that provokes "a sharp discord with the visual images."[54] However, Burnett's pairings of sound and image work not to establish counterpoints—to build contrast—between these sites of difference, but rather to provoke open-ended associations between them. In this sense, they are properly considered surrealist.

Burnett's surrealist gestures also work on the image track. The most palpable instance occurs at the beginning of *Killer of Sheep,* in a series of riveting images of Stan's daughter, Angie (played by Burnett's niece, Angela Burnett), wearing a rubber dog mask that bears a preposterously forlorn expression (fig. 10.8). She first appears in the kitchen, where, silent and masked, she observes her father as he simultaneously repairs the floor and talks to a friend who has stopped by unexpectedly. Stan Jr. swoops into the frame and grabs her by the snout, and his violent play syncs with the off-screen voice of Stan's friend, who coolly greets the young boy with the words, "Hey, killer." Stan rises to scold Stan Jr., but the boy darts out of the house. The scene in the kitchen continues to unfold, and Burnett returns briefly to Angie a few moments later: still wearing the mask, she slumps against a chain-link fence and looks, vacantly it seems, at a small boy who has joined her outside. We could of course interpret these images as a distanced and potentially ironic critique of a society that treats humans, and particularly human children, like animals. But much more is contained in this gesture. Inexplicably grafted onto Angie's small frame, the mournful dog mask calls attention to its own act of effacement; we cannot but question what exactly is being veiled here and why. The splicing of human and animal in Angie's mask produces an inscrutable image, yet one that we can at least begin to read in the context of the film's sustained acknowledgment of an incalculable human-animal reciprocity. The image of Angie and her mask spurs my comparison to surrealism as it recalls ironic works such as René Magritte's inverted mermaid and even Man Ray's *Minotaur.* While the splicing of human and animal in visual art dates to antiquity, a resolute inscrutability binds this image of Angie specifically to the half-breeds and hybrids of surrealism. To put it another

Fig. 10.8

way, these figures are alike in their resistance to overt metaphorization or narrative causality.

The images of Angie also recall surrealism insofar as they contribute to the film's thickening of the boundary between waking and dreaming life. Clifford Thompson is the sole critic who considers the film's dreamlike texture in any depth, and his attention to this register prompts him to connect the film with surrealism. In an early piece for *Cineaste*, he asserts, "Stan's true problem is not that he can't get to sleep but that he seems to be in one long, tiresome dream from which he can't rouse himself; episodes in the film, as in a dream, don't conclude so much as blend into different episodes."[55] He refined that view a decade later, explaining in a follow-up article, "It now seems to me that the foray into the world of dreams in *Killer of Sheep* is deeper and more deliberate . . . deeper, even, than that in such surrealist films as Luis Bunuel's *Un Chien Andalou* or *L'Age d'Or*."[56] Thompson may well have been thinking of the introductory scene in Stan's kitchen when he made his revision, as it demonstrates the film's disturbance of the boundary of dreams on the level of both narrative and style. At one point,

Stan holds his teacup against his cheek and compares its warmth to the feeling you get "when you're making love to a woman." His reverie inserts a distinctly Proustian moment into the narrative: like Marcel's nibble on a *petite madeleine*, Stan's caress of the teacup lends him access to involuntary memory and the world of dreams. While I agree with Thompson's rereading (and would note that the fact that he revised attests to the film's lasting effects), I hesitate over his choice of words on several counts. He describes the film's slippage into the world of dreams as a "foray," yet this movement (here and elsewhere) does not, as that word suggests, express itself as a sudden incursion—as a fantastical exercise in style. That is, the film does not transgress any clearly marked boundaries, as is typically the case with dream sequences. Burnett's approach here closely resembles cinema verité: the scene in Stan's kitchen, for example, unfolds principally in extended static shots with seemingly little directorial intervention, and Burnett favors awkward angles and close framing, effectively rendering the setting confining and the characters confined. These qualities lead me to my second disagreement with Thompson's wording: where Thompson describes the film's slippage between waking and dreaming life as a "blending," I insist that it is a flattening. In this scene in particular but also in other moments, the film expresses the same urge toward flattening that is evident in abstract art, from Gauguin to Cézanne to the cubists. Burnett, who was the cinematographer for *Killer of Sheep*, generates this effect by combining a number of peculiar cinematographic choices: he allows shots to protract and extend just to the point of directionless tedium; he films from extremely high and low angles and sometimes from canted ones; he frequently uses a telephoto lens in the exterior scenes; he tends to move the camera frenetically or to not move it at all; he frames shots of human figures so that heads and limbs are lopped off; and he dispenses with point-of-view shots.[57] I agree that the film's framing and editing create ambiguity but argue that something more specific is at stake. By flattening the image's affective and compositional properties, Burnett graphically "populates the limits" between his human and animal actors. To put it another way, he brings into focus the kaleidoscope of connections and boundaries that run between Stan, his family, and the human and nonhuman beings in their surrounds.

This is not to say that Burnett's formal movements foster a chaotic or muddled cacophony—quite the contrary. Over the course of my analysis, I have circled back several times to the early scene of Stan and Bracy drinking tea in Stan's kitchen. This scene concludes with a jarring, high-angle shot over Stan's wife's shoulder that reveals that the two men are playing dominoes. The inclusion of this shot can be read to adumbrate the film's formal structure and the concomitant mode of reading it obliges. That is, it serves as a miniature model of the film's construction and thereby guides our reading of it. While there are numerous ways to play dominoes, the game essentially entails culling tiles—which, coincidentally, are referred to as "bones"—from a stock or "boneyard" and arranging them in mutually productive configurations. Players take turns aligning the tiles so that their values correspond; those correspondences generate new combinations, and so on. *Killer of Sheep* can productively be understood as working in an analogous fashion.[58] On my first viewing of the film, I was discomfited by its loose structure—by the way its scenes and disparate threads bump up against one another according to an unexplained logic—and my instinct was to insist on identifying causal links between the different strands. Yet I soon gave myself over to discerning transversals—that is, to distinguishing through lines and appreciating the interdependence of the fragments and their subjects. In this way, viewing the film is akin to playing the interactive and regenerative game of dominoes. Burnett's idiosyncratic use of sound and image, as well as his cinematography and editing, effect a continuous slippage between adjacent elements and thus unsettle a series of frontiers—waking and dreaming, human and animal. This slippage, at once breathtaking and understated, imbues everyday life with the terror that humans daily inflict on animals; that is, it effectively brings this violence home. It also disallows spectators a stable entry point and instead obliges them to constantly look anew at the relationships that, to recall Derrida's definition of *limitrophy*, complicate the lines between the film's actors and spaces.

I conclude by returning to my opening premise that *Killer of Sheep* undoes the way we have been trained to look at animals and animal slaughter and loosens the visual field to accommodate an ethical recognition of the ways in which the killing of animals imbues everyday life. As I have demonstrated, the film brings together or abuts a series of peculiar layers—incongruous sounds and images, flattened compositional and affective planes, eerie matches on action, and graphic rhymes. The film's limitrophic treatment on these planes, moreover, enables it to access alternative ways of visualizing relationships between perceptual modes of experience, waking and dreaming life, and humans and animals. In this way, *Killer of Sheep* not only strips away the centuries-long accretion of assumptions that inform our understanding of what humans and animals mean to one another but also underscores the immense value to be had in reconfiguring these relationships. In summary, the film undresses us, and it also urges us to redress our relationship to animals and to animal slaughter.

Notes

1. Jacques Derrida, "The Animal That Therefore I Am (More to Follow)," David Wills, trans., *Critical Inquiry* 28 (2002): 382.
2. Ibid., 369.
3. Walter Benjamin, "On Some Motifs in Baudelaire," in *Illuminations: Essays and Reflections*, Hannah Arendt, ed., Harry Zohn, trans. (New York: Schocken Books, 2007), 175.
4. Derrida 2002, 369.
5. Steve Baker, *The Postmodern Animal* (London: Reaktion Books, 2000), 93.
6. Derrida 2002, 372.
7. Adam Lowenstein, "Films Without a Face: Shock Horror in the Cinema of Georges Franju," *Cinema Journal* 37, no. 4 (1998): 41.
8. Ibid. Meanwhile, Jonathan Burt cites Franju's perambulatory view of Paris and La Villette, the suburban slaughter complex that fed the city from the 1860s to the 1960s, as a rare exception to the slaughterhouse aesthetic, the name he gives to the conventions by which cinema regularly sets slaughter apart. Although Franju begins his film by emphasizing the abattoir's enforced exile from the metropolis (the title on the first frame reads "Auz portes de Paris"), he proceeds to weave together the industrial site of slaughter and the desultory urban landscape, suggesting that the two are only outwardly at odds. As Burt puts it, "By moving between the invisible practice of slaughter and the highly visible city, his film follows a more transgressive course by making killing more than merely a confined act." He furthermore observes that *Le sang des betes* bares a "tension between images of networks and fragmentation." Jonathan Burt, *Animals in Film* (London: Reaktion Books, 2002), 176. The limitrophic movements I identify in *Killer of Sheep* achieve a similar effect, binding and loosening the connections between human life and animal death.
9. Eduardo Kac, *Telepresence and Bio Art: Networking Humans, Rabbits, and Robots* (Ann Arbor: University of Michigan Press, 2005), 236.
10. George Kouvaros, "'We Do Not Die Twice': Realism and Cinema," in *The SAGE Handbook of Film Studies*, James McDonald and Michael Renov, eds. (Los Angeles, CA: Sage Publications, 2008), 377.
11. Ibid., 381.
12. Sergei Eisenstein, "The Dramaturgy of Film Form (The Dialectical Approach to Film Form)," in *The Eisenstein Reader*, Richard Taylor and William Powell, trans. (London: British Film Institute, 1998), 108.
13. Ibid., 199.
14. Ferdinand de Saussure, *General Course in Linguistics*, Wade Baskin, trans. (New York: Columbia University Press, 2011), 115–166.
15. Jacques Derrida, "'Eating Well,' or The Calculation of the Subject," in *Points: Interviews, 1974–1994*, Avital Ronell, trans. (Stanford, CA: Stanford University Press, 2005), 278.
16. Paula Massood, "An Aesthetic Appropriate to Conditions: *Killer of Sheep*, (Neo) Realism, and the Documentary Impulse," *Wide Angle* 21, no. 4 (1999): 20–32.

17. Kate Stables, "*Killer of Sheep*," *Sight and Sound*, 19, no. 1 (2009): 94.
18. Ntongela Masilela, "The Los Angeles School of Black Filmmakers," in *Black American Cinema*, Manthia Diawara, ed. (New York: Routledge, 1993), 107.
19. Ibid., 111.
20. Clifford Thompson, "Good Moments in a Tough World: The Films of Charles Burnett," *Cinéaste* 33, no. 2 (2008): 32–24.
21. Massood 1999, 22–23.
22. Ibid. Citing Burnett's own affirmation, "*Killer of Sheep* is supposed to look like a documentary." Massood here provides a meticulous account of how the film brings together conventions from fictional and documentary models to represent what Grierson called "the drama of the doorstep." Ibid., 24–29.
23. Ibid., 38–39.
24. Ibid., 28, 35–36.
25. Inez Hedges, "Signifyin' and Intertextuality: *Killer of Sheep* and Black Independent Film," *Socialism and Democracy* 21, no. 2 (2007): 133–143.
26. Ibid., 138.
27. Jeffrey Skoller, *Shadows, Specters, Shards: Making History in Avant-Garde Film* (Minneapolis: University of Minnesota Press, 2005), 119.
28. Ibid., 119, 129.
29. Cary Wolfe, *Before the Law: Humans and Other Animals in a Biopolitical Frame* (Chicago, IL: University of Chicago Press, 2012), 43. Wolfe is referencing Foucault's discussion of race and biopower in *"Society Must be Defended": Lectures at the College de France, 1975–76*, Mauro Bertani and Alessandro Fontana, eds., David Macey, trans. (New York: Picador, 2003), 80.
30. Ibid., 43.
31. Massood 1999, 37.
32. Derrida 2002, 397.
33. Limitrophy is not specific to Derrida's "question of the animal" but is, rather, among the fundamental ambitions of his lifelong project of tracking *différance*. Ibid., 398.
34. Thomas More, *Utopia* (London: Forgotten Books, 1960), 57.
35. Upton Sinclair, *The Jungle* (New York: New American Library, 1960), 23.
36. Notably, the hitchhiking younger brother tells the friends that he did not work at the slaughterhouse with his brother and grandfather. Rather, he accompanied the older men to work, where he marveled at the "wonderful efficiency of it all" and took photographs. The film thus connects violence against humans not only to the age-old practice of animal slaughter but also to the modern practice of viewing animal slaughter.
37. Massood 1999, 35.
38. This reading also surfaces in a number of reviews of *Killer of Sheep*. Aida Hozic remarks that Stan's "existence is as bounded by invisible threads of hopelessness as that of the sheep that he is forced to kill each day." Aida Hozic, "The House I Live In: An Interview with Charles Burnett," *Callaloo* 17, no. 2 (1994): 471–491. Clifford Thompson likewise illuminates the "subtle and even brilliant ways" that Burnett connects the people in Stan's community and domestic life to the animals in his workplace. Thompson recounts, for example, the aforementioned scene in which one of the thugs attempts to justify his recourse to violent crime with the assertion "animal's got its teeth, man's got his fists," a statement Thompson reads as indicative of what he takes to be the film's message—that "for these characters, morality is synonymous with staying alive, and whatever it takes to do that." Thompson 2008, 32–34.

39. Skoller 2005, 122. Skoller adds that "the black and white of the film creates a much more abstract and metaphorical world than a realistic one. There is no clearer instance of this than the graphic quality of the white sheep disappearing into the black space of the chute in the slaughterhouse. The contrast between black and white is made even more potent when the image of the white sheep going to slaughter is reversed in the viewers' mind—through the film's central metaphor—into the black skins of the film's subjects." Ibid., 125. If we press on Skoller's logic, it breaks down: within the metaphor (the Black characters are like the white sheep), does Stan figure among the sheep (the Black community), or does he remain the leader (the one who leads to slaughter)? If it is the latter, then does Stan lead his children, his community, to death? Is this not precisely the damning critique of Black masculinity the film works so hard to resist?

40. Armond White, "*Killer of Sheep*: 'More than a Masterpiece,'" DVD promotional materials for *Killer of Sheep* (Los Angeles: Milestone Film and Steven Soderbergh, 2007).

41. The comparison provokes extreme discomfort precisely because slavery entails putting the trope of animalization into practice on a vast, industrialized scale. As Mark Roberts explains, the American slave trade's particularly "egregious abuse and exploitation of humans" was licensed by "the Aristotelian reduction of the slave to human property and the subsequent equating of humans and domesticated animals." Mark S. Roberts, *The Mark of the Beast: Animality and Human Oppression* (West Lafayette, IN: Purdue University Press, 2008), 66.

42. Hedges, "Signifyin' and Intertextuality," 140.

43. Cary Wolfe, *Animal Rites: American Culture, the Discourse of Species, and Posthumanist Thought* (Chicago, IL: University of Chicago Press, 2003), 101.

44. Cary Wolfe, *What Is Posthumanism?* (Minneapolis: University of Minnesota Press, 2010), 101.

45. Massood 1999, 34.

46. Ibid., 35.

47. André Bazin, "The Evolution of Film Language," in *What Is Cinema?*, Timothy Barnard, trans. (Montreal: Caboose, 2009), 104. Burnett does use duration. As Skoller puts it, "The formal style [of *Killer of Sheep*] is constructed around major kinds of shots: the long shot, in which the entire object shown is contained in the frame; and the long take, in which the duration of the shot is continuous. These shots emphasize complete actions and images of whole objects. These types of shots emphasize the real-time continuity of an action rather than the expansion or elision that results from putting together individual shots to make up a whole action." Skoller 2005, 121–122.

48. André Bazin, "Editing Prohibited," in *What Is Cinema?*, Timothy Barnard, trans. (Montreal: Caboose, 2009), 81.

49. Bazin 2009, "Evolution," 101.

50. Jennifer Fay, "Seeing/Loving Animals: André Bazin's Posthumanism," *Journal of Visual Culture* 7 (2008): 41–64.

51. Adam Lowenstein, "The Surrealism of the Photographic Image: Bazin, Barthes, and the Digital Sweet Hereafter," *Cinema Journal* 46, no. 3 (2007): 54–82.

52. Massood 1999, 24–29.

53. Ibid., 35.

54. Sergei Eisenstein, Vsevolod Pudovkin, and Grigori Alexandrov, "Statement on Sound," in *Film Theory & Criticism*, Leo Baudry and Marshall Cohen, eds. (Oxford: Oxford University Press, 2009), 113–114.

55. Clifford Thompson, "The Devil Beats His Wife: Small Moments and Big Statements in the Films of Charles Burnett," *Cineaste* 23, no. 2 (1997): 24–27.

56. Thompson 2008, 32.

57. I owe these last two observations to Hedges 2007, 138.

58. Different versions of the game may of course adumbrate very different formal structures—even homogenizing ones. In his reading of *Amélie* (Jean-Pierre Jeunet, 2001), Dudley Andrew identifies a masterful series of shots of tumbling dominoes as emblematic of the film's neat storyboard aesthetic and of director Jeunet's way of "clicking off" brief shots: here the dominoes "model the overall strategy of one shot falling into the next, which brings its neighbor to fall until the entire suite renders the pleasure of patterned reality. Of course, the dominoes have to be milled to be homogenous, then lined up just so." Dudley Andrew, *What Cinema Is! Bazin's Quest and its Charge* (West Sussex: Wiley-Blackwell, 2010), 49.

SCREENPLAY

Killer of Sheep

1. Front room near the kitchen. Night.

Slow fade in to a close-up of a child's face. The boy is almost paralyzed with fear. At first, the man who is talking to the boy doesn't seem to be speaking clearly. However, his voice becomes clearer with its meaning and its emotional impact on the child.

Image of child's face

>   MAN'S VOICE. You let anyone jump on your brother and you just stand and watch, I'll beat you to death. I don't care who started what. If he is winning or losing, you pick up a stick or a god damn brick,

Camera pulls back to include man's face

>   MAN. . . . anything, and knock the shit out of whoever is fighting your brother because if something happens to me and your mama, you ain't got nobody in the world except your brother. And this goes for him too.

Cut to:

Woman standing in the kitchen holding her other son, who is crying.

>   MAN. He knows but it's you who comes up with this off-the-wall bullshit about Henry started it. And if the son of a bitch is too big for you, come get me. Look, you're not a child anymore; you'll soon be a god damn man. So start learning what life is about now, son.

Woman standing in the kitchen doorway holding her other son releases the boy and walks toward the child who has just been cursed out by his father. She slaps the boy across his face.

Fade out.

Second titles

Fade to black:

2. Vacant Lot. Day.

A boy's face is peeping out from something that looks like a moving wall. The boy picks up a bottle and throws it at a group of kids standing on a dirt mound. It is a rock fight. Two groups come together throwing dirt rocks almost at point blank. One kid picks up a handful of dirt and sprays everyone with dirt rocks. Clouds of loose dirt settle. One kid picks up a hard rock and throws it and hits another kid in the head, knocking him to the ground.

    VOICE. Wait a minute. Wait a minute. I think he is hurt.

Someone picks up another handful of rocks and throws them at the hurt boy on the ground. Several kids continue to throw rocks, pretending not to hear anyone saying to stop.

    BOY #1. Are you all right? Which one of you hit him with a rock?

    BOY #2. I didn't. Let me see.

He intentionally tries to hurt him by pretending to look but slaps him hard on his injured spot.

    BOY #2. Ah, that didn't hurt.

    INJURED BOY. You poopbutt.

    BOY #2. Who are you calling a poopbutt?

A new fight breaks out and everybody is on the ground struggling to take advantage of the other man. A train passes and everyone is excited about the train.

    BOY #3 (STAN JR.) Get off of me; here comes a train.

    Everyone gets up to go throw rocks at the passing train. After the train passes, they all sit on the train tracks trying to think of something else to do.

    BOY #4. Let's go stand in front of the Vicksburg Club and watch the whores go in and out.

    BOY #5. No, if anyone tells Moms that they saw me even on the same block as the Vicksburg Club, my ass is hers. They will have to call the police to drag her off me.

Cut to:

3. Close-up of boy laughing.

Half of his body is under a box car. He is shouting to the other boys to try and push the box car over his body.

    BOY #4, Push, push, you guys ain't pushing.

Cut to:

Stan Jr., who is walking away from the box car.

> BOY #6. Stan Jr., where are you going?

Stan Jr. stops to tie his shoes.

> STAN JR. I'm going home to get my bee-bee gun.

Cut back to:

> BOY #4. Push, push, say man, what are you doing to my shoes?

4. Stan Jr. walking down an alley.

Just as he passes a white fence, two men climb over the fence carrying a TV they have just stolen. They put the TV on the ground to rest.

> MAN #1. Man, you broke the antenna.

> MAN #2. Don't worry about it.

Just as the two men pick up the TV, they discover that an old man who is watering his grass is watching them.

> MAN #2. Hey, what are you looking at? I'll kick your heart out!

> MAN #1. Oh man, let's go.

The two men walk down the alley, about to pass Stan Jr.

> MAN #1. You ain't seen nothing.

Stan Jr., combing his hair, looks back and sees that the old man has run into the house.

> STAN JR. Say, man, he has gone to call the police.

One of the men puts his end of the TV down and starts back after the old man. His friend catches up with him and tries to stop him.

> MAN #2. I told that punk that I was going to kick his ass. I'm going to mess him up.

> MAN #1. Let the man alone and let's go.

> MAN #2. No man, I'm going to mess him up.

He persuades him to drop the stick and to forget about trying to get the old man. They pick up the TV and take off running down the alley.

5. Stan's kitchen.

Two men talking. One is on his knees [laying linoleum] while the other man is standing. A little girl is standing in the doorway with a rubber mask on with her hands behind her back, sort of rocking against the door jamb, listening to the two men.

>STAN. I have worked myself into my own hell; unable to close my eyes, I can't sleep at night, no peace of mind.
>
>OSCAR. Why don't you kill yourself, then you'll be a lot happier. Go out like Johnny Ace.

Slowly a smile appears on Stan's lips.

>STAN. No, no, I won't kill myself but I got the feeling that I might have to do somebody else some harm.

He looks at the little girl in the doorway.

>OSCAR. When was the last time you've been to church?
>
>STAN. Back home; since then, I've done a lot of things but nothing yet to make the devil blush.
>
>OSCAR. I don't have any trouble sleeping. I ain't ashamed of nothing I can't help.

Stan Jr. comes into the kitchen and heads to the bedroom.

>OSCAR. (To Stan Jr.) What's going on, killer?

Stan Jr. goes into the bedroom, looks all over for his bee-bee gun; he stomps out of the bedroom into the kitchen and takes his anger out on his little sister.

>STAN JR. Where is my bee bee gun?
>
>LITTLE GIRL. Mama threw it away.
>
>STAN JR. How come you didn't tell me?

Stan Jr. grabs her by the mask and pulls, causing the little girl to cry out.

>STAN. Hey boy, you better stop acting like you ain't got no sense!

Stan Jr. keeps pulling on the girl's mask, ignoring his father. Stan looks around for something to pick up and throw at him. He picks up a towel and chases him out the back. Stan Jr. runs into the arms of Charles Bracy, who comes up the driveway with Ernest Cox.

BRACY. Young man, what's going on?

Stan Jr. breaks away from Bracy.

STAN JR. Ah man, I got to go.

BRACY. Man, that cat is something else.

Oscar, inside the house, hears Bracy and Ernest coming up the driveway.

OSCAR. Here come Bracy and Ernest Cox. I don't want them asking me for any money; I'm going out front.

The two men knock on the back door, then walk in. Ernest pulls on the girl's mask as he passes through the door.

BRACY. I see the wife got you towing the cart. I see Oscar must have been here.

STAN. How do you know?

BRACY. He is the only one I know who uses that Old Spice aftershave.

STAN. (to Ernest) Say man, if you want to catch Oscar, he just left.

Ernest hurries out the door.

STAN. Say man, do you want some coffee?

The little girl standing in the door hears someone call her name; she runs outside to see who it is. A little boy standing next to a fence, too shy to say any more, just waits for the little girl to make the next move. Inside the house, Stan pours Bracy a cup of coffee and then serves himself a cup. Stan stares at his cup, deep in thought.

STAN. What does this remind you of, when you hold it next to your cheek?

BRACY. Not a damn thing but hot air.

Stan takes the cup back and places it near his cheek.

STAN. Doesn't it remind you, when making love, how warm her forehead get sometimes?

Stan holding the cup next to his cheek.

STAN. Just like this.

BRACY. Myself, I don't go for women who got malaria.

Stan puts the cup down and changes the subject.

    STAN: What have you been doing?

    BRACY. Walking the streets all night. We passed here about three last night; saw the light on but we thought it best we keep going.

    STAN. You should have stopped; I'm always awake.

    BRACY. Counting sheep.

The two men are sitting at the table playing dominoes. Their attention is turned to the outside. A dog is barking like it is attacking someone. It stops barking and the men turn back to their game of dominoes. Stan's wife come into the kitchen and gives Bracy a rather cold greeting. It is morning; someone outside is trying to get their car started. Bracy checks his watch.

    STAN. It's time for me to get ready to go to work.

    BRACY. Maybe me and Earnest can luck up on a slave if we's lucky.

6. A day at the job.

We don't see the sheep being killed; Stan is working, noise of the machines, etc. . . .

7. Stan's house.

Stan's wife is in the kitchen cooking; she goes into the bathroom to make herself pretty for Stan; the little girl, Angela, is on the back porch singing to a record while her mother is putting on her make-up.

8. Later that same evening.

Stan and his wife and daughter Angela are sitting at the kitchen table. His wife would like to be alone with him but the little girl will not leave them alone.

    STAN'S WIFE. Why don't you try to get some rest?

The mother looks at the girl, hoping to get her to leave. They stare at each other. The little girl gets mad and storms out of the kitchen.

    STAN'S WIFE. You never smile any more. Doesn't anything make you happy anymore?

Stan ignores what his wife is saying and gets up to start work on the floor again.

9. Little kids are playing in a rather dangerous area where workmen have been tearing down houses.

Cut to:

10. Back at Stan's workplace.

The men getting ready to slaughter the sheep. The scene ends with the sheep coming up the ramp following Judas goats.

11. Saturday morning.

A black car drives up and comes to an abrupt stop. Two men get out of the car laughing like they were kids and did not have a care in the world.

    SCOOTER. Hey, Stan, can you come out and play? Ah, he's my hope to die buddy.

They knock on the door.

    SCOOTER. Come on out of there, turkey. We know you're in there.

Stan opens the door.

    SMOKE: *(to Stan)* Say man, loan me a buck.

Stan slams the door in their faces.

    SMOKE: Open up, Stan; we want to talk to you.

Stan opens the door and comes out. Smoke puts his arms around Stan's shoulders.

    SCOOTER: Jive turkey. Tell him your plan.

    SMOKE: We need a third man and someone recommended you, Stan.

    STAN: I don't want to hear it.

    SMOKE: Just be cool.

    STAN: I don't want to hear it.

    SCOOTER. Now let me tell you off hand that it is a five-to-life proposition. Me and him face a dark day if we go before the magistrate, but . . .

    STAN. Look man, I don't want to hear it!

Stan's wife comes to the door to hear Smoke tell her husband that they will do the killing; that they just need him for the unnecessary details.

> SCOOTER. Hum, well look here, do you know anybody who will keep their mouth shut and won't blush at murder?
>
> STAN. You know more of those kinds of people than I do, and who in the hell told you that I'll help you do away with somebody?
>
> SCOOTER. A friend of yours.
>
> STAN. Who?
>
> SCOOTER. Never mind who. Let me borrow your roscoe.
>
> STAN. I ain't got no gun.

Stan's wife comes out on the porch and everyone gets quiet.

> STAN'S WIFE. Why do you always want to hurt somebody?

Scooter looks around to see if she might be referring to someone else.

> STAN'S WIFE. Yes, you.
>
> SCOOTER. That's the way I was brought up, god damn me. I mean, an animal got its teeth and a man got his fist. A man got scars on his face for being a man. And ain't nobody going to run over this nigger, just dry long so.
>
> SMOKE. Right on.
>
> SCOOTER. Now me and Smoke are going to take our issue. You can be a man if you can, Stan.
>
> STAN'S WIFE. You wait just a minute! You talk about being a man if you can. Where do you think you are? In the bush or some damn where? You are here. You use your brain; that's what you use. You're not an animal. And both of you nothing ass niggers got a lot of nerve coming here to ask him to do something like that. *(Looking at Stan)* And who are you to sit there and let them do this.
>
> SMOKE. Look, all we trying to do is help the nigger.
>
> STAN'S WIFE. If you wanted to help him, you wouldn't have come up here in the first place.
>
> SMOKE. Look, look, look . . .

SCOOTER. Forget it, man.

SMOKE. Look what has Stan got? He don't even have a decent pair of pants. All we trying to do is help, nigger. You can't live if you are afraid of dying. Am I right? Am I right?

SCOOTER. Forget it, man.

The two men walk off. Stan goes back up on the porch. The kids come out and the little girl isn't wearing any shoes. The little girl starts to play in the dirt. The boy, Stan Jr., is trying to get up enough nerve to ask his mother something.

STAN'S WIFE. Come back in this house and put your shoes on, girl. If you get sick, I ain't got no money to take you to the doctor.

The little girl goes back into the house. The boy finally gets up the nerve to ask his mother a question.

STAN JR. Mot dear, can I have a dollar?

Stan gets mad because his son refuses to stop calling his mother "mot dear," which sounds so backwards.

STAN. Say old long headed boy, didn't I tell you about calling your mother mot dear? You ain't in the country.

12. An alley.

Stan's girl is standing with a group of other girls in an alley. A little boy on a bicycle rides into the group of girls who snatch him off his bike, which is too big for him. One of the girls kicks in his spoke and one tears his shirt. While his back is turned the girl that he pushed kicks him in the butt.

BOY. I'm going home to get my big brother.

GIRLS. Is he cute? You better take yourself home. You better come get this raggedy thing. You better take it home.

The boy runs away, leaving his bike.

13. Stan's little girl runs home.

She skips around the corner of the house to see her father talking to some men, Gene and Bracy. Stan's wife sees her listening to her father and his friends talk dirty.

STAN'S WIFE. Girl, come in this house! Haven't I told you about listening to grown people talk?

The little girl runs into the house.

> BRACY. What do you niggers want with another raggedy ass car for?
>
> GENE. Trying to get ahead.
>
> BRACY. I suppose now you think that you are middle class.
>
> STAN. I ain't poor. I give things to the Salvation Anny and you can't give things away and be poor. We may not have a damn thing some of the time but if you want to see someone who is poor, go around to Walter's and they live like chickens; they be sitting over an oven with their coats on, newspapers under their feet, rubbing their knees, all day eating nothing but wild greens picked out of a vacant lot. That ain't me and damn sure won't be. *(to Gene)* Tomorrow after I cash my check, let's go over to Silbo's and buy that motor and put it in.

14. Inside the house.

The little girl is putting on her clothes. When she finishes, she goes into the kitchen where her brother is sitting at the table, pouring sugar in his bowl of corn flakes. She joins him at the table. Stan Jr. looks at his sister as if he doesn't like her.

> STAN JR. I need some money.
>
> GIRL. What?
>
> STAN JR. I need some money.

15. Close-up of a woman's face.

She is obviously wearing a wig and is upset about something. She begins to talk to someone she doesn't care too much for.

> WOMAN. You better stay in line!

She walks into the camera. Cut to wide angle shot of her getting into a car full of people; the man she has just spoken to is bracing himself by holding on to the wall of the liquor store. He staggers to the car, gets in, and throws out a beer can. A kind of crazy laughter comes from the car. A woman inside is telling a man to get her a drink.

> WOMAN'S VOICE. Get out this damn car and go buy us a Johnny Walker and leave that damn cheap Ripple and shit at the counter.

One of the men sitting in the car reaches through where the front window of the car would be and picks up a can of beer that was sitting on the hood of the car.

> MAN'S VOICE. Ah, baby, I bees tired.

WOMAN'S VOICE. Get your ass up. Don't roll your eyes at me.

MAN'S VOICE. I bees tired.

The man is struggling to get out of the car when Stan and Gene drive up in a pickup truck and both car doors bang into each other. Stan getting out of the truck:

STAN. Hey mister, you want to watch that car door.

MAN. Ah mister, don't get mad. I'm sorry.

Both men walk toward the liquor store entrance.

16. Interior of Liquor store.

MAN. *(with check)* Can I get this check cashed?

MAN. *(behind the counter)* This your check here?

MAN. *(with check)* Yes.

MAN. *(behind the counter)* This here is your check?

The man behind the counter looks around for the owner of the store and calls her.

MAN. *(behind the counter)* Oh, Jerry.

Jerry comes and grabs the check out of his hand and pushes him to one side and studies the check and the man.

JERRY. Hell, no!

The man takes the check back and walks out the door. As he leaves, Stan comes in. Jerry sees Stan coming in and starts to smile. She likes Stan very much.

JERRY. Hello, Stan. What can I do for you?

STAN. Ah, ah, can you cash a check?

JERRY. I might; why don't you come and work for me?

STAN. Liquor stores get robbed too much and I don't want to get shot in no hold-up.

JERRY. I'll protect you; you can work in the back with me. He takes care of the register.

The man behind the counter doesn't take to the idea of Stan moving in. Jerry sees that he is upset.

>JERRY. What's the matter?

The man just shakes his head, too afraid of Jerry to say anything. Stan looks at the man and smiles.

>STAN. It's a warm proposition, but . . .

>JERRY. You think about it.

Jerry clutches his arm and takes a deep breath, and, with sad, appealing eyes, rings the cash register to cash his check. A man in the background gets a carton of milk from the freezer and puts it on the counter.

17. Outside a house. Same day.

The truck, gears screeching, comes jerkingly to a stop. Stan, Gene, and Stan's little girl are in the truck. Stan and Gene are counting their money, not wanting to show it to the people inside the house. Gene gets out of the truck first and Stan puts money in different pockets and leaves the girl in the truck.

17a. Interior of the house.

A woman, Delores, sitting at a table with a little girl resting her head on the woman's lap. Silbo, sitting at the far end of the table with a deck of cards in his hands, stares out of the window. On occasion, he glances into the mirror in front of him on the table. Another man is sitting at the table across from Delores; he is picking his toes. There is a man lying on the floor with a bandage on his head. Gene is standing in the doorway; his attention is drawn to the man with the bandage on his head.

>GENE. Who beat you up?

>JAMES MILES. *(man on the floor)* None of your damn business.

>MAN. *(sitting at table picking his toes)* Adolf and Boulevard jumped him.

Stan comes up the stairs, out of breath. He knocks on the door. Stan enters the room and gives everyone a nod.

>MAN. *(picking his toes)* What's happening, old dude?

Stan looks at the man on the floor.

>STAN. Who has been beating on you?

GENE. Adolf and Boulevard kicked his ass.

STAN. Who kicked you in the face?

JAMES. Adolf.

STAN. Why did he do that?

JAMES. Because he had nothing else to do with his hands and feet.

STAN. He kicked you ass for being smart.

JAMES. Wait till I get on my feet.

The little girl who was resting her head on her mother wants to go outside.

LITTLE GIRL. I'm just going outside.

DELORES. OK, baby.

17. Outside the house.

Stan's little girl Angela is resting in the truck; the little girl coming out of the house sees her and sneaks down the steps to surprise her.

LITTLE GIRL. Boo!

Angela jumps and sees that it is her friend.

ANGELA. How come you don't come to school?

LITTLE GIRL. I have been sick.

Cut back to:

17a. Inside the house.

Silbo is shuffling cards and looks around for someone to play with. He asks the woman next to him.

SILBO. You play cards?

DELORES. Solitaire.

SILBO. Suit yourself.

James, the man with the bandage on his head, wakes up, looks around; stares at the car motor sitting in the front room.

>JAMES. What is this, a side show?

17. Outside the house.

The kids are sitting by the car, chewing gum.

>Cut back to:

17a. Inside the house.

Delores is chewing gum but making it pop between her teeth. The man who was picking his toes is playing with a pencil and watching Delores put lotion on her legs. James is also looking at Delores. His look is very obvious.

>JAMES. How come me and you ain't never got together?

>DELORES. And what would you do?

James smiles and sticks his tongue out in a rather obscene manner.

>JAMES. I wouldn't know what position to take, mama.

>DELORES. You dirty dog. You ought to find yourself a place to stay instead of sponging off my sister.

>JAMES. This is my uncle's house, too.

Silbo, trying to keep some kind of order . . .

>SILBO. Please, please.

>DELORES. Well, tell this nigger to shut up then.

Stan and Gene are resting on the floor beside the motor; Stan is trying to get Gene to ask Silbo about the motor.

>GENE. All I got is fifteen dollars.

>JAMES. Don't sell them nothing, uncle, nothing.

>STAN. Say man, why don't you be cool? [Quiet]

Delores is busy staring at Stan. She kind of likes the way he looks.

>DELORES. You know, you would be a good-looking fellow if you didn't frown so much.

James, thinking that she is talking to him, jumps in the conversation before Stan can say anything.

>JAMES. Who me? Some sister [woman] told me that I look just like Clark Gable.

>DELORES. *(visibly upset)* You about as tasteless as a carrot.

>JAMES. You are always in a nasty frame of mind.

>DELORES. You are just a regular hardship case. Someone is always trying to revive your poor ass or giving you first aid. Always feeling sorry for yourself.

>JAMES. If don't, nobody else will and you are just an all day sucker, Bitch . . .

Before James can finish the sentence, Delores kicks him in the head. Stan rushes to his aid and Gene tries to keep Delores from hitting him anymore.

>GENE. *(to Delores)* Why did you have to kick the son of a bitch in the head? *(to Silbo)* Hey Silbo, you better come see about your nephew.

Silbo at the table, still playing cards, looks in the mirror.

>SILBO. I got more important things to worry about; my damn hair is falling out.

>STAN. Hey Silbo, you better come see about your nephew. He is bleeding.

>SILBO. Can't you see that I don't give a damn? He shouldn't have been running his damn mouth so much. You want the motor, give me fifteen dollars for it.

Stan and Gene struggle to get the motor out of the house. They have a hell of a time trying to take it down the back stairs. They carry the motor to the truck and put it on the bed of the truck. However, Gene gets his finger caught under the motor. He gets his finger out from under the motor and refuses to help any more in pushing the motor back on to the truck.

>GENE. Leave it there. It will stay.

>STAN. No it won't, man.

>GENE. Yes it will.

Delores's little girl gets out of the truck and Gene and Stan get in. Gene starts the truck; it jerks forward and makes the motor fall off the back. Both men jump out of the truck to see what damage is done to the motor.

>GENE. The block is busted.

They get into the truck and drive away, leaving the motor in the street.

18. Street scene.

Looking up between apartments, kids are jumping across. The camera pans down to show Gene and Stan drive up. Kids are playing in the back of the apartments, throwing rocks at each other. One of the kids is hit by a rock and starts to cry. Cut to a man running out of an apartment. He is wearing an army uniform. The man goes back to the entrance of the hallway and looks upstairs. He starts to go back up but a woman with a gun chases him back down the stairs. There is a group of kids sitting on the stairs watching what is taking place between the man and the woman. Gene and Stan walk up to see what is taking place. Cut to inside of the house. A woman is holding a gun; she is obviously attempting to protect herself and her children. The man at the bottom of the stairs shouts up to her.

> MAN. Throw me my god damn shades.

The woman looks at her kids, holding the gun in her hands, ready to use it on the man. The woman throws the man the sunglasses, which break. The man picks up the broken glasses and throws them down and looks up the stairs.

> MAN. You can forget about living when I catch you. The only thing looks good dying is a rose.

Stan looks around to see Truman Doyle walking by. Stan chases after him.

> STAN. Hey, Truman Doyle.

He grabs Truman by the arm.

> STAN. Hey Truman Doyle, is that you?

> TRUMAN. Who the shit does it look like?

> STAN. Like someone who owes me money!

> TRUMAN. Well, I ain't got nothing but my good looks.

> STAN. Do you know where we can get a few bucks?

> TRUMAN. Ya, go rob a damn liquor store.

> STAN. You look better going than coming anyway; so get on, nigger.

18a. Gene's house.

Stan and Gene walk to Gene's house where his wife, Dian, is standing in the door with no shoes on. The two men sit at the bottom of the steps. Gene looks up at his wife.

> GENE. Why don't you go put some shoes on.

19. Stan's house.

Stan and his wife are dancing; she is trying to get him to respond to her but he seems like he is in another world, a world of no feelings. The record ends and Stan leaves her standing on the floor. She goes to the window.

>STAN'S WIFE. Memories that don't seem mine, like half eaten cake and rabbit skins stretched on the backyard fences. My grandmother, mother dear, mot dear, mot dear, dragging her shadow across the porch. Standing bare headed under the sun, cleaning red catfish with white rum.

Close-up of hands picking up baby shoes.

20. Sheep in pens, looking into the camera. All of a sudden they start to run.

21. Stan's house, porch.

There are boys doing hand stands against the porch wall. One boy is sitting counting, while the others stand on their heads.

>BOY #1. 507, 508, 509, 410, 411, 512, 4, no, 513 . . .

>BOY #2. Can't you count?

>BOY #1. Count yourself then.

Two small girls pass by.

>BOY #1. Look at them old ugly girls.

>GIRLS. Your daddy is ugly.

>BOY #1. You want to fight?

Stan comes home, walks up on the porch, and knocks down the kids who were standing on their heads.

>BOYS. What did you do that for?

22. Kitchen.

The family is sitting at the kitchen table, having just finished dinner. The boy, Stan Jr., gets up from the table and bangs the chair to the table. Stan Sr. is too tired to say anything to him. The little girl, Angela, takes the dishes off the table.

>STAN. *(to his wife)* What did you do today?

With her head, she indicates that nothing unusual took place.

> STAN. I got to find another job.

Angela at the kitchen sink, getting water, looking at her father and mother.

> STAN'S WIFE. Tomorrow is Saturday.

She looks at Angela, then back to Stan.

> STAN'S WIFE. Let's go to bed.

Stan does not answer; she gets mad and leaves the table. The little girl goes over to her father and rubs his neck. Stan's wife is sitting in the living room looking at Angela and Stan and wondering why she cannot get near him.

23. Outside.

A little girl is hanging up clothes outside. Some small boys crawl out of a hole in a garage door. They see the girl hanging out some freshly washed clothes, pick up handfuls of dirt, and throw it on the clothes. Cut to Judas goats in the sheep yards. The two of them are alone; the sheep are all gone.

24. Gene's house late in the evening.

Gene and his wife are in front of the house. Gene is working on his car. There are some kids playing nearby.

> DIAN. Gene, we need food in the house; you shouldn't have spent your last dime to get this car fixed. That ain't right.
>
> GENE. Don't worry about it; if things get worse we can always sell it.

Stan walking up with a can of peaches under his arm. He takes five dollars out of his pocket.

> STAN. Here, take part of this. Miss Sally gave me five dollars for cleaning up behind her garage. She gave me a can of peaches.
>
> GENE. Thanks, I'll pay you back.

Dian, staring at the peaches.

> STAN. Here, you can have half.
>
> DIAN. No thank you.
>
> GENE. It's getting late. Let's go have some coffee and see how my guests are doing.

25. Inside Gene's house that same evening.

A man is kissing a girl who is sitting in a chair; she smiles when she looks up into his face. The man, putting his hand in his pockets, starts to walk away toward what appears to be a dice game outside on the back porch. He comes back and kisses her again; he starts to leave again, makes a quick turn, picks her up out of the chair, and kisses her again.

> MAN. I love you; let's get married.

She nods her head with a slight sigh. He sets her down and goes out where the dice game is. Gene, Stan, and Dian walk into the kitchen. Dian goes to the woman who is sitting down.

> DIAN. Are you happy now?

The woman in the chair nods yes. Stan and Gene are watching the men on the floor play dice. Bracy, who is dressed up in a new suit, throws the dice down and walks away.

> MAN #1. Why don't you two brothers get in the game?

Gene and Stan shake their heads. Cut to another man who is throwing the dice.

> MAN #2. Nine.

26. Saturday.

Stan, Bracy, Stan's wife, Angela, Gene, and Dian. Everybody is moving about getting ready to take a trip to the country. Consequently, no one is concerned about Bracy's chatter. He is trying to explain to anybody who will listen. Gene slams the hood down. The wives are looking around to see nothing is left. Stan is carrying Dian's baby. Bracy is trying to get everybody's attention.

> BRACY. It was some time in the A.M. when I dropped my last red. The moon had stopped over the street sign. All I could think is that I gots to get the blood to my head. All I could see was Alma Jean wearing that cascade that looks like a fruit stand on her head, yelling S.O.B.s at passing cars until her Boulevard, as she calls him, fire to her jubs. Then Boulevard said, "We best be thinking at sometun to eat." Boulevard, thinking we can get food and music together, kept circling the block looking for the Five-Four Ballroom; I said, "Alma Jean, tell this nigger of yours that while he was looking at fifteen years for being felonious and other things, we changed."
>
> DIAN. Go on, Bracy, I ain't got time.
>
> GENE. Come on, Bracy, get in the car.
>
> BRACY. Ah shit.

The car leaves with everyone in it.

26a. In car.

> BRACY. If I had a few bucks, I would bet on this son of a bitch in the ninth race at Los Alomitos.
>
> DIAN. What are the odds?
>
> BRACY. 9 to 1.
>
> DIAN. 40, 50 to 1, those are the long shots.

27. Out in the country.

The car is parked on the side of the road with a flat tire. Gene sticks his head out of the car to survey the damage.

> BRACY. Look man, I got to get to this race at Los Alomitos. Look, look, I told you not to go nowhere without spare. Look, man, I told you that I got to get to this race out at Los Alomitos. I got some money on a horse in the ninth race that I know is going to come.
>
> GENE. I ain't got no spare.
>
> BRACY. *(this part is not supposed to make sense)* I told you to keep a spare but you're a square. I'm out here singing the blues, got my money on a horse that cannot lose, and you're on a flat. You are a square. Now how are we going to this there.
>
> GENE. I ain't got no spare. I guess we'll have to ride back on the rim.

They all get back in the car.

28. Late in the afternoon, the same day.

Stan, his wife, and Angela come in the door. His wife calls to Stan Jr.

> STAN'S WIFE. Stan Jr. . . . Stan Jr. . . . If that boy's left this house open again, I'll kill him.

She goes over to the window and Stan sits down while the little girl, Angela, looks out the door at the sky.

> STAN'S WIFE. It's going to rain and the roof still needs fixing.
>
> ANGELA. Daddy, what makes it rain?
>
> STAN. It's the devil beating his wife.

29. Next day.

Stan's wife comes out of the back door looking for her son.

>STAN'S WIFE. Stan Jr. . . . Stan Jr. . . . Boy, you hear me calling you? I know that boy hear me calling him.

She goes back into the house. Stan Jr. and his friends are on the roof. On the front porch is a group of girls. Walking up the steps is a young crippled girl. She knocks on the door and goes in. Stan's wife comes to meet her at the door. The crippled girl whispers to Stan's wife. There are two other women sitting on the sofa.

>WOMAN #1. *(to the crippled girl)* Well, well, look who is visiting.

>WOMAN #2. Tell us why you have that pretty smile on your face.

>STAN'S WIFE. Girl, she is going to have a baby.

>WOMAN #1. Well, I thought her old man was shooting blanks but I see he is dropping bombs on occasion, I guess.

There is a close-up of the crippled girl's stomach. The next scene is dissolved over. The music of Dinah Washington comes in. Stan is herding sheep to the killing floor. The picture ends with a close-up of the sheep all trying to get on the killing floor.

THE END

BIOGRAPHY

Charles Burnett was born in Vicksburg, Mississippi, in 1944, but, following the path of many African American families in moving from the rural South to Northern and Western cities, the Burnetts relocated to South Los Angeles in 1947. Following the separation of his parents shortly after their arrival in Los Angeles, Burnett was raised by his grandmother. His subsequent work reveals a ubiquitous admixture of homespun Black Southern language and folklore with the cosmopolitan concerns and sensibilities of everyday life in a large industrial city. After studying electronics at Los Angeles Community College in the mid-1960s, Burnett enrolled in the film program at UCLA, where he met other filmmakers who would go on to have similarly distinguished careers, such as Billy Woodberry, Larry Clark, Haile Gerima, and Julie Dash. Taken together they would become the core group of filmmakers known as the LA Rebellion. Emerging directly out of this experience as his MFA thesis project, *Killer of Sheep* was first released in 1977 and revealed the powerful aesthetic and political concerns that would characterize much of his career. This career has been enviably long, wide-ranging, and celebrated, with Burnett receiving grants, awards, and accolades from numerous organizations over the years, including the Film Society of Lincoln Center, the Rockefeller Foundation, the NEH (National Endowment for the Humanities), and the MacArthur Foundation's "Genius" award. In 2017, he was a recipient of the Academy of Motion Pictures Governor's Award, the "honorary Oscar" bestowed upon individuals for a significant lifetime achievement in cinema. Notwithstanding this long and lauded career, Burnett has remained largely unknown to a wider public beyond the world of independent cinema.

SELECTED FILMOGRAPHY

Several Friends (1969, short)
The Horse (1973, short)
Killer of Sheep (1977)
My Brother's Wedding (1983)
To Sleep with Anger (1990)
America Becoming (1991, TV documentary)
The Glass Shield (1994)
When It Rains (1995, short)
Nightjohn (1996)
The Wedding (1998)
Dr. Endesha Isa Mae Holland (1998, short documentary)
Selma, Lord Selma (1999)
The Annihilation of Fish (1999)
Olivia's Story (2000, short)
Finding Buck McHenry (2000)

Nat Turner: A Troublesome Property (2003, TV documentary)
The Blues: Warming by the Devil's Fire (2003, TV documentary)
Namibia: The Struggle for Liberation (2007)
Quiet As Kept (2007, short)
Relative Strangers (2009)
Mulatto Saga (2012, short)
Power to Heal: Medicare and the Civil Rights Revolution (2018)

INDEX

Academy of Motion Pictures Governor's Award, 2
Across 110th Street, 57, 58
Adams, Faye, 171
African-American Symphony (a.k.a. Afro-American Symphony), 179, 191
Afrofemcentric. *See* Dash, Julie
Agee, James, 187
Alea, Tomás Gutiérrez, 70, 72, 82, 150
Alexander, Elizabeth, 89
Alexandrov, G. V., 237
Algerians, 56, 83
American Film Institute, 132
Anderson, Lindsay, 22
Anderson, Madeline, 68
Anderson, Steve, 132
Andrieux, Pierre, 106, 107
Anger, Kenneth, 60, 141
Angie (a.k.a. Angela), 10, 43, 155, 161, 162, 164, 187, 188, 189, 190, 194, 195, 196, 197, 198, 199–200, 228, 237–38
Animal Liberation, 227
Animalization, 216, 217, 219; as trope, 223–24, 226, 242n41
animalséance, 216
Annihilation of Fish, 106
Anstey, Edgar, 150
Anti-Chinese riots, 126
Anticipation of the Night, 137
Antonioni, Michelangelo, 270
Armstrong, Louis, 171, 199
Arthur, Paul, 138
As Above, So Below, 73
Ashes & Embers, 73
As Long as Rivers Run, 62
Audiences, 4
Avant-garde, 136, 139–40, 222

Bailey, Philip, 135
Baise-Moi, 90–92
Baker, Steve, 216

Bakhtin, Mikhail, 151, 163
"Ballad for Americans," 144n25. *See also* Robeson, Paul
Bamako, 117
Bambara, Toni Cade, 71, 100, 185
Banham, Reyner, 122–23, 130, 131, 139, 143n19
Baraka, Amiri, 50, 68
Barren Lives, 17
Battle of Algiers, The, 17
Baudrillard, 122
Bazin, André, 217, 235–36
Bazin-Eisenstein debate, 130
Beckett, Samuel, 6, 33
Bell, James, 171
Benjamin, Walter, 215
Benning, James, 205
Berger, John, 121
Berlin International Film Festival, 221, 144n23
Bicycle Thieves (*Ladri di bicicette*), 17, 27, 152, 153, 177, 207
Biggest Picture of All, The, 137
Bird, Stewart, 55
Birth of a Nation, The, 67, 147, 174
Birth of a Race, The, 68,72
Biskind, Peter, 3
Black aesthetic, 49–50, 63n3, 102, 148, 220
Black Arts Movement, 49–50, 68, 83, 101, 148
Black Atlantic, 65, 66, 84
Black bohemianism, 52
Black family, 11–12, 25–27, 52, 77, 83, 103–4, 131, 149, 159, 172, 176, 183, 184, 187, 200, 205, 218
Black independent filmmaking, 51–52, 65, 89, 93, 104, 105, 112, 185, 220, 221
Black Journal, 83
Black masculinity, 6, 10, 27–29, 31, 60, 83, 147, 149, 158–59, 193, 196–97, 210, 219
Black Nationalism. *See* Karenga, Ron, 133
Black Panther [film], 53, 55

269

Black Panther [newspaper], 55, 56
Black Panthers: A Report, The, 54, 57
Black Panther Party, 53, 56–57, 133, 148; Chicago, 54–56; Oakland, 53–55; Los Angeles, 33–34
Black Panthers, The, 55
Black Power, 49, 53, 59, 60, 82, 93, 213, 219
Black Power, We're Goin' Survive America, 53
Black revolutionary cinema (obstacles to), 61–63
"Black Shirts," 168. *See also* Nazis
Black trope, 28–29
"Black urban realism," 149. *See also* realism
Black womanhood, 12–13, 30–33, 78–79, 80, 82–83; nation building, 81–82. *See also* Stan's wife
Blade Runner, 139
Bless Their Little Hearts, 132, 148, 155, 192
Blaxploitation, 4–6, 8, 29, 57–58, 60, 61, 83, 89, 91, 104, 131–32, 135, 147, 152, 157, 171, 176, 192, 220, 223; neo-blaxploitation, 8
Blood of the Beasts (*Le sang des bêtes*), 216
"blue devils, " 169
Blues music, 35, 169–70, 171, 172, 174, 175, 177–78, 179, 230
Bourne, St. Clair, 68, 101
Boyz n the Hood, 8, 91–92, 132, 142n11, 163
Bracey, 37, 155, 160, 163, 190, 191, 199, 224, 227, 228–29, 239. *See also* Stan
Bracey, Charles. *See* Bracey
Brakhage, Stan, 60, 137
Breakfast for Children, 53
Brent, Bill, 55
British New Wave, 22
British Social Realism, 18, 35–36, 41
Brody, Richard, 27, 175
Buddy, 157
Bunuel, Luis, 95, 236, 238
Burnett, Angela. *See* Angie
Burnett, Charles, 1, 2, 3, 4, 6, 7, 8, 9, 12, 13–14, 15, 17, 19, 20, 22, 23, 25, 26, 28, 30, 31, 33, 34–35, 43, 51, 65, 72, 73, 74–78, 80, 81, 83, 89, 90, 91, 93, 99, 107, 108, 117, 130, 132, 134, 136, 139, 146, 147, 148, 149, 150–51, 152, 153, 154, 155, 157, 159, 161, 162, 163, 164, 167, 168, 169, 170, 171, 172, 173, 174, 175, 176–77, 183, 184, 185, 186, 187, 188, 189, 190, 191, 192, 193, 194, 195, 196, 198, 199, 200, 202, 203, 205, 206, 210, 211, 212, 214, 217, 219, 220, 221, 223, 224, 226, 227, 228, 229, 230, 232, 233, 234, 235, 236, 238, 239; biography, 267, close-up, 74–78; filmography, 267–68
Burns, Carol, 62
Burton, Julianne, 69
Bush Mama, 51, 73, 80–82, 90, 94, 95, 133, 148, 152. *See also* Gerima, Haile

Cabral, Amílcar, 148
Cahiers du cinema, 172
Caldwell, Ben, 8, 51, 132
California Institute of the Arts, 110, 140
Cannes Film Festival, 106
Capitalism, 11, 15, 50, 61, 219
Carmichael, Stokely, 53, 54, 55
Cézanne, 239
Chaplin, Charlie, 176
Chappelle, Dave, 96–97
Chappelle Show, 96–97
Cherry, Eugene. *See* Eugene
Chicago Guerilla Theater, 62
Chicago Tribune, 56
Chicano Moratorium, 127
Child of Resistance, 80, 81
Chinatown, 124, 139
Chong, Kim, 137
chronotope, 163–64. *See also* Bakhtin, Mikhail
Churchill Films, 100
CiBy 2000, 107
Cine-memory, 66, 72–73, 77–78, 82
Cineaste, 238
Cinema Novo, 69, 90, 149, 186
Cinema verité, 149, 160, 169, 220
Citizen Kane, 167
Civil Rights Bill (1964), 53
Civil Rights Movement, 113, 175, 213
Clarke, Shirley. *See Cool World, The*
Clark, Larry, 51, 73, 90, 93, 133, 147, 220
Clark, Mark, 56
Class, 10–11, 56
Cleaver, Eldridge, 53, 55, 74
Cleopatra Jones, 58
Clutsam, George H., 184
Coalition Against Blaxploitation (CAB), 147

Coffy, 58
Colon, 56
"Concerning Violence." *See* Fanon, Frantz
Conditions in Los Angeles, Calif, 127
Conference of Studio Unions (CSU), 127
Constitution (US), 25
Cool World, The, 6, 52, 53
Corman, Roger, 60
Corporation for Public Broadcasting (CPB), 112
Cosby, Bill, 60
Cotton Comes to Harlem, 57
Cox, Ernie, 190
Crazy Kill, 115
Cripps, Thomas, 203–4
Cuban cinema, 149
cultural ecologies, 130
cultural landscape. *See* Sauer, Carl Ortwin
Cummings, Michael, 74

Dali, Salvador, 236
Dargis, Manohla, 187
Darrow trial, 127
Dash, Julie, 4, 51, 65, 72, 73, 80, 82, 83, 84, 93, 104, 132–33, 147, 175, 185, 192, 220; close-up, 78–79
Daughters of the Dust, 78, 82, 84, 90, 185, 192
Davis, Ossie, 57
Davis, Zeinabu Irene, 147
Death Certificate, 93
Defiant Ones, The, 7
Demps, John, 109
Denby, David, 171
Derrida, Jacques, 215, 216, 218, 219, 223, 228, 240
De Santis, Giuseppe, 168
De Sica, Vittorio, 17, 152, 168, 171, 176, 207, 221
Despentes, Virginie, 89, 90–91
Devil in a Blue Dress, 163
Dian, 193, 197, 198, 199
Diary of an African Nun, 78–79, 83
Diawara, Manthia, 153, 185
Diegues, Carlos, 150
Dixon, Ivan. See *Spook Who Sat by the Door, The*
documentary, 22, 127, 150, 151, 152, 157, 160, 164, 169, 205, 210, 221

Dodge, Kim, 70
dogmask, 24, 42, 189, 190, 237. *See also* Angie
Dolores, 190, 195, 196
Dorothy. See *Bush Mama*
Drake, Francis, 138
dressage, 215–16
Drifters, 152
Driving Miss Daisy, 7
Drummond, Jack. *See* Stan Jr.
Duff. See *Nothing But a Man*
Dupree, Mignon, 79, 80, 82
Dvorak, Antonin, 201, 229

Earth, Wind & Fire, 95, 135, 170, 191
Easy Rider, 152
Eclipse, The (*L'Eclisse*), 207
Ecologies. See Banham, Reyner
Eisenstein, Sergei, 136, 217, 236
Ellison, Ralph, 43
Elton, Arthur, 150
Empire Marketing Board, 151
End of Day, 124
Enginemen, 23
Enrico, Robert, 137
Erikson, Kai, 211–12
Ernest, 190
Espinosa, Julio García, 70, 94
"Esthetic of Hunger, An," 69, 90, 95, 96, 97
Eugene, 177
Every Day Except Christmas, 22
Exiles, The, 127

Fanon, Frantz, 57, 69, 72, 80, 94, 96, 97, 148
Fascism, 168; antifascist cinema, 174
Fay, Jennifer, 235–36
Feininger, Lyonel, 96
Fellini, Federico, 168
Ferro, Marc, 68
Field, Allyson Nadia, 74
Film Society of Lincoln Center, 2
Finally Got the News, 53
Fireworks, 60
Foot, Horton, 112–13
"For an Imperfect Cinema," 70, 94
Foucault, Michel, 124, 125, 138
Four Women, 51, 78, 83
Fox Searchlight, 3

Foxy Brown, 58
Fragments of Keeping, 60
Franju, Georges, 216, 240n8
Franklin, Carl, 163
Fred Hampton, 54–55
Free Cinema, 1, 18, 22, 23; manifesto, 23
"Free Huey" (rally), 55
Freeman, Morgan, 117
Freire, Paulo, 57
French New Wave, 149, 150
From Dusk to Dawn, 127
Fruchter, Norman, 53
Frye, Marquette, 146
Fulson, Lowell, 179

G, 121
Gable, Clark, 190
Gabriel, Teshome H., 72
Ganja and Hess, 6, 51, 185
Gant, Cecil, 189
Garcia, David, 127
Gates, Henry Louis Jr., 221–22
Gauguin, 239
Gehr, Ernie, 203
Gene, 11, 37, 41, 161, 193–94, 195, 196, 197, 198, 199
geo-cinematic hermeneutic, a, 121–22, 128–29, 130
Gerima, Haile, 51, 66, 70, 72, 83, 84, 90, 93, 94, 101, 132, 147, 148, 149, 152, 175, 220; close-up 79–82
Gershfield, Burton, 60
Gershwin, George, 170, 178
Gessner, Peter, 53
Getino, Octavio, 17, 69, 94
G.I. Jose, 62
Gillespie, Dizzy, 179
Glass Shield, The, 4, 89, 93, 97, 106, 111, 115
Glover, Danny, 109, 116, 117
Godard, Jean-Luc, 133, 205
Godzilla, 124
Going Home, 35, 230
"Going Home." *See* Dvorak, Antonin; Robeson, Paul
Gone with the Wind, 175
Gordon, Avery F., 202, 212
Graduate, The, 124

Gramsci, Antonio, 27
Grant, Cecil, 189
Grant, Leila, 82
Grant, Nathan, 28, 33, 160, 162
Greaves, William, 68, 101
Grierson, John, 150–51, 152, 160, 221. *See also* documentary
Griffith, D. W., 67, 75, 147, 174
Grisby, Michael, 23
Groupe Dziga Vertov, 133
Guerrero, Ed, 4
Guess Who's Coming to Dinner, 6, 7, 51, 149
Gunn, Bill. *See Ganja and Hess*

Hall, Stuart, 66
Halstead, Fred, 128
Hamlet, 171
Hampton, Fred, 54, 55–56, 57, 133
Hanrahan, Edward V., 56
Harrington, Curtis, 60
Hartman, Saidiya V., 96
Harvard Film Archive, 68
Harvey, David, 122
Haskell, Aaron, 137
Hayward, Susan, 16
Hedges, Inez, 221–22, 223, 225–27
Heller, Paul, 106, 110
Henney, Leonard, 53
Henry Gale Sanders. *See* Stan
Himes, Chester, 115
Hinton, James, 68
Hollywood, 3, 4, 6, 7, 18, 22, 27, 28, 30, 44n16, 51, 59, 62, 69, 70, 72, 78, 79, 80, 82, 83, 89, 100, 102, 104, 105, 117, 122–25, 127, 131, 133, 139, 140, 141, 147, 148, 149, 150, 152, 153, 171, 172, 174, 175, 176, 177, 184, 185, 200, 204, 207, 219, 220
Hollywood Lockout!. *See* Conference of Studio Unions
Holocaust, 226
Honorary Oscar, 2, 44n7
Hooper, Tobe, 224
Hopper, Dennis, 152
Horse, The, 19–21, 22, 76–77, 89
Hour Glass, 80
Hour of the Furnaces, The, 17
"House I Live In, The," 161–62, 228, 229

Housing Problems, 150, 151
House Un-American Activities Committee (HUAC), 133
Hughes, Albert and Allen, 132
Hughes, Langston, 132

I and I: An African Allegory, 51
Ice Cube, 93
If He Hollers Let Him Go, 115
Illusions, 79, 82, 133
"imperfect" cinemas, 133. *See also* "For an Imperfect Cinema"
Indiana University Cinema (IU), 116
In the Event Anyone Disappears, 53
In the Street, 187
Inside Bedford-Stuyvesant, 83
International Critics Prize. *See* Berlin International Film Festival
Interview with Bobby Seale, 53
Israel, Frank, 123
Italian neorealism, 1, 17, 18, 133, 150, 171, 174, 177, 205, 221
"I Wonder," 189

James, 195
James, Alex, 80
James, David E., 11, 18, 49–64
James, Elmore, 171
Jeeter, Ester, 79, 80, 82
Jim Crow, 27, 68
John D. and Catherine T. MacArthur Fellowship, 167
Johnson, Lyndon, 26
Jones, James Earl, 106
Joplin, Scott, 171, 196
Josie. See *Nothing But a Man*
Jost, Jon, 133
Jungle, The, 224

Kac, Eduardo, 217
Kader, Abd El, 83
Keaton, Buster, 176
Kes, 41
Killer of Sheep, 1, 2, 4, 6, 7, 8, 9, 10, 12, 13, 15, 16, 17, 18, 20, 22, 23, 26, 27, 28, 34, 35, 37, 41, 43, 51, 75, 77, 82, 83, 89, 91, 93, 94, 95, 96, 97, 103, 108, 113, 114, 115, 116, 121, 126, 130, 131–32, 134, 135, 139, 144n23, 146, 148, 149, 150, 151, 152, 153–54, 159, 161, 162, 163, 164, 167, 168–69, 170, 171, 172, 173, 174, 175, 176, 177, 178, 181, 184, 185, 186, 187, 188, 190, 191, 202, 203, 204, 205, 206, 207, 210, 211, 212, 213, 214, 216, 217, 218, 219, 220, 221, 222, 223, 224, 225, 226, 232, 233, 234, 235, 236, 237, 238, 239; 240; in relation to Third Cinema aesthetic, 94–96; organizing principles, 9–16; screenplay, 245–65
King, Martin Luther Jr., 6, 53
King, Oliver, 182
Kouvaros, George, 217
Kramer, Stanley, 149

Lacy, 11, 41
Lady Sings the Blues, 57
L'Age d' Or, 238
L.A. Plays Itself, 124, 128
LA Rebellion, 8, 16, 23, 65–67, 68, 69, 70–71, 72, 73, 78, 79, 81, 83, 84, 100, 101, 147–48, 149, 152, 164, 174–75, 220; exilic and diaspora cinema, 84; naming of, 66–67, 84n5; orientation and organizing principles, 71–72, thematic concerns, 71–72
Larkin, Sharon, 93, 147
Lathan, Stan, 101
League of Black Revolutionary Workers, 53
Lee, Spike, 2, 4, 44n1, 104
Leigh, Mike, 41
Lenin, Valdimir, 50
Levitt, Helen, 187
limitrophy, 239, 241n33
Little Red Book, 55
Loeb, Janice, 187
Lookout Mountain Films, 140
López, Ana M., 70
Los Angeles, 18–19, 60, 65, 93, 122, 123, 124, 125, 126, 127, 128, 129, 130, 131, 132, 133, 134, 136, 137, 139, 141, 143n16, 146, 159, 163, 168, 172, 175, 184, 185, 192, 206, 214, 218, 219
Los Angeles Film and Photo League, 127
Los Angeles Newsreel, 53
Los Angeles Rebellion, 93
Los Angeles School of Black Filmmakers. *See* LA Rebellion
Los Angeles Times, 127, 128

Los Siete, 62
Lost Command, The, 137
Lowenstein, Adam, 216, 236
"Lullaby," 183
lumpen-proletariat, 6, 19, 77

MacArthur Foundation, 2
Machover, Robert, 53
Mack, The, 4, 5, 57
Mackenzie, Kent, 127
"Ma Curly-Headed Baby," 183
Madea, 185
Magritte, René, 237
Malcolm X, 6, 53
Mandingo, 29
Marsalis, Wynton, 177
Martin, Adrian, 190
Martin, Michael T., 1–46, 44n3, 65–88, 99–117
Marxism, 10, 53, 55, 68, 81
Masilela, Ntongela, 23, 66, 71, 147, 148, 149, 220
Maslin, Janet, 167
Massood, Paula, 17, 18, 146–66, 221–22, 223, 225, 228, 229, 235–36, 237
Mayday, 53
Mazzetti, Lorenza, 23
McCarthy, Todd, 106–7
McCullough, Barbara, 128
"Mean Old World," 230
Mehlinger, Keith, 35, 167–81
Menace II Society, 8, 132
Merritt, Bishetta D., 18
mesocosm, 138
Meyer, Russ, 60
Micheaux, Oscar, 148–49, 174
Mike Gray Associates, 54
Milestone Films, 168, 185, 190
Minotaur, 237
Miramax Company, 3
"Miss Sally," 193–94
Moholy-Nagy, László, 96
Moo Moo, 59–60
Moore, Kayce, 186, 192–93, 227. See also Stan
More, Thomas, 224
Morrison, Toni, 185
mouton, 216–17, 218
Moynihan Report, 26, 159, 219

Murder of Fred Hampton, The, 54, 57, 64n8
Murray, Albert, 167, 172, 177
My Brother's Wedding, 3, 83, 103
My Left Foot, 106

Naficy, Hamid, 84
Namibia: The Struggle for Liberation, 76, 83, 107–9, 112
Naremore, James, 19, 24, 26, 35, 182–201
National Association for the Advancement of Colored People (NAACP), 51
National Endowment for the Humanities, 2, 140
National Film Registry, 1, 2, 44n1, 167, 221
National Film Theatre, 22
National Society of Film, 167
National Society of Film Critics, 2
Nat Turner: A Troublesome Property, 93–94
Nazis, 168
Neal, Larry, 68, 101
Negro Family: The Case for National Action, The, 26
neorealism, 16–17, 77, 146, 149, 150, 151–52, 153, 155, 162, 164, 168, 169, 174, 175, 176, 205, 206–9, 214, 235; American neorealism, 53, 174
New American Cinema Group, 52
"New Black Cinema," 206–7
New Latin American Cinema, 70
New Line, 3
New Jack City, 8, 91
Newton, Huey, 54, 55, 56, 57, 59
New Yorker, 174
New York Times, The, 167
Nichols, Mike, 124
Nightjohn, 4
9/11, 107
Noble, John W., 68
"Notes on Trauma and Community," 211
Nothing But a Man, 6, 26, 34, 52, 53, 159
Nujoma, Sam, 108

Oasis Cinema, 140
O'Brian, Sarah, 43, 214–44
Obsession (Ossessione), 17
Occurrence at Owl Creek Bridge, An, 137
October Films, 3

Olivadados, Los, 95
Oliver, King, 183, 199
Ollie, 195
O'Neal, Ron, 58
O'Neill, Pat, 60–61, 130, 136, 137–38, 139, 140, 141
Ongiri, Amy Abugo, 7, 89–98
Oprah Winfrey Productions, 4
Original Gangsters (OGs), 173
Orion Classics, 3
Oscar, 188, 189
Otis, Clyde, 197
Overby, David, 173
Owens Valley Project, 137, 139

Paisan, 177
Pan-Africanism, 68, 81, 203; Pan African cinema, 203
Paramount Studio, 124, 126
Parks, Gordon, 58, 147
Passing Through, 51, 90, 133
Peazant family. See *Daughters of the Dust*
"peculiar institution." *See* slavery
Pena, Richard, 185
Penick, Thomas, 74
Perry, Tyler, 106, 185
Petty, Lori, 107, 115
"Piano Concerto Number 4." See Rachmaninoff
Poitier, Sidney, 6, 57, 149
Polanski, Roman, 124
Poltergeist, 139
Pontecorvo, Gillo, 17
protopos, 138a
Powell, William, 217
Prentice, John. See *Guess Who's Coming to Dinner*
"Problems of Form and Content in Revolutionary Cinema," 69
Proust, Marcel, 239
Pudovkin, V.I., 136, 237
Pueblo Se Levanta, El, 62

"race movies," 83
Rachmaninoff, 170, 178, 183, 197
Rafferty, Terrence, 168
Raisin in the Sun, A, 51

Ramaka, Joseph Gai, 65
Rape Me. See *Baise-Moi*
Ray, Man, 237
realism, 34, 149, 205, 206, 216, 235; Bazinian realism, 217, 235–36; "kitchen sink realism," 22; "poetic realism, 23–24, 150; "subtle realism, 150
"Reasons." *See* Earth, Wind & Fire
Redgrave, Lynn, 106
Redgrave, Vanessa, 106
Reflections on Black, 60
Reid, Mark, 90
Reisz, Karel, 22
Renoir, Jean, 172
Requiem 29, 127
Return of the Jedi, 139
revenons à nos moutons, 214, 217–18
Reynaud, Bérénice, 172
Robeson, Paul, 35, 135, 162, 170, 172, 173, 179, 183, 184, 201, 229–30
Rocha, Glauber, 69, 90–91, 97
Rockefeller Foundation, 2
Rockwell, Norman, 173
Rodia, Simon, 185
Roemer, Michael. See *Nothing But a Man*
Roizman, Owen, 2
Roma, citta aperta (Rome, Open City), 16, 152, 177, 207
Rompiendo Puertas, 62
"roscoe," 192
Rossellini, Roberto, 16, 134, 152, 168, 171, 176, 207, 221
Russell, Luis, 171

"Sad Lover Blues," 171
Salazar, Ruben, 128
"Same in Blues." *See* Hughes, Langston
Samuel Goldwyn Company, 3
Sanders, Henry G. *See* Stan
Sandhu, Sukhdev, 2, 6
San Francisco Newsreel, 53, 55
Sanjinés, Jorge, 69
Sankofa, 81, 84
Santos, Nelson Periera dos, 17
Saturday Night Fever, 135
Sauer, Carl Ortwin, 121, 130
Saugus Series, 136

Saussure, Ferdinand de, 217–18
Say Brother, 83
Schoenberg, Arnold, 123
Schroeder, Carolyn, 107
Schwarzenegger, Arnold, 124
Scooter, 157–58, 162, 192–93
Scott, A. O., 175
Senghor, Leopold, 50
Senso, 17
Several Friends, 74–75, 76, 186
Shaft, 4, 5, 57, 58, 147, 176
Shaft in Africa, 57
Shaft's Big Score, 57
Sheep, 13–15, 34, 36, 41, 42, 105, 184, 186, 210, 214, 216–18, 219, 223–24, 225, 226, 230–31, 232, 233; in relation to Stan, 241n38, 243n39
Sidewinder's Delta, 136
Signal-Germany on the Air, 203
Silbo, 195
Simone, Nina, 78
Sinclair, Upton, 224
Singer, Peter, 227
Singleton, John, 132, 163
"Sixty-Mile Circle." *See* Soja, Edward
69 Pickup, 74
Skoller, Jeffrey, 11, 19, 202–13, 222, 223, 226
Slaughter, 57
Slaughter's Big Ripoff, 57
slavery, 19, 25, 50, 78, 84, 93, 96, 203, 212, 222, 226
Sleep with Anger, To, 83, 93, 97, 103, 105, 112, 116, 117, 178
Smoke, 157–58, 162, 192–93
Soderbergh, Steve, 168
Soja, Edward, 126, 142n6
Solace, 196
Solanas, Fernando, 17, 69, 94
Solano Meat Company, 176, 229
Song of Ceylon, 114
Songs of Innocence and Experience, 128
Sony Classics, 3
Soul and Latin Theater, 62
Soul on Ice, 53
South Central, 132
South West Africa People's Association (SWAPO), 107–8
Speaking Directly, 133

speciesism, 227
Spiegel, Marjorie, 226
Spook Who Sat by the Door, The, 6
Spriggs, Edward, 68
Sragow, Michael 2
Stam, Robert, 69
Stan, 9, 10–13, 15, 16, 18, 19, 22, 24–25, 26, 2728, 30–34, 35, 41, 42, 43, 77, 132, 135, 148, 153, 154, 155, 157, 158, 159, 160, 161, 163–64, 167, 171, 172, 175, 177, 186, 187, 189–90, 191–92, 193, 194, 195, 196, 197, 198, 199, 200, 210, 204, 205, 207, 209–10, 211, 218–19, 221, 222, 223, 224, 225, 227–28, 229, 230, 232, 235, 236, 237, 238; internal colony, 14; metaphor, 15; Stan Jr., 10, 22, 161–62, 163, 186, 187–88, 198, 200, 218, 223–24, 237; Stan's wife, 10, 11, 12, 24, 31–33, 156–59, 163, 164, 171, 173, 176, 177, 191–92, 193, 196–97, 198, 199, 200, 205, 210–11, 227, 228–29, 233, 238, 240. *See also* Angie
Stepin Fetchit, 175
Still, William Grant, 179, 191, 228–29
Strike, 217
Student Nonviolent Coordinating Committee (SNCC), 53
Studies in Cinema of the Black Diaspora, 1
Sundance Film Festival, 3
Superfly, 4, 5, 57, 58, 59, 175–76
Superfly T.N.T., 57, 58
surrealism, 216, 234, 236, 237–38
Survival of the American Indian Association, 62
Sutherland, Donald, 2
Sweet Sweetback's Baadasssss Song, 6–7, 45n23, 58–59, 60–61, 132, 147, 149, 171
"Symphony No. 1: Afro-American," 228–29

Taylor, Clyde, 78, 100, 206
Taylor, Richard, 217
Teach Our Children, 53
Teatro Campesino, 62
10 Point Program, 55
Texas Chainsaw Massacre, The, 224
Teza, 79, 83, 84
Thi, Coralie Trinh, 92
Third Cinema, 1, 17–18, 22 26, 69, 70, 71, 73, 82, 83, 89, 91, 94, 95, 96, 149, 152, 163, 164–65, 219, 220

Third Eye Symposium—On Third World
    Cinema, 82
Third World, 56, 69, 128
Third World Cinema, 82, 150, 151, 205
Third World Film Club, 149
Third World Newsreel, 53–54, 55
"Third Worldist," 54, 79, 81, 83
"This Bitter Earth," 24, 135, 156, 170, 197,
    201, 232
"This Old Man," 160, 229
Thompson, Clifford, 238, 239
Together, 23
To Kill a Mockingbird, 51
Toronto Film Festival, 173
Toussaint Louverture, 117
"Towards a Third Cinema," 94, 96
Trick Baby, 57
Troublemakers, 53
Truck Driver, 58

Umberto D, 177
Un Chien Andalou, 137, 236, 238
Underclass. *See* lumpen-proletariat
"Unforgettable," 197
University of California, Irvine, 138, 143n18
University of California, Los Angeles
    (UCLA), 1, 8, 23, 51, 66, 70–71, 78, 79, 93,
    99–100, 101, 102, 107, 114, 132, 134, 139,
    143n18, 144n20, 147, 148, 149, 150, 151, 174,
    220–21
University of Southern California (USC),
    124, 127
Unnamable, The, 33
Utopia, 224

Van Peebles, Melvin, 6, 58, 60, 132, 147,
    149, 171
Varda, Agnes, 2, 54, 55, 57
Vietnam, 63, 81, 125, 133, 190
Vietnamese, 56
Visconti, Luchino, 16–17, 168
Vorkapich, Slavko, 139
Voting Rights Act (1965), 53

Walker, Alice, 78–79, 185
Wall, David C., 1–46, 66, 85
Waller, Greg, 116–17
Walter, 37

Walter, Little, 171, 230, 234
Warner Brothers, 58
"War on Poverty." *See* Johnson, Lyndon
Washington, Dinah, 24, 135, 156–57, 171, 197,
    201, 232
Water and Power, 130, 136, 138, 139, 140, 141
*Water Ritual #1: An Urban Rite of Purifica-
    tion*, 128
Watkins, Sean Davis, 28
Watts, 16, 53, 89, 90–91, 146, 151, 153, 159,
    160, 161, 162, 163, 164, 168, 171, 173, 175,
    176, 185, 186, 188, 190, 194, 214, 218, 219,
    221, 224, 225
We Are the Lambeth Boys, 22
Wedding, The, 4, 117
Weinraub, Bernard, 4
Weinstein, Harvey, 3
"West End Blues," 199
"What Is America to Me?" *See* Robeson, Paul
Where Others Wavered, 108
White, Armond, 6–7, 226
Will. *See Horse, The*
Willeman, Paul, 163
Wills, David, 216
Winfrey, Oprah, 117
Winkler, Tony, 106
Wolfe, Cary, 222, 227
Wolfe, Frank E., 127
Woodberry, Billy, 65, 81, 93, 132, 147, 148, 155,
    175, 192, 220
Working class, 10, 22, 50, 131–32, 142n11, 149,
    228–29; Black, 10, 26, 58, 80, 132, 168, 171,
    172, 173, 175, 176, 187, 204, 205, 219; laboring
    class, 77, 126; Native American, 127; Third
    World, 138; trans-ethnic, 126; White, 132;
    proletarian film, 63, 127
Worth, Sol, 62
WPA, 126
Wright, Basil, 23, 114, 151

Yamasaki, Minoru, 96
"Yankee Doodle Dandy," 193
Young, Linda, 78

Zavattini, Cesare, 168, 169
Zedong, Mao, 55
Zeitgeist, 3
"zoot suiters," 126

www.ingramcontent.com/pod-product-compliance
Lightning Source LLC
Chambersburg PA
CBHW041311240426
43661CB00065B/2897